JONSONIANS

Jonsonians explores the theatrical traditions within which Ben Jonson was working, investigates the ways in which his work has influenced and informed the development of theatre from the early seventeenth century to the present day, and examines Jonson's theatre in relation to twentieth and twenty-first century traditions of performance. It argues that although Jonsonian traditions are rarely acknowledged, they are vibrant and powerful forces that are very much alive today in the theatre of writers and directors as diverse as Caryl Churchill, David Mamet, Spike Lee, John Arden, Alan Ayckbourn and Peter Barnes.

The book opens with essays on *Poetaster*, *Sejanus*, *Bartholomew Fair*, *The New Inn* and *The Magnetic Lady* – each of which interrogates, in a variety of ways, the notion of 'Jonsonian' theatre and considers the relationships of Jonson's theatre to classical traditions, to his contemporaries in England and Europe, and to modern performance practice and theory. The second section of the book includes essays on The Sons of Ben (including Richard Brome) Aphra Behn and Daughters of Ben (women working in the theatre in the post-Restoration period). The book concludes with an extensive section devoted to modern day Jonsonians, exploring how reading their work as Jonsonian might alter perceptions of contemporary theatre, and how seeing them as contemporary 'Jonsonians' might affect our understanding of Jonson's theatre.

The book has resonance for students of Early Modern Drama and of contemporary theatre in performance; specialists in English, Drama and Theatre Studies; theatre practitioners; and theatre goers with an interest in Jonson and Early Modern Theatre in performance.

T0347478

Studies in Performance and Early Modern Drama
Series Editor: Helen Ostovich

This series presents original research on theatre histories and performance histories; the time period covered is from about 1500 to the early 18th century. Studies in which women's activities are a central feature of discussion are especially of interest; this may include women as financial or technical support (patrons, musicians, dancers, seamstresses, wig-makers) or house support staff (e.g., gatherers), rather than performance per se. We also welcome critiques of early modern drama that take into account the production values of the plays and rely on period records of performance.

Other Titles in the Series

Jonsonians
Living Traditions

Edited by
BRIAN WOOLLAND
University of Reading, UK

Routledge
Taylor & Francis Group

LONDON AND NEW YORK

First published 2003 by Ashgate Publishing

Reissued 2018 by Routledge
2 Park Square, Milton Park, Abingdon, Oxon OX14 4RN
711 Third Avenue, New York, NY 10017, USA

Routledge is an imprint of the Taylor & Francis Group, an informa business

A Library of Congress record exists under LC control number: 2003040359

ISBN 13: 978-1-138-71068-9 (hbk)
ISBN 13: 978-1-138-71065-8 (pbk)
ISBN 13: 978-1-315-19915-3 (ebk)

Contents

PART III: JONSONIANS IN THE MODERN PERIOD

List of Plates and Figures

List of Contributors

Peter Barnes is a playwright, screenwriter and director. His plays include: *The Ruling Class, The Bewitched, Laughter!, Red Noses, Sunsets and Glories, Dreaming, Jubilee.* Productions he has directed include: *Bartholomew Fair, Antonio, Lulu, The Frontiers of Farce.* He has written and directed numerous films and television series. Oscar nominated, winner of Olivier Award, Television Drama Award, Best Radio Play of the Year Award, Evening Standard Award.

John Bull is Professor of Film and Drama at the University of Reading, and is a past Chair of the Standing Conference of University Drama Departments. He has published extensively, particularly in the field of modern and contemporary drama, and his books include: *New British Political Dramatists; Stage Right: Crisis and Recovery in Contemporary British Mainstream Theatre* and *Vanbrugh and Farquhar.* He is currently editing a six volume project, *British and Irish Dramatists Since World War II.*

Richard A. Cave is Professor of Drama and Theatre Arts at Royal Holloway, University of London. He has written extensively on aspects of renaissance drama (especially Jonson and Webster), nineteenth-century and modern theatre, Anglo-Irish drama, forms of dance theatre and the study of the body as a medium of expression. He has edited the plays of Yeats and Wilde. While general editor of *Theatre In Focus*, he contributed monographs on Terence Gray and Charles Ricketts to the series.

Alison Findlay is Reader in Renaissance Drama at Lancaster University. Her publications include *Illegitimate Power: Bastards in Renaissance Drama* (Manchester University Press, 1994), *A Feminist Perspective on Renaissance Drama* (Blackwell, 1998). She is co-director of an interdisciplinary research project on early modern women's drama, and co-author of *Women and Dramatic Production 1550–1700* (Longman, 2000). She is currently working on *Women in Shakespeare*, for the Athlone Shakespeare Dictionaries series, and *Macbeth* for the Arden 'Shakespeare at Stratford' series.

Claudia Manera has a PhD in Drama from the University of Reading, where she has been a part-time lecturer in Drama and a language teacher for a number of years. The research topic for the PhD is a comparative study of Dario Fo, Franca Rame and Caryl Churchill. Research interests include contemporary physical theatre and performance, street theatre, feminist performance, political theatre, women and comedy. Claudia has also performed as clown and is currently refining workshops in clowning and Commedia dell'Arte.

Stephen Lacey is a Principal Lecturer in the Department of Contemporary Arts at Manchester Metropolitan University. He has written about post-war British theatre, in particular realist theatre of the late 1950s and 1960s, and has a long term admiration for the work of John Arden. He is currently involved in research into television drama from 1960 to 1980 and has published in this area.

Julie Sanders is Reader in English at Keele University. She is the author of *Ben Jonson's Theatrical Republics* (1998), *Caroline Drama* (1999) and *Novel Shakespeares* (2001). Currently editing Jonson's *The New Inn* for the *Cambridge Edition of the Works of Ben Jonson*, she is also carrying out research on the 1630s.

Carolyn D. Williams is a lecturer in the School of English and American Literature at the University of Reading. She has published *Pope, Homer, and Manliness* (1993), as well as many articles on various aspects of early modern life and literature. She has directed university productions of Gay's *Beggar's Opera* and Aphra Behn's *The Rover*.

Brian Woolland is a Senior Lecturer in the Department of Film, Theatre & Television at the University of Reading and also works as a theatre director and playwright. He has edited *The Alchemist* (Cambridge University Press, 1995) and co-authored *Ben Jonson and Theatre* (Routledge, 1999). He has directed *The Magnetic Lady*, *Epicœne*, *The Devil is an Ass* and (most recently) *Sejanus*. His own plays have been produced and toured in several European countries. His monograph, *Dark Attractions:The Theatre of Peter Barnes* is to be published by Methuen in 2004.

A Note on Editions

For the sake of consistency Jonson's plays are referred to in the relevant *Revels Plays* edition.

The convention has been to use Arabic numerals wherever appropriate in references to Acts, Scenes and lines (thus 4.8.12). Roman numerals are used to indicate Volumes (as in editions of *Collected Works*). This convention was not followed in the chapter on *Poetaster*, where it is more appropriate to use Roman numerals in references to the work of Latin poets and, for the sake of consistency within the chapter, Acts and Scenes are referred to using Roman numerals (thus IV.viii.12).

Details of the editions used appear in the endnotes for each chapter.

Acknowledgements

In my introduction to this volume I acknowledge Helen Ostovich's observations about Jonsonian cinema; but I would also like to thank her for the interest and enthusiasm she showed in this project from the moment I first mentioned it to her. My thanks also to Erika Gaffney, the commissioning editor at Ashgate, for her prompt and positive responses at every stage of the development of the volume; and to my colleagues in the Department of Film, Theatre & Television (formerly the Department of Film & Drama) at the University of Reading, who have been unfailingly supportive throughout the development of this project.

My thanks to Professor Edward Braun, whose generous reply to my rather vague query about Meyerhold led me indirectly towards Eisenstein and the notion of a 'Jonsonian Cinema'. I am grateful to Stevie Simkin for the stimulating conversations we enjoy about Renaissance Theatre; and to all those who have contributed to the seminars held after each of the Jonson productions I have directed at Reading.

It is, perhaps, unusual to thank those who have contributed to a volume of essays such as this one, but I would like to register my appreciation to all – for their essays, which I have much enjoyed reading, and for their generous contributions to the lively colloquium held at Reading in July 2001, where we discussed Jonsonian theatre so vigorously and openly. In particular, I would like to thank Richard Cave, whose own interest in Jonson has been so stimulating, and whose continuing encouragement and advice has been most influential in focusing my interest in Jonson's theatre.

I owe a substantial debt of gratitude to the Reading University students who participated in and assisted with my productions of *The Devil is an Ass*, *The Magnetic Lady* and *Epicœne*. In this context, I would particularly like to thank the cast of both the workshop and the fully realised productions of *Sejanus His Fall*, staged in December 2001 and December 2002 respectively.

Finally, I owe the greatest debt of gratitude to my partner, Hilary Garrett, for her love and support through the process of developing and realising this project.

General Editor's Preface
Helen Ostovich, McMaster University

Performance assumes a string of creative, analytical, and collaborative acts that, in defiance of theatrical ephemerality, live on through records, manuscripts, and printed books. The monographs and essay collections in this series offer original research which addresses theatre histories and performance histories in the context of the sixteenth and seventeenth century life. Of especial interest are studies in which women's activities are a central feature of discussion as financial or technical supporters (patrons, musicians, dancers, seamstresses, wig-makers, or 'gatherers'), if not authors or performers per se. Welcome too are critiques of early modern drama that not only take into account the production values of the plays, but also speculate on how intellectual advances or popular culture affect the theatre.

The series logo, selected by my colleague Mary V. Silcox, derives from Thomas Combe's duodecimo volume, The Theater of Fine Devices (London, 1592), Emblem VI, sig. B. The emblem of four masks has a verse which makes claims for the increasing complexity of early modern experience, a complexity that makes interpretation difficult. Hence the corresponding perhaps uneasy rise in sophistication:

Masks will be more hereafter in request,
And grow more deare than they did heretofore.

No longer simply signs of performance 'in play and iest', the mask has become the 'double face' worn 'in earnest' even by 'the best' of people, in order to manipulate or profit from the world around them. The books stamped with this design attempt to understand the complications of performance produced on stage and interpreted by the audience, whose experiences outside the theatre may reflect the emblem's argument:

Most men do vse some colour'd shift
For to conceal their craftie drift.

Centuries after their first presentations, the possible performance choices and meanings they engender still stir the imaginations of actors, audiences, and readers of early plays. The products of scholarly creativity in this series, I hope, will also stir imaginations to new ways of thinking about performance.

Chapter 1

Introduction

Brian Woolland

There have been some very fine revivals of Jonson's plays in recent years;[1] and, although the great 'middle period' comedies[2] are still by far the most popular of his plays, some of the lesser known plays have also enjoyed exuberant and intelligent theatrical productions.[3] Jonson's theatre may be better known to theatre goers now than it was thirty years ago, but whilst there is still a tendency amongst the majority of academic critics to approach Jonson's work as literature,[4] it seems that most journalistic theatre critics continue to be taken by surprise by the effectiveness and modernity of the plays as theatre. This book focuses exclusively on the theatricality of Jonson's dramatic output, interrogating that theatricality by relating it to a variety of contexts across the years between the first production of the plays and the present day.

Although it is now more than thirty years since an edition of *Gambit* largely devoted to the topic *Ben Jonson and the Modern Stage* was published, the arguments and assertions it contains are still surprisingly pertinent. In his editorial introduction, Irving Wardle wrote:

> Jonson is neglected: but the odd thing is that while very little of his work reaches the stage, no dramatist of the past exerts a greater or more continuous influence on the modern repertory. ... One can speak of Jonsonian actors and writers, as one cannot speak of any Shakespearean equivalents.[5]

Wardle's assertion was provocative in 1972, and remains so today. But, in spite of the growing attention paid to Jonson's work in the theatre and the academy, he is still neglected. Whether Jonson truly exerts the power of influence that Wardle claims, the use of the term 'Jonsonian' begs significant questions of definition. What characteristics do 'Jonsonian actors' or writers share? What, indeed, is Jonsonian theatre? These would be rather dry questions if they did not open up debates about the nature of theatre itself and about theatre's relationships to changing traditions of performance.

The word 'tradition' is, as Raymond Williams has noted,[6] a surprisingly difficult one in modern English usage. Ultimately, the root of the English word is the Latin *tradere*, to hand over or deliver. This meaning still informs its current meanings, which have developed into two dominant senses: knowledge handed down, and the passing on of doctrine. But it is misleading to deduce from either of those senses that tradition is necessarily static and that working within a tradition makes one a passive recipient of knowledge, skills and attitudes. Although there is undoubtedly a dismissive and even a pejorative sense to the word in its current usage – the traditionalist is resistant to innovation and change – when traditions are examined carefully it becomes evident that they are not so much fixed bodies of knowledge as active and evolving processes.

The paradigm of the Master craftsman (I use the patriarchal model consciously) and the apprentice, who in turn becomes a Master, may be appealing for its apparent certainties and stability, but even the 'traditional' skills of the thatcher and the blacksmith evolve in relation not only to developing technology, but also to broader cultural changes. Even if a blacksmith living in the early twenty-first century in a picturesque English village were still working on the same anvil and in the same forge that he had inherited from his great-great-grandfather, and the bulk of his work was still shoeing horses, the meaning of his work – socially, personally and culturally – would be very different to that of his father. The thatcher who 'carries on the traditional craft' may use the same tools that had been used in the nineteenth century, but the ideological function of his work has massively changed.

Where the blacksmith and the thatcher work alone or with a very small hierarchically ordered team, theatre is by its very nature a collaborative art; and, as Stephen Orgel has demonstrated,[7] even a text such as *Sejanus his Fall* (which appears to be so determinedly single-authored) is a product of collective interaction, not only between Jonson and his much vaunted classical sources, but also between himself and theatrical institutions, audiences, actors, publishers and subsequent editors. Jonson was acutely aware of the diverse traditions within which he was working, but his interests in theatrical traditions are always plural and interactive. And, similarly, if present day theatre practitioners are seen as Jonsonian, the term should be seen as implying a plurality of inter-related practices, rather than as constraining and definitional.

Each of the various essays in this volume attempts to examine not only what the term 'Jonsonian' might mean, but also to ask what Jonson's theatre means to us in the early twenty-first century and further, by extrapolation, to examine what the 'Jonsonian' tells us about our own theatre.

This book is divided into three Parts. The first of these, *Jonsonian Theatre*, interrogates the term 'Jonsonian' by asking how five of Jonson's own plays might themselves be considered Jonsonian. This might seem to be potentially tautological, but the term 'Jonsonian' carries a wealth of meanings and implications. Peter Barnes's celebratory account of *Bartholomew Fair* energetically proposes a view of the play as life-enhancing in its theatricality. His assertions about the play are, however, far more contentious than they might at first seem. The enthusiastic audience responses to George Devine's 1949/1950 revival of *Bartholomew Fair*[8] were not matched by generally hostile critics, whose responses are indicative of a generic response to Jonson's theatre which is almost as common now as it was half a century ago.

> It is very brave of the Old Vic to disinter Ben Jonson's 336 year old *Bartholomew Fair*, which has been but once revived since 1731. There is good reason for its neglect. It is a documentary picture of London life of Jonsonian times, of ancient Smithfield as it was with its show folk. ... It is in fact anything but a play.
>
> (*The Star*, 19 December 1950)

> The play as Jonson wrote it is defeated by its own perfection. ... If life is all you want, why go to the theatre? ... Ben Jonson ... is honest and superfluous.
>
> (Harold Hobson, *The Sunday Times*, 24 December 1950)

> It is many years since Jonson's *Bartholomew Fair* was given in London, and it is very easy to see ... why. ... The play itself seems to me ... to be the most crashing bore. ... It is a realistic comedy. ... It is really more like a vivid and comprehensive piece of descriptive reporting than a play...
>
> (*New Statesman*, 30 December 1950)

What each of these critical responses to the play reveal is a denial, or even a refusal to see the play on its own terms – a refusal, even, to see the play as theatrical. Barnes delights in precisely those qualities which these newspaper critics decry: the play's social specificity, its multiplying narratives and its shifting points of view. To claim that *Bartholomew Fair* is not a play implies that such a thing has a stable identity and can be recognised. What the essays on *Poetaster*, *Sejanus his Fall*, *The New Inn* and *The Magnetic Lady* reveal is that whatever apparent certainties Jonson expressed in various epistles, dedications, inductions and prologues, his relationship with theatre was dynamic and changing. His work for the theatre was restlessly experimental. Although he was acutely aware of the various traditions from which the theatre of the late Elizabethan period had emerged, he did not see these traditions as static.

The metatheatrical qualities of Jonson's theatre have been discussed at length in terms of the way in which he uses theatrical tropes with which an audience would be familiar in order to subvert that audience's expectation and to encourage it to interrogate its own responses to the unfolding drama. The essays in Part I reveal Jonson to be constantly interrogating his own practice; to be using the theatrical tradition(s) within which the particular play was conceived as a starting point and a framework from which (and within which) to challenge his own assumptions about the forms and functions of theatre. Jonson's vehemently expressed authorial intentions should not be mistaken for the meaning of the plays; they comprise part of a developing dialectic about theatre, and indeed about authorship itself. Whatever the term 'Jonsonian' might mean, it was never a generic formula. The following extract from the Induction to *Every Man out of His Humour* exemplifies the point:

MITIS   Does he observe all the laws of comedy...?

CORDATUS ... O no, these are too nice observations.... If those laws ... had
            been delivered us *ab initio*, and in their present virtue and
            perfection, there had been some reason of obeying their powers;
            but ... that which we call *Comœdia* ... (has)... changed ... in
            Menander, Philemon, Cecilius, Plautus and the rest, who have ...
            altered ... augmented it with all liberty, according to the elegancy
            and disposition of those times wherein they wrote. I see not then,
            but we should enjoy the same license, or free power to illustrate
            and heighten our invention, as they did; and not be tied to those
            strict and regular forms which the niceness of a few... would
            thrust upon us.

Every Man out of His Humour Induction

Each of the five plays discussed in this first section has been written off as unstageable, or at the least untheatrical. At the time of writing, although *The New Inn* was revived by the RSC in 1987[9] and *Bartholomew Fair* may now be firmly re-established in the repertoire, neither *Poetaster*, *The Magnetic Lady* nor *Sejanus his Fall* has enjoyed a professional revival in at least three hundred years.[10] Each of the essays on these asserts the play's theatrical strengths by first addressing the question: what are the theatrical terms on which it demands to be seen? But there is another reason for focusing on these less well known plays. It might be argued that *The Alchemist*, *Volpone* and *Epicœne* are the most influential of Jonson's plays and, for that very reason, there are frequent references to them elsewhere in the volume. Discussing what it is that makes these relatively less well-known plays characteristically 'Jonsonian' constitutes not only an attempt to make the term both broader and more specific, but also to open up the Jonson canon. Furthermore, devoting two chapters to the relatively early Roman plays and another to two of the late Caroline comedies highlights amongst other things the diversity of Jonson's appropriation of classical sources and his increasingly experimental use of theatrical space.

Part II, *Sons and Daughters of Ben*, investigates and problematises relationships between Jonson's theatre and the work of Nathan Field, Richard Brome, Aphra Behn and some of the significant number of women working in the theatre in the post-Restoration period. Jonson's influence on male playwrights of the immediate post-Restoration period is well documented elsewhere,[11] which is why two of the three essays in this section focus specifically on women working in the post-Restoration theatre. The significance of Jonson's theatre for male playwrights of this period is, however, alluded to in the essays on Aphra Behn and the 'Daughters of Ben'. Each of the essays in this section clearly demonstrates that from the early part of the seventeenth century, while theatre practitioners have found Jonson's influence an inspiration, a challenge and a provocation, they subverted and challenged his work as much as they appropriated and developed it. Richard Cave's essay on the 'Sons of Ben', the first in this section, opens by discussing and problematising the issue of 'influence' (a central concept throughout the second and third sections of the book) relating it to intertextuality and arguing that 'influence' is rarely a one-way process. Although his focus his specifically on the early seventeenth-century playwrights, Nathan Field and Richard Brome, his argument has far broader implications and includes a particularly fruitful discussion of gender and misogyny. Carolyn D. Williams considers the work of Aphra Behn and its relationships with Jonson's theatre. In doing so she vividly evokes the rather fractious theatrical culture of the post-Restoration period and demonstrates how Behn sought to establish her own identity as a playwright through interactions with her contemporaries and complex and highly problematic negotiations with the pervasive influences of Jonson and Shakespeare. Aphra Behn may have been the most prominent female playwright of the post-Restoration period but, as Alison Findlay's wide-ranging essay, 'Daughters of Ben', demonstrates, a growing number of women were working in the theatre, and attitudes towards women (both in the theatre and in society at large) were changing rapidly. The essay – which includes a witty and informative discussion of the transvestite tradition – refers to a wide range of Restoration plays by women, relating them both directly and indirectly to the works of Jonson.

The final section of the book, *Jonsonians in the Modern Period*, explores the relationship of Jonson's theatre to twentieth- and twenty-first-century traditions of performance. In exploring possible meanings for the term 'Jonsonian' it asserts theatrical traditions that are vigorous and invigorating, challenging and provocative; and, although rarely acknowledged, exert vibrant and powerful forces that are very much alive today. Each of the essays adopts a different approach to their subject. It is in the spirit of Jonsonian theatre that meanings are contested, and that readers (off the page or in the theatre) are thereby encouraged to reflect on their own responses to the dramatic and theatrical experiences. There are inevitably tensions between the different interpretations of the term 'Jonsonian'; and it is hoped that these tensions create a productive dialectic rather than a fudged consensus. The intention here is not to assert a conscious Jonsonian tradition but, rather, to consider how thinking about what might constitute 'Jonsonian' theatre sheds new light both on Jonson's theatre and on practitioners whose work is not normally thought of in that way (and some of the playwrights whose work is discussed here do not – or did not – perceive of themselves as 'Jonsonians'). Put in another way, 'How does thinking of them as Jonsonian affect both our reading of them, and our contemporary understanding of the possibilities of Jonson's theatre? The usefulness of such comparisons is in how it allows a modern reader to see Jonson's theatrical methods in contemporary terms.

The decision to focus on the theatre of John Arden, Joe Orton, Peter Barnes, Caryl Churchill and Alan Ayckbourn was made to exemplify the *different* ways in which these playwrights and their plays can be thought of as Jonsonian; and should not be read as indicating a view that these are the modern playwrights whose work most closely resembles Jonson's. The term, at least in this volume, does not imply homogeneity. Arden and Barnes have both acknowledged a considerable debt to Jonson, although that debt is manifest in their plays in diverse ways. Their work may have become rather unfashionable, and these two essays both attempt to redress that balance, arguing that Arden and Barnes have each produced plays whose significance goes far beyond their immediate cultural impact; but that is not the prime concern of either essay. Stephen Lacey argues that Arden's admiration for Jonson's craftsmanship – his complex plots, assured narrative control, use of humour and characterisation – informs our understanding of theatricality and moral purpose in each playwright's work. Brian Woolland discusses the limits and functions of comedy, drawing parallels between Barnes and Jonson in an essay which also considers the way that Barnes's use of montage structure sheds light on some of Jonson's formal theatrical strategies. John Bull's essay on Orton is concerned with issues of narrative closure and the boundaries of farce, relating Jonson and Orton back to Aristophanes, and addressing the question whether each is a moral satirist or an amoral 'realist'. Claudia Manera, on Churchill, is also concerned with boundaries; focusing on the carnivalesque. *Serious Money* has often been termed a modern Jonsonian comedy (and Manera refers to it both directly and to the complex cultural phenomenon surrounding its reception); but her discussion is far more wide ranging, including provocative and challenging discussions of language, the 'grotesque body', social transgression and use of classical sources. In her essay on *The New Inn* and *The Magnetic Lady*, Julie Sanders relates Jonson's evocation of an off-stage social world to Alan Ayckbourn's. Richard Cave's essay on Ayckbourn develops this discussion of theatrical space; but his approach to issues of theatricality is very different to the earlier essays in the volume. Taking as his starting point Peter Hall's assertion that Ayckbourn's farce, *Absurd Person Singular*, is a 'cruel' play, he discusses the meaning and the implications of cruelty in Ayckbourn's work by relating it to the highly problematic notion of *darkness* in Jonson's comedies. After examining intertextuality (as it is referred to by current critical theorists), he returns to the complex problem of moral purpose in satire.

Although the choice of playwrights in this section was far from arbitrary, there are many others that might have been included. Mark Ravenhill's dark urban satires, for example, display a Jonsonian fascination with shifting vocal registers and the metamorphic qualities of language, whilst examining the commodification of human exchange. Whilst the plots of *Shopping and Fucking*[12] and *Some Explicit Polaroids*[13] bear no resemblance to anything in the Jonson canon, the sexual anarchy is prefigured in Jonson's *Epicœne*; and the instability of Ravenhill's tone (which veers between the comic and the shocking) echoes Jonson's. The immense theatrical energy of much of Tony Kushner's work[14] has many Jonsonian characteristics: montage-like structure (*Angels in America*, *Bartholomew Fair*, *Poetaster* and *Every Man in His Humour* can all be thought of as 'fantasias' on a theme); dark humour in the service of socially driven satire; an extraordinarily rich and self-reflexive use of language; the awareness of theatre as an 'educative' force (in the broadest sense); and, again, an acute awareness of the commodification of human relations.

It is tantalising to consider the related fields in which the Jonsonian thrives. Should Swift, Dickens and Joyce, for example, be thought of as Jonsonian? Not only did Swift's *A Tale of a Tub* share the same title as Jonson had used for his play, but the projectors in *Gulliver's Travels* seem to have been schooled by Meercraft and Engine in *The Devil is an Ass*.

There is no doubt that Dickens's characterisation owes a debt to Jonson (in appropriating and developing the tradition of Humours) and Jonson certainly owes a posthumous debt to Dickens, whose revival of *Every Man in His Humour*[15] was referred to regularly in publicity for the rare productions of Jonson's work in the first half of the twentieth century. Christopher Murray[16] has noted the references to Jonson in *Ulysses* and *Dubliners*. But this volume confines itself to theatre, and it is regrettably beyond its scope to consider Jonson's influence on the development of the novel or to examine those forms which can be traced back to the Jacobean and Caroline court masques: ballet, pantomime, opera and, perhaps even companies such as Welfare State International.

This section of the book concludes with my own essay on *Jonsonian Cinema*, for which I acknowledge a debt to Helen Ostovich,[17] who has compared *Bartholomew Fair* to Fellini's *Amarcord* (1974), relating the festive carnival atmosphere of *Amarcord* to *Bartholomew Fair's* brilliant montage structure in order to demonstrate how Jonson attacks authority, hypocrisy and pretentiousness. In doing so, whilst not specifically making this point, she shows how Jonson prefigured the development of cinematic montage, and might well (as I argue in the essay) have indirectly influenced it. The Russian theatre director, Vsevolod Meyerhold, developed the concept of the 'montage of attractions' in collaboration with Sergei Eisenstein (at one time his pupil). In montage, meaning is created as much through juxtapositions as through the individual units of meaning. It is in the spirit of creating meaningful juxtapositions that these essays in the last section of the volume have been written; in the hope that the collisions between Jonson and these diverse modern practitioners will create incendiary sparks, whose effects may not be entirely predictable, but which will, I hope, not only reignite an interest in Jonson's theatre in its own right, but also in his influence on changing and developing theatre forms.

Notes

[1]   In particular I am thinking of *The Alchemist*, directed by Sam Mendes for the RSC (first at the Swan in Stratford-on Avon, and subsequently The Barbican in London); *Bartholomew Fair*, directed by Laurence Boswell, also for the RSC; several productions of *Volpone*, including one by Matthew Warchus for the Royal National Theatre and a radical touring production, adapted and directed by Xavier Leret for Kaos Theatre.

[2]   *Volpone, The Alchemist* and *Bartholomew Fair* are regularly revived. *Epicœne, the Silent Woman*, certainly a 'middle-period' comedy, is, however, less well known in the modern period – although very popular in the seventeenth century. See note 10 below.

3   The RSC has revived *Every Man in His Humour, Epicæne, The Devil is an Ass* and *Eastward Ho!* with considerable success – both critically and at the Box Office.

4   Cambridge University Press recently published a Cambridge Companion to Ben Jonson (2000). The publisher's introduction opens with the following sentence: 'Ben Jonson is, in many ways, the figure of greatest centrality to literary study of the Elizabethan and Jacobean period'.

5   Irving Wardle in *Gambit* (1972, p. 3). This edition of *Gambit* (No. 22) included essays on Jonson and his work by John Arden and Ian Donaldson, and the transcription of a debate between the Gambit editors and Peter Barnes, Colin Blakely (who had recently played Volpone in Tyrone Guthrie's National Theatre production) and Terry Hands (who had directed an RSC revival of *Bartholomew Fair*).

6   Raymond Williams, (1976), *Keywords: A vocabulary of culture and society*, revised and expanded 1983, pp. 318–20.

7   Stephen Orgel, (1981), 'What is a Text?', *Research Opportunities in Renaissance Drama*, 26: 3–6. In this essay, Orgel uses *Sejanus* to demonstrates that even where a playwright has tried to exorcise the spirit of his collaborators, the written text that we receive is the product of collective work.

8   The production was staged for the Old Vic Company at the Edinburgh Festival in 1949, and revived in London the following year. It played to capacity houses in both venues. This is the production that Stephen Lacey refers to in his essay on John Arden (Chapter 10).

9   The RSC production of *The New Inn* was first performed at The Swan Theatre, Stratford on Avon, 4 November 1987. It was directed by John Caird.

10 Although William Poel's 1916 revivals of *Poetaster* were seen in London, Pittsburg and Detroit, he was working with amateur and student casts. Details of the 1996 revival of *The Magnetic Lady* at the University of Reading can be found in Richard Cave, Elizabeth Schafer, and Brian Woolland, (1999) *Ben Jonson and Theatre*, pp. 130–35. The play was also revived at the University of Bristol in 2001. Details of semi-professional and amateur revivals of *Sejanus* – it has not been revived in a fully realised professional production since the seventeenth century – can be found in Chapter 3.

11 It is likely that *Epicæne* was the first play to be performed after the reopening of the theatres following the Restoration in 1660, when Pepys saw it many times, once referring to it in his diary as 'the best comedy, I think, that was ever wrote' (see also p. 107 of this volume). At least forty-two performances are recorded between 1711 and 1748; Dryden thought of as 'the greatest and most noble of any pure unmixed comedy in any language'. *Epicæne* became the prime model for Restoration comedy, for which it provides the prototypes of numerous characters: in Congreve's *The Old Bachelor*, Heartwell is based on Morose, Haughty and the Collegiates are the models for Lady Fidget and her companions in Wycherley's *The Country Wife*, Farquhar used La Foole as his model for Captain Brazen in *The Recruiting Officer*; and the descendants of Truewit, the dashing young gallant who is not quite as alert as he thinks himself to be, can be found throughout Restoration comedy. For specific discussion of the relationship between *Epicæne* and Restoration comedy see J.B. Bamborough, (1970) *Ben Jonson*, pp. 93–5. *Bartholomew Fair* was revived with great regularity from 1661 to 1731; *The Alchemist* and *Volpone* were also very popular and influential in this period. For detailed stage histories, see Herford and the Simpsons (1950), Volume IX.

12 *Shopping and Fucking* (or *Shopping and ****ing* as it was billed on its first national tour) was first produced by Out of Joint Theatre Company in association with the Royal

Court Theatre, directed by Max Stafford-Clark. It was premiered at the Royal Court
Theatre Upstairs in September 1996. It is published (1996) by Methuen, London.

[13] *Some Explicit Polaroids* was first produced in 1999 by Out of Joint Theatre Company,
directed by Max Stafford-Clark. It is published (1999) by Methuen, London.

[14] Here I am thinking particularly of Kushner's *Angels in America, Hydriotaphia, Slavs!*
and *Homebody / Kabul.*

[15] In 1847 Charles Dickens revived *Every Man in His Humour* (with an amateur cast) for
the benefit of Leigh Hunt. The production was so successful that it was mounted again,
this time at the Theatre Royal, Haymarket, London. Charles Dickens played Bobadil and
Dickens's brothers, Frederick and Augustus, Young Knowell and Thomas Cash
respectively. There is a certain irony in the fact that the Theatre Royal revival was in aid
of a fund to endow the curatorship of Shakespeare's house in Stratford.

[16] Christopher Murray gave a paper at the *Ben Jonson and the Theatre* Conference held at
Reading University in 1996 entitled *Teaching Jonson in University College, Dublin.* He
talked about introducing his students to Jonson (with whose work they would be totally
unfamiliar) by noting some of the various references and allusions to Jonson in the work
of James Joyce. 'For Joyce as for Jonson', he noted in one of several examples,
'Character is defined and discriminated by the choice of words employed, whether
voiced publicly or internalised. The opening of *Ulysses*, where Buck Mulligan parodies
the opening of the Mass as he bids good morrow to the day with his shaving bowl on the
roof of the Martello Tower at Sandycove invites direct comparison with the opening
scene of *Volpone*.' See also: Richard Cave, Elizabeth Schafer, and Brian Woolland
(1999), *Ben Jonson and Theatre*, p. 127, 135n. 1, 204n. 10.

[17] In her essay on *Bartholomew Fair*, Helen Ostovich writes: 'If Jonson had written the
play 360 years later, it might have become a shooting script for Fellini, whose *Amarcord*
(1974) relies on a similarly panoramic pastiche of intertwining lives.... In its treatment of
place as magic space, Jonson's play also resembles Victor Fleming's film *The Wizard of
Oz* (1939).' Ostovich (1997a), p. 43.

Part I

Jonsonian Theatre

Chapter 2

Poetaster:
Jonson and his Audience

Richard A. Cave

The most distinctive Jonsonian quality about *Poetaster* is the playwright's characteristic awareness of the precise audience for which he was creating his drama. Because the play is fundamentally about representation and reception, inevitably that audience has a defined role to play in the proceedings. Representation is bound up with questions of artistic conventions within a given medium; and those same conventions when too firmly rooted in an audience's expectations can become limiting determinants of their modes of reception, leading to slack judgements of the work being observed. Representation risks, therefore, being culturally determined. Jonson in *Poetaster* devises strategies to make spectators think deeply about why they are present in a theatre engaging in a performance (playgoing for Jonson is never a simple matter of being entertained). But more questions accrue around this central issue. What are spectators' exact expectations of a play? What precisely motivates their laughter (since this is a comedy) and how would they define the *tone* of that vocal response? What function does drama as an art form serve in their daily lives? To what degree might they describe themselves as culturally conditioned? These might seem very cerebral lines of enquiry about the activity of merely sitting at a play, but Jonson was writing in this particular instance for a highly educated audience. The likely composition of that audience in large measure determined the *cultural* questioning at the heart of this play (rather than the preoccupations with gender, morality or class, which fuel Jonson's later comedies).

Poetaster was written for performance at the Blackfriars Theatre in 1601 by the company known as the Chapel Children, a troupe of boy actors under the management of Henry Evans.[1] The Blackfriars being an indoor theatre was more costly to enter than the open-air theatres on Bankside (prices ranged from 6d for basic entry to the galleries to 2s 6d for a box). This inevitably made for a wealthy, upper-class clientele, which included a sizeable proportion of members of the Inns of Court. Given the tenor of much of the repertory designed for performance at the venue, it is safe to suppose the theatre attracted spectators with some refinement of taste, a good education and a developed knowledge of contemporary theatrical culture. The company had its rivals, not only amongst the adult troupes on Bankside, but also, and more importantly, a second company of boys based in the precinct at St. Paul's, which, in being again relatively expensive to attend, attracted audiences of a similar composition: learned, informed, culturally aware. The two companies of boy players were quick to turn the potential for rivalry to profit. Satire that was topical and increasingly hard-hitting became their staple fare, often directed at each other's repertory. That they prospered with such a line of business argues *knowing* audiences, quick to interpret the significance of what was offered. Over a period the satire turned inward as with the Poetomachia or 'War of the Poets' when what one might term the 'house' dramatists of the rival establishments began to lampoon one another. They ridiculed each other's dramaturgy, styles of expression and (in time) social, moral and literary standing, as cultural critique elided subtly with personal abuse. Jonson, as sole champion of the Blackfriars troupe, was in the thick of the fray with, interestingly, two one-time collaborators, Marston and Dekker, his opponents. (They appear thinly disguised as Crispinus and Demetrius in *Poetaster*, where Jonson presents himself in the role of Horace, victim of their scandal-mongering and abuse.) Clearly audiences relished the animus and scandal involved until the authorities put a stop to the unseemly wrangling, after the Paul's staging of Dekker's *Satiromastix* late in 1601. But though *Poetaster* was one skirmish in the ongoing battle, it emerges from a study of all the various works contributed to the 'war' by Jonson and his rivals as more than animated lambasting. Despite its rapid fifteen-week composition (surprising for Jonson, who tended to labour diligently over his plays) it is nothing less than a studied defence of the art of theatre when it fulfils certain cultural conditions. There is a high seriousness to this comedy (his detractors doubtless found Jonson's agenda pretentious). That seriousness anticipates the confidence with which Jonson collected and edited his plays and published them in 1616 as his *Works* in frank imitation of the way that plays of the classical dramatists were currently made available, anthologised in collected editions. What is *different* about this play is established right from the start and Jonson devised a characteristically challenging strategy to make his spectators sit up and take due note.

Beginnings or Inductions are often a tease in Jonson's plays, putting one on one's mettle; and *Poetaster* is one such.[2] Before the sounding of the third trumpet which conventionally preceded the start of a play, a hideous figure erupts up onto the stage from the central trap; it is Envy, whose speech quickly exposes how she is as monstrous within as her appearance without. She begins to tempt the audience to consume the snakes that deck her head and arms and so take on her characteristics and ways; but her bold, confrontational stance is discomfited on discovering where the play is set: Rome. Three times she repeats the word with mounting exasperation and horror. Till now the plays within the poets' war had been situated in the here and now to make the satire immediately accessible; but, given the Roman location, Envy cannot determine what Jonson is doing. Frustrated, she seeks to depart but cannot descend through the trap before the Prologue arrives with the sounding of the third trumpet. He is armed (the image is of his playing Perseus to her Medusa) and forces her to bow her head beneath his foot: the stage picture forms the traditional icon or emblem representing Victory over Evil. It is a strange start to the play, juxtaposing time past (Rome) with time present (the device of the prologue and its embodiment in the armed actor; the theatre audience who are consciously addressed as such; the expectations that Envy has of the drama). This double prologue is wholly unexpected and yet in allegorical terms it contains the germ of the drama that is to follow, while in that final triumphant image it anticipates the play's actual conclusion.[3] Though initially a surprise, this beginning in retrospect seems wholly appropriate. Most importantly, Envy's shocked perception that this play is to be *classical* prepares the audience for a play in which the satire can be appreciated only by reading modern experience in the light of ancient precedents. It is the Roman emphasis, which indicates Jonson's high seriousness.

This is the first of three Jonsonian plays with Roman settings, but *Poetaster* carries its wealth of classical knowledge with an effortless wit and brilliance whereas in the tragedies, *Sejanus* and *Catiline*, the learning which underpins the drama is more self-consciously on display. To read the notes to their edition offered by Herford and the Simpsons is to realise how virtually all the situations and characters in *Poetaster* have a precise classical source.[4] Horace's encounter with the boring and boorish Crispinus (III.i–iii) derives from the Roman poet's *Satires* (I.ix), while Ovid's poem that challengingly opens with an address to Envy (I.i.43–84) is based on Christopher Marlowe's translation of *Amores* (I.xv). The emetic to purge Crispinus of his clumsy, infelicitous diction (V.iii) is modelled on Lucian's *Lexiphanes*. The banquet where mortals impersonate the gods is adapted from Suetonius's *Augustus* (70) where the emperor as Apollo (and not Ovid as Jupiter) initiates and presides over what is a markedly aristocratic event. Virgil (V.ii.56–97) recites from his *Aeneid* (IV.160–88) in Jonson's translation, while his modesty about his masterpiece, as voiced in this scene, decorously refers to his known wish expressed in dying that the poem should be burnt, since he had not fully revised it. Many of the speeches assigned to Horace carry glancing echoes and resonances of his poems, mostly from the *Satires*. Augustus, Maecenas, Horace, the Ovids (father and son), Gallus, Propertius, Aristius, Hermogenes, Tibullus, Aesop the tragedian, Julia, Cytheris (Lycoris) and Plautia (Delia): all have their place in Roman political, literary and cultural history. So too do even Laberius Crispinus and Demetrius Fannius, but they are clever Jonsonian compounds linking in two characters the names of four feeble artists, whom Horace and his contemporaries refer to with acid contempt. Significantly, this leaves only the characters that populate the underbelly of Roman society in the play (Albius, Minos, Histrio, the Pyrgi, Lupus, Tucca and Chloe) as wholly of Jonson's invention.

With the notable exception of the two hack writers, the known classical figures all inhabit a precise decorum in their lifestyles and expression: it is generous, genteel and gracious, eloquent, considerate and urbane. And it is above snobbery or envy, though not above judgement when the values making for that decorum are set at risk. Much of the comedy arises from situations where that serene tone is disrupted. (Structurally these episodes imitate the pattern that occurred in the play's beginning, when the confident, open-minded relations normally established between Prologue and audience were forestalled and challenged by the arrival of Envy hectoring and insisting that spectators take on her vicious, closed opinions.) Ovid Senior (I.ii) has no time for his son's versifying and insists he get down to his legal studies, think about his future career and strive to make a name for himself (which is ironic from a modern perspective, given Ovid's eminence among Latin poets). Caesar's repose is continually being invaded by Lupus bringing warnings of ever more heinous threats to Augustus's state and person yet his stupidity and officiousness are the prime force for social disruption in each case. Two more complex episodes need fuller exploration.

In the first three scenes of Act Three Horace is beset by the tedious Crispinus, who cannot take a politely phrased hint to be gone but hangs in there like a ferret in pursuit of game. Poor Horace is seriously discommoded, but to our amusement cannot bring himself to be downright rude. Even when abandoned by his friend, Aristius, who thinks the set-up a huge joke, Horace never loses touch with what is here proved an innate decorum: for all his frantic asides, he never *openly* loses his 'cool', however forcefully his dignity is assailed. The scene does much to humanise Horace and the decorum he represents; but Jonson uses the episode also to dissect Crispinus's shortcomings with a rare precision through the sharply contrasting verbal registers of the two men. Jonson's ear for an appropriate register exactly to sum up and *place* a character is unerring in its invention (it is one of the recurring excellences of his dramatic craftsmanship that his characters *live* in a spectator's or reader's imagination with great immediacy through the medium of their diction). This scene is exemplary of his skill, particularly when Crispinus manipulates the conversation till it engages with the issue of patronage (a subject dear to the ever-impoverished Jonson's heart):

CRISPINUS And how deals Maecenas[5] with thee? liberally, ha? Is he open-handed? Bountiful?

HORACE He's still himself, sir.

CRISPINUS Troth, Horace, thou art exceeding happy in thy friends and acquaintance; they are all most choice spirits, and of the first rank of Romans: I do not know that poet, I protest, has used his fortune more prosperously than thou hast. If thou wouldst bring me known to Maecenas, I should second thy desert well. Thou shouldst find a good sure assistant of me, one that would speak all good of thee in thy absence, and be content with the next place, not envying thy reputation with thy patron. Let me not live, but I think thou and I, in a small time, should lift them all out of favour, both Virgil, Varius, and the best of them: and enjoy him wholly to ourselves.

(III.i.228–242)

Crispinus's verbosity in marked contrast to Horace's dry succinctness makes immediately apparent their wholly different value-systems: the one crudely mercenary and divisive, the other appreciative, respectful, honest. There is no hint of flattery about Horace's depiction of Maecenas as 'still himself' and, though it is not in fact judgmental as uttered, the observation exposes the distinct want of self-knowledge in Crispinus. He stands revealed as one so wrapped up in his own self-importance that he does not *listen* to Horace's reply; if he had, he would know how totally out of place are his proposed machinations to influence Maecenas's affections and purse. The longer Crispinus stays with Horace, the more his inherent vulgarity stands revealed. His own verbal posturing shows he has no place where decorum rules and where verbal felicity is the mark of a cultivated moral scruple. Though Horace is challenged by the deliberately prolonged comedy of the scene, ultimately the values he represents go unscathed. That Crispinus's punishment eventually is to be made to vomit forth his tortured diction is poetic justice in every sense of the term: mouth, mind and morals need a rigorous disinfectant. As Peter Womack wryly observes: '...the insistence on the materiality of the signifier could hardly be more negative'.[6] He is referring to the emetic scene, but the comment could equally well be applied to all of Crispinus's diction and the underlying intention behind his speech. Whether he is addressing Chloe, a married woman for whom he conceives a poetical passion, discussing Horace's standing with his patron, writing songs or satire, Crispinus focuses only on himself, his physical needs, his reputation, his envy of artists better than himself. His motives for writing are wholly material and grounded in vaunting expression of his own ego; writing is invariably a means to an end concerning his (misplaced) sense of his own worth, status and quest for power. There is nothing celebratory or generous, nothing socially or morally perceptive about his utterance as there is about Horace's or Virgil's at their every appearance: the style is as self-conscious and self-centred as the man.

The second episode deserving close attention, Caesar's disruption of Ovid's banquet of the gods (IV.v–vi), is more intricate. Till now the pattern since the clash of Envy and the Prologue has been for authority to be challenged by some unexpected subversive force; here it is authority with armed support, which bursts into Ovid and Julia's party, dispenses a seemingly harsh justice and dispels the prevailing mirth. It is a display of the power of absolute rule. The episode is the more startling for anyone familiar with Jonson's source, since in Suetonius's account it is Augustus himself who on a whim commands such a banquet, though the diners partaking in the charade are notably different from Ovid's guests.[7] But the fact of that *difference* is a characteristic Jonsonian strategy; it invites a spectator to ponder the likely thematic purpose underlying the change. Noticeably though Caesar generally respects the opinions of the likes of Maecenas and Horace, he here firmly rejects their plea that he show mercy and magnanimity to Ovid and Julia. Horace later describes the feast and the diners' impersonation of the gods as 'innocent mirth /And harmless pleasures, bred of noble wit' (IV.viii.12–13). But this seems more aptly to describe Caesar's banquet as recounted in Suetonius than Ovid and Julia's enterprise: a flight of imperial fancy offering temporary respite from the responsibilities of rule. Horace would seem to be judging by the outward show (the jolly jape of mortals dressing up as gods) but the audience knows that the party has a more particular agenda. From the first Ovid as Jupiter ordains how 'It shall be lawful for every lover – To break loving oaths – To change their lovers, and make love to others, – As the heat of every one's blood – And the spirit of our nectar shall inspire' (IV.v.31–35). And several of the guests present are quick to seize the opportunity to indulge in covert wife-swapping or at least in making overtures with that aim in mind.

Donning costumes to act a role becomes, for the likes of Tucca and Chloe, an excuse to throw aside restraint: acting paradoxically reveals them for what they truly are.[8] Several poets like Gallus and Tibullus use the situation to pay court in fleshly earnest to lovers they have previously idealised in their verses. Strangely, Ovid and Julia, though finally in each other's company, stay firmly within the prescriptions of their roles as Jupiter and Juno and sustain a jealous wrangling, threatening each other with dire punishments because she dares to criticise his philandering. For passionate lovers, this is a perverse tone to pursue.[9] The awesome majesty of the gods as shapers of destiny is forgotten at this banquet; instead they are represented as temperamental, unprincipled or creatures of unbridled lust. The whole carnival is threatening to get wildly out of control just as Augustus makes his entrance.

What impresses next is how, despite his rage and the summary justice he dispenses, Augustus makes subtle discriminations between the various offenders. Tucca and his page are allowed to slink away, while Albius, Chloe and Crispinus (the remaining lower-life characters), once they have identified themselves, are ignored as beneath his contempt. Gallus and Tibullus will in time be restored to Caesar's favour. Sentence is reserved for the architects of the affray: Julia is imprisoned because, by her impious behaviour in reducing Juno to a wanton 'cotquean' and by consorting freely with the underworld of Roman society to give rein to her pleasures, she is undermining her father's authority. Ovid is exiled for the abuse of his imagination as poet in devising this rout. Augustus has a high regard for poets (as is manifest throughout the play) but poets who are worthy of their calling; and Ovid has no conception, seemingly, of poetry serving any function but the expression of personal romantic ardour. Like Crispinus, Ovid is the victim of his own high self-regard. Jonson has devised a series of linked strategies (involving Ovid, Horace, Maecenas, Virgil and Crispinus) throughout the play but centring on this episode which demonstrate his understanding of what is required of one in the vocation of poet, as classical Rome determined that office. (Virgil's reception by Augustus (V.i–ii) makes it clear that for the emperor poetry rightly pursued is to be deemed an office of the state.)

What Jonson has achieved through the pattern of comic or serious disruptions in these scenes is a meticulous and lengthy dramatisation of that defence of poetry, which earlier he ardently voiced as *statement* through the character of Lorenzo Junior in the first version of *Every Man in His Humour* (acted 1598). Lorenzo, called upon by his father and Doctor Clement to justify his constant versifying, carefully distinguishes between 'brainless gulls' who 'utter their stol'n wares' and 'a true poet; than which reverend name / Nothing can more adorn humanity'(V.iii.318–325).[10] In *Poetaster* Jonson is taking an idea briefly expressed in the closing moments of the earlier drama and making it the whole subject of his new work. That he rendered the writing of poetry fit material for theatrical representation is made possible by his working with classical Latin examples, which illustrate his belief that the particular quality of a poem is reflective of the particular mind that conceived and composed it. Framing experience in judiciously chosen diction is a *self*-revealing art, exposing the ideological, aesthetic and moral dimensions of a poet's mind-set. Poetry by this means becomes a direct exposition of *character*, on which drama is founded. None of this would have been possible, however, but for the precise, educated audience, which Jonson could expect at a performance by a company of boy players. To appreciate its subtlest effects, the play invites spectators who are *in the know*; but, typical of Jonson, the result both flatters and challenges their specialist knowledge. His audience cannot sit back, confident in their superior insight: they are required to observe and judge. Jonson would appear to be demonstrating to his audience how there are responsibilities, which must accompany a classical education. If (to use T.S. Eliot's terms) one sees oneself as inheriting a classical tradition, then one must accommodate one's individual talent to its particular values.[11] Closely bound up with this conception is the whole issue of translation and plagiarism, which is voiced sufficiently often within the drama to draw attention to it as of urgent relevance.

The representation in the Elizabethan theatre of figures that peopled Augustan Rome is in itself a kind of translation, particularly when, as in all the episodes just discussed, there are literary or recorded historical precedents for the action now staged. Horace is indicted by his rivals, Crispinus and Demetrius, of treason, which is easily refuted, and of plagiarism, a more subtle accusation to resist. As Horace is presented very much as an alter ego for Jonson within the play and Jonson is presenting the poetry of Ovid, Horace and Virgil in translation by himself and others, the issue of plagiarism is acute. But there is a distinction to be drawn here. Whereas Crispinus tries (IV.iii.) to pass off a poem of Horace's as his own work ('Why, the ditty's all borrowed; 'tis Horace's: hang him, plagiary!'), Jonson offers translations of the works of Latin writers but in contexts where it is clear to anyone with or without a classical training who precisely the originating authors are. Translation is not plagiarism but a means of representing a work of literary art in another language and as such it is an act not of wilful appropriation but of respect. This is equally true when Jonson, in offering Ovid's poem, 'Envy, why twit'st thou me my time's spent ill' (I.i.43–84), deploys Marlowe's translation of *Amores* (I.xv) but incorporating over thirty emendations of his own. Jonson is refining a known translation the better to make it a fit and felicitous representation of Ovid's excellence. Jonson is not here traducing or plagiarising Marlowe in offering 'improvements' to his text, rather he is acknowledging for the alert audience that they are all (Ovid, Marlowe, Jonson, the educated spectator) part of an inherited and shared, cultural tradition, which embraces ancient and modern modes of expression. Throughout the play and by diverse means Jonson, chiefly through his dramatising himself as Horace, shows the extent to which he *inhabits* that culture, especially in the act of creativity as poet and dramatist. There is nothing snobbish, vainglorious or pretentious about the claim (though his detractors were subsequently to argue otherwise in *Satiromastix*). Jonson is cogently arguing that, if socially the Elizabethan era vaunts the excellence of a classical education, then the values of that educational system should inform, shape and to a large degree determine the age's thinking, expression and behaviour. What is remarkable is that Jonson, by deliberately exploiting the particular audience present at a performance of his play, can render such a complex of ideas as engaging *theatre*. Though *Poetaster* is full of lively and varied comic incident, that action continually expounds and develops the inner thematic life of the drama, shaping it to achieve an organic unity. (Jonson's control over his inventive powers in structuring the play is exemplary.) It is here that the low-life scenes are seen to have their relevance as more than comic contrast.

Several of the characters that people the low-life scenes such as Lupus, Albius and Chloe, while nicely characterised and a source of some social comedy, exist primarily to advance the plot. Crispinus and Demetrius are poet-dramatists who consort with the actor, Histrio, and the soldierly backbiting parasite, Tucca. All four are the means whereby a wealth of allusions to contemporary Elizabethan writing enters the text, though only to be weighed in the balance with Latin culture and found distinctly wanting. Marston and Dekker (as Crispinus and Demetrius) are parodied; their styles and temperaments are deconstructed and held up to question as wanting in a fundamental decorum. Dekker is dismissed as a mere hack and made to wear the motley suit of a fool. Marston, as an educated man who needs properly to learn the value of what he has been taught, is believed to be capable of reformation, if his 'purging' has its desired effect. As one who, given his background, ought to know better, he is to be allowed a second chance. (As with the judgements meted out to the participants at Ovid's banquet, Jonson takes care invariably to discriminate between degrees of blame.) Dekker's verse is graceless doggerel, his satire lacking in acuity and his sense of metrical scansion crude:

And, but that I would not be thought a prater,
I could tell you he were a translator.
I know the authors from whence he has stole,
And could trace him too, but that I understand 'em not full and whole.

(V.iii.304–7)

Marston's verse is ruined by its pretentiously over-wrought style; it is all self-conscious artiness, quite devoid of matter:

Ramp up my genius, be not retrograde,
But boldly nominate a spade a spade.
What, shall thy lubrical and glibbery muse
Live, as she were defunct, like punk in stews?

(V.iii.269–272)

Beside the Latin poets whose works, quoted in the play, have a clarity and immediacy, despite their age, these lines are either obscure or dim-witted and decidedly wanting in taste. By the *sound* of their verse alone, Marston and Dekker stand judged as inferior.

Both poets, however, have pretensions to be playwrights (Jonson chooses to ignore Marston and Dekker's established careers) and their scene with Tucca and Histrio allows him to make considerable fun of contemporary popular tastes in theatre. Tucca is served by two bright, cheeky pages (the Pyrgi), who have got the measure of their master and his various tricks to gull the men he preys on of their cash. They immediately would call to mind for an audience (especially in the context of performances like this of a company of boy players) the pairs of pages that often appear in Lyly's plays to afford a measure of earthy comedy. A couple of such likely lads turn up, for example, in *Endymion* (1588), making fun of the old man whom they serve and acting generally as the sharp voice of satire in the drama. Though Tucca's pages criticise him, he exploits them for his private gain, offering them to Histrio as valuable additions to his troupe. To prove his point, Tucca has the lads perform for the actor, Crispinus and Demetrius. What they choose to act is a series of recognisable snippets from the popular early Elizabethan repertoire (Preston, Kyd, Peele, and Chapman), mostly from plays that were still regularly revived by companies like the Admiral's at the Rose. Beside Jonson's own dialogue, the speeches (though delivered with relish) seem like so much melodramatic fustian. These lads have the energy of Lyly's pages, but none of their critical powers. The irony in all this would not be lost on Jonson's audience. Lyly was associated for much of his career with the boy players situated at St. Paul's as (amongst other functions) their house-dramatist, the situation a decade later now occupied by Marston and Dekker. Lyly had been the great innovator of courtly, romantic comedy but he had continually found a place in his work for a critique of uncourtly, anti social or downright foolish behaviour. He, in other words, had a sure sense of that aesthetic and social decorum which his successors are consistently shown to lack. Within the tradition of Elizabethan playwriting they are seen to stand in need of a proper talent:

> Detraction is but baseness, varlet,
> And apes are apes, though clothed in scarlet.
>
> (V.iii.315–6)[12]

Jonson's later plays explore manifestations of evil in society, political expediency, obsessive materialism and power-hunger rather than questions of cultural excellence. But, as Anne Barton has shown, most of Jonson's plays demonstrate an acute awareness of what is currently fashionable in theatrical taste and his own works engage in constant critical dialogue with dramatic conventions and popular subjects which he finds morally dubious.[13] *Poetaster* is the play in which Jonson establishes the high standards by which he thought contemporary literature and drama should be judged, including his own endeavours; and the standards which should determine spectators' response to performance. In retrospect it appears a seminal work for a number of reasons. *Poetaster* shows Jonson devising dramatic strategies to encourage an audience not only to experience a theatricalised world but also to meditate upon that world and to discriminate its strengths and limitations. The strategies were to grow more subtle and insinuating but Jonson's agenda respecting the ideal reception of his plays remained constant. Caesar's abrupt, thrilling and authoritative dispelling of the riotous carnival that is Ovid's banquet set a pattern that recurs in the Court Masques whenever the unruly forces of the anti-masque need quelling. Though Jonson was not for some years to give an uncontested voice to authority in his plays (except in the Masques), he did return to that tone of absolute command over the self with Lovel's disquisition on the nature of love in *The New Inn*.

However the one character in *Poetaster* who really heralds the way in which Jonson's comic invention was to thrive is Captain Tucca. Jonson had previously explored the *miles gloriosus*, the braggart soldier of Roman comedy, with Bobadil in *Every Man in His Humour* (1598), whose verbal threats vaunt a prowess he cannot sustain physically. But though Tucca possesses many of the verbal characteristics of his predecessor, he is altogether a darker creation, chiefly because Jonson chooses to blend into one individual qualities of both the braggart soldier and that other recurring type in Latin comedy, the parasite (a term that he interprets in its most pernicious manifestation). As a result Tucca is a complex figure, in many ways the most complex in the comedy: he can manipulate anyone into giving him cash; he can malign people who are absent and be sickeningly sycophantic of people in his presence; he attempts to seduce Chloe, familiarly calling her his 'punk', in her husband's house (IV.iii); he rips off Maecenas's chain of office in front of Augustus, when he thinks he has evidence that Maecenas and Horace are traitors, and later he inveigles himself on to the panel of judges at the poetasters' trial in an effort to swing matters in their favour (V.iii). Throughout he acts as if he is above the law, a source of riot not only in himself but through others whom he inspires. Were Tucca only characterised in these terms, he would be easy to place morally. However Jonson makes him a challenge for spectators: he offsets these disturbing qualities by endowing Tucca with huge resources of energy, verbal and physical. Tucca is irrepressibly loquacious, never at a loss for words; and he continually reinvents himself, usually to save his neck in difficult situations. All in all (and unlike Bobadil), he has the makings of a crafty shape-changer, and as such he anticipates those more brilliant adepts at the art: Tiberius, Mosca, Face, Quarlous and Meercraft. It is in these characters who, living precariously by their wits, both delight and disturb that Jonson next positioned his test of a spectator's sensibilities; but the test now was moral not cultural. The change signified a different audience, socially more complex in its composition, less uniform in its trained tastes. That change exemplifies precisely why it is right to judge as characteristically Jonsonian the playwright's awareness of the specific audience for which he was creating a particular drama. All Jonson's finest plays problematise the issue of their proper reception.

Notes

[1] I am indebted for information about the companies of boy players, their performance history and repertory to Andrew Gurr (1970), *The Shakespearean Stage*, Cambridge University Press, Cambridge; and Reavley Gair (1982), *The Children of Paul's: The Story of a Theatre Company*, Cambridge University Press, Cambridge.

[2] Ben Jonson, *Poetaster*, ed. Tom Cain (1995), The Revels Plays, Manchester University Press, Manchester and New York. All references in the text are to this edition.

[3] Most of Jonson's Inductions draw attention to the organising theme of the ensuing play in this way. Interestingly, *Bartholomew Fair* also confronts audience expectation and issues of judgement respecting the dramatic conventions surrounding stage realism.

[4] See C.H. Herford, P. Simpson and E. Simpson (eds) (1925–52), *Ben Jonson*, Clarendon Press, Oxford. Volume IX (1950), pp. 533–85.

[5] Jonson spells the name of Horace's patron as 'Mecoenas'. Cain in his edition for The Revels Plays, which is cited here, prefers the more traditional spelling of 'Maecenas'.

[6] Peter Womack, *Ben Jonson* (1986), Basil Blackwell, Oxford and New York. p. 101.

[7] Suetonius's account of the banquet or 'Feast of the Divine Twelve' is morally ambiguous. The incident is presented at first satirically but what is stressed is less the impiety of the event than that it caused an outrage for its ostentatious prodigality, since Rome was undergoing a food shortage at the time. But the matter is included within a listing of Augustus's defects as expressed by some critics at the time. Characteristically Suetonius then offsets this negative view by stressing how Augustus disproved many of the accusations made against him on moral grounds and how in many ways the emperor led an exemplary (even Spartan) life-style. Confronted by conflicting evidence, it is Suetonius's method to lay out all the facts as he received them and leave his reader to make the final judgement. Augustus's harsh treatment of his daughter, Julia, is repeated frequently throughout Suetonius's account of Caesar's life: she was exiled to an island prison for much of her life for what Augustus deemed gross immoral conduct. Suetonius may also have provided Jonson with details of the lives of Virgil and Horace, through the fragments that survive of another work, *Illustrious Writers*.

[8] This is a recurring theme in Jonson's comedies both for ill and good ends. It is perhaps seen at its most challenging in the dressing up of Pru, the waiting-maid, in *The New Inn* as Queen of the Revels, a role which allows her to reveal depths of integrity and political astuteness.

[9] For all their vaunted passion and longing to be in each other's company, we never see and hear Ovid and Julia in a truly romantic encounter. Their final scene after Caesar has passed judgement on them has a curiously edgy tone: even though it echoes Romeo and Juliet's balcony scene and the later scene of their parting after their wedding night, the sequence never rises to any emotional height. Indeed the spatial appearance of the scene with her situated on high at a window in her prison and he below in the street serves to emphasise the social and class differences which occasion Caesar's anger. The uncertain tone can be played as if grief at parting is awakening each of them to a sense of responsibility. But Jonson never dramatises their relationship as *loving*. Given the context of dressing up and acting that prevails at the banquet, the lasting impression is that for both Ovid and Julia passion is a pose, a charade, a performance rather than an experience of deep-rooted feeling.

[10] Ben Jonson, *Every Man in His Humour: A Parallel-Text Edition of the 1601 Quarto and the 1616 Folio*, ed. J.W. Lever, Regents Renaissance Drama Series (1972), Edward Arnold, London.

[11] It might be argued that it is an elitist audience that Jonson is writing for and, given the precise circumstances of the initial performances, that is true. Much of my argument in this section of the essay is influenced by participating in a workshop conducted by Michael Walling with actors from Border Crossings Theatre Company at a conference on 'Ben Jonson and the Theatre' held at the University of Reading in January 1996. The audience found the actors' performances hugely funny and entertaining. On this occasion that audience was composed of theatre practitioners, students and academics, who together possessed trained responses to drama in performance and to the study of Jonson's plays, even if they had not experienced the classical education that might be

supposed in most of the original spectators. They were an elite of a kind, but crucially they shared an open mind towards what the play might offer.

[12] Throughout the summer of 1906 the poet W.B. Yeats read Jonson's work extensively while staying at Coole Park. That his reading included *Poetaster* is evident from a letter he wrote to his publisher, A.H. Bullen, who was also a Renaissance scholar of some distinction. The letter, dated 21 September, 1906, informs Bullen how Yeats is 'deep in Ben Jonson' and how he is anxious to acquire a copy of *Satiromastix*, since he is contemplating writing an essay 'upon the ideal of life that flitted before the imagination of Jonson and the others when they thought of the Court'. He wonders whether 'Jonson meant Shakespeare not Chapman by the character of Virgil' and asks how he might research information about the dedicatees of Jonson's plays and the ladies 'one lights upon' in the Masques. The terse epigrammatic couplets with which *Poetaster* concludes may have continued to resonate in Yeats's imagination since similar qualities begin to characterise many of the poems printed in *From 'The Green Helmet' and Other Poems* (1910) and *Responsibilities* (1914). These were poems composed when Yeats found himself, several of his friends and many of his aesthetic, political and social values objects of detraction by his enemies and sought in himself to find forgiveness, though 'all my priceless things / Are but a post the passing dogs defile'. Reading Jonson's *Poetaster* may have influenced his revisions at this time to his play *The King's Threshold* in which a poet, Seanchan, goes on hunger-strike in protest against King Guaire's decision to deprive poets of their right to a seat on the governing council of his kingdom. Poets have a central place in Augustus's court as portrayed by Jonson, which may have been why Yeats considered writing about how Renaissance poets conceived of court life and their place within it. Yeats had his problems with the nationalist movements in Ireland, particularly over their rather limited conception of the role of art and the artist in helping forge an independent Irish state. Jonson's art offered Yeats the kind of useful precedent that classical literature had afforded Jonson.

[13] See Anne Barton (1984), *Ben Jonson, Dramatist*, Cambridge University Press, Cambridge. Barton examines many of the plays staged in the same period as Jonson's various works, showing the extent to which he engaged in dialogue with other dramatists and their literary and social values. Jonson emerges from her study as a dramatist both decidedly of his age and yet, viewed from a different perspective, a writer who was independently minded.

Chapter 3

Sejanus his Fall:
Does Arruntius Cry at Night?

Brian Woolland

During rehearsals for a workshop production of *Sejanus* at the University of Reading[1] the student actor playing Arruntius[2] asked: 'Does Arruntius cry at night?' The question might have been slightly mischievous, and it certainly provided a very welcome moment of light relief, but it is more than a whimsically inappropriate musing about the actions of a character outside the fictional world of the play (along the lines of 'How many children and/or miscarriages had Lady Macbeth?') for it gets at crucial issues relating to the theatrical realisation of *Sejanus*: how does the play explore Arruntius's state of mind and how does this, in turn, relate to the state of Rome. The question is useful, moreover, because it encourages a shift in emphasis away from Sejanus and those in positions of power towards those on the margins of this profoundly corrupt society, towards those affected by the power struggles of those at the top of the hierarchy. *Volpone* and *Sejanus* are frequently thought of as closely related; the central characters are equally self-obsessed and determined to push themselves to the very limits of their powers. Of all Jonson's extant plays, however, only *Sejanus his Fall*, *Catiline his Conspiracy* and *Volpone* boast eponymous central protagonists;[3] the more characteristic Jonsonian strategy is to focus on the activities of social groups. That these groups are frequently socially incohesive and fragmented is an essential part of the Jonsonian dramatic project. I will argue in this essay that one of the most significant Jonsonian characteristics of *Sejanus* is that it, too, is as interested in the social and political environment as it is in the man himself.

For a play which has been performed so rarely, *Sejanus* has attracted a considerable amount of critical attention. That criticism has, unsurprisingly, tended to focus on the rise and fall of Sejanus himself and on the Machiavellian subterfuges of Tiberius. This approach has been immensely useful in developing our understanding of Jonson's complex analysis of the workings of state power.[4] In this essay, however, I do not propose to explore those aspects of the play which have received close attention elsewhere, nor to attempt to emulate Herford and the Simpsons, whose superb scholarly edition[5] gives a detailed analytical account of how Jonson uses his classical sources. I intend, rather, to consider how issues of theatricality illuminate political readings of the play: reflecting on why the play has been so seldom performed in the theatre; discussing how it might work as theatre in the early twenty-first century; and considering, therefore, how it might be conceived of as Jonsonian theatre. And that, I will argue, relates closely to our perception of Arruntius.

The early performance history of *Sejanus* is puzzling. The text that has come down to us is Jonson's revision of an earlier work 'wherein a second pen has a good share'.[6] There has been considerable speculation as to who Jonson's collaborator might have been on that first stage version of the play.[7] What is certain, however, is that the play was unpopular at its first performance(s); and that Jonson revised the text substantially in preparation for publication. There are indications that it was subsequently revived to acclaim some time before 1654, when an anonymous writer noted: 'I amongst others hissed *Sejanus* off the stage, yet after sat it out, not only patiently, but with content and admiration.'[8] There might have been a revival soon after the Restoration, but there is no firm evidence for any production of the play between the early seventeenth-century production at The Globe and William Poel's 1928 revival of the play at the Holborn Empire Theatre, although in 1752 Francis Gentleman offered Garrick his own revised version of the play, somewhat ambitiously entitled *Sejanus, a Tragedy, as it was intended for the Stage*. Garrick rejected what Herford and the Simpsons refer to as a 'worthless adaptation'. In the late twentieth century the play has been revived by several student groups at universities (at Sussex and Cambridge in the 1970s, at Merton College, Oxford in 2000 and at Reading in the workshop production to which I refer in this essay). It was also given a rehearsed reading at the Globe Education Centre in November 1997,[9] but there have been no professional productions since Poel's in 1928.[10] That realisation referred obliquely to the 1603 production by the King's Men, dressing Arruntius as Ben Jonson and Cordus as William Shakespeare. Although this costuming refers partly to Shakespeare's appearance[11] as an actor in the first production of the play, this particular post-hoc example of 'application' relates to the commonly held view that Arruntius acts as a kind of Jonsonian chorus, voicing something akin to the author's position. It also seems to suggest that whereas Shakespeare would die for his art, Jonson might have been an acerbic social commentator but was also a survivor. 'The play, as Mr. Poel saw it, was not written to give prominence to any individual character in it, but to show the sudden rise and fall of a people's favourite; it was political satire.'(H&SS, Vol. IX, 1950: 192). Whatever the strengths or weaknesses of Poel's production, this interpretation reveals at least some of the reasons underlying the play's unpopularity. It defies conventional definitions of tragedy: not only is it difficult to find any sympathy for Sejanus, but the focus of the play shifts constantly. We may not 'sympathise' with Macbeth, Titus Andronicus or even Lear; but we are actively engaged with their situation. The fall of Sejanus occurs not from a position of nobility, but from a self-erected pedestal whence he may exercise power, but upon which he has become an object of loathing. The play opens with two of Sejanus's most active opponents heaping derision upon his political methods. From the outset, an audience is positioned to actively seek his fall.

The likely outcome of Poel's reading is that Arruntius becomes the character who engages our interest in the play; but Arruntius is powerless. He makes no decisions that affect the turn of events. Indeed, when Tiberius and Sejanus discuss how they are going to deal with dissent, Sejanus states that they should leave Arruntius unscathed: 'He only talks' (2.299). Arruntius may be central to our perception of the events of the play (and he is certainly given some of the play's finest *sententiae*); but his weakness as an agent of change compounds the sense that the structural dynamic of the play is problematic. But 'problematic' and 'flawed' are not necessarily synonymous; and I will argue that those aspects of the play which are most problematic are not only its most Jonsonian characteristics but are also a key to understanding how it might work effectively in the theatre of the twenty-first century.

Anti-theatricality

In reading the play off the page, it often seems almost perversely anti-theatrical. It is tempting to interpret this as a symptom of the specific history of the production of the text that we now have, acknowledging that Jonson rewrote the play for publication in book form rather than to be staged, and perhaps dismissing it as a manifestation of Jonson's attempt to reinvent a more 'pure' dramatic form, which harks back to Seneca. I would prefer to consider how this apparent anti-theatricality has the potential to be highly productive of theatrical meaning. Most of the major events of the play take place off-stage and are subsequently described by characters: the death of Drusus; the killings of Cordus and Sabinus; Tiberius's 'strange and new commented lusts, / For which nature hath not left a name' (4.400–

01); the destruction of Sejanus's statue and the terrifying 'popular rage' that tears Sejanus limb from limb. This relative absence of spectacle and dramatic action results in a play which focuses to a large extent on reaction, on responses to corruption, on complicity with an insidiously abusive body politic. Whilst this refusal to represent theatrically the dreadful violence and abuse that characters forcibly describe in the course of the play may be characteristic of Jonson's classicism, it does draw our attention to those mechanisms of corruption that we do see: entrapment, misrepresentation, libel, slander, bribery, flattery, betrayal and brutalisation. In general, an audience is protected from observing at first hand the violence that Tiberius and Sejanus deal out; but the effects of that brutality are shown. The public suicide of Silius is a notable exception to this apparent austerity. This is all the more remarkable given Jonson's divergence from his classical sources at this point. The historical Silius did commit suicide (Tacitus, *Annals*, IV. xix.: 'Silius anticipated the impending condemnation by a voluntary end') but not in the Senate. Jonson's decision to stage a public suicide at the exact centre point of the play[12] is hugely significant. Silius's suicide is shown as a noble act; but it also provides a benchmark against which the degrees of complicity of others can be measured. His suicide speech construes his own death as a challenge to any who would resist the political hegemony:

> Romans, if any be here in this Senate,
> Would know to mock Tiberius' tyranny,
> Look upon Silius, and so learn to die.

> (3.337-9)

The syntax elegantly challenges the senators' Romanness whilst simultaneously alerting any who would criticise Tiberius's regime to the likelihood of their imminent death. Mock Tiberius, and you will die. Watch me, and I will show you how to die.

If Arruntius represents Jonson's image of himself, he looks over his own shoulder with a degree of self-mockery. No sooner is Silius dead than Arruntius declares: 'My thought did prompt him to it' (3.342). This may represent approval, but it is also a fine example of the play's wry and extraordinarily dark comedy. Arruntius is not deliberately self-mocking here or elsewhere in the play; but the juxtaposition of Silius's death and Arruntius's self-aggrandising claim draws attention to the latter's inaction. Throughout the play, Jonson dramatises inaction,[13] or at least the failure to find an active response to tyranny. Now this is a very risky theatrical strategy. In performance, if an inappropriate tone is found – both here and elsewhere – not only is the dark humour of the moment denied, so too are its implications and its wider significance.

As many critics have noted,[14] in writing *Sejanus*, Jonson was as indebted to Machiavelli as he was to Tacitus and Suetonius: his examination of Tiberius's control and manipulation of both Sejanus and the Senate is an exceptionally astute analysis of the workings of Machiavellian state-craft. As Richard Cave has argued,[15] Jonson's purpose in exploring these uses and abuses of power is to mount a critique of the very notion of power for its own sake. At the heart of Machiavelli's analysis of political authority was an understanding of the power of the vacuum. Jonson's Tiberius knows precisely how to control those who would rush in to exploit what they see as a black hole. Thus Jonson uses Tiberius's deliberate creation and devious exploitation of a political void as a self-reflexive metaphor in his own dramatisation of a world bereft of moral values, for what is so profoundly disturbing about *Sejanus* is its depiction of the moral vacuum within which Tiberius and Sejanus operate. In this moral climate, suggests Silius, any Roman worthy of the name should be prepared to follow his example. None do, although Cordus does use his arraignment before the Senate to defend himself and his honour as a historian and a poet with great vigour. But Cordus's spirited defence again calls attention to Arruntius's responses to these events. He is certainly witty: 'My thought did prompt him to it. Farewell Silius!' (3.342) is followed by his wry comment a few lines later on Tiberius's claim that Silius's suicide forestalled his own mercy: 'Excellent wolf! / Now he is full he howls.' (3.347–8). The actor playing Arruntius is presumably to deliver this line as an aside, and he may well get a laugh from it; but if Arruntius is a choric figure, he is a complex one with many functions. He informs the audience about narrative developments, advises how to read many of the other characters – 'This Lepidus / Is grave and honest. ....' (3.367–8). Whatever Sejanus may say, Arruntius does not 'only talk'. He is a witty commentator, an entertainer, a go-between within the action and outside it; he draws us in to the play and distances us from it, engaging our interest with his wit and disengaging us by forcing us to interrogate our responses both to him as a character and to the play itself. Given the complexity of the role, it would be a mistake to make too simple a judgement on the character (in the way that Sejanus himself does when he persuades Tiberius to allow his dissident view to be heard), but it would be equally inappropriate to ignore his position within the politics of the play and see him only as a choric figure. This duality in the role is one of the characteristic fascinations of Jonsonian theatre. His reference to Tiberius as an 'Excellent wolf' is likely to arouse laughter in an audience partly because here (and, indeed, throughout the play) his wit is so ready and so succinct, but also because the metatheatrical game makes him safe from Tiberius's wrath. At one level, what keeps Arruntius alive is his dialogue with the audience. As in Beckett's *Endgame*, 'What is there to keep me here? The dialogue.'[16] We know that the play needs to keep him alive; but the character is implicated in the events of the play. He may be always ready to articulate his criticism of the appalling political regime and of the senators' own complicity with those who currently hold power, but he is never willing to follow the example of Cordus or Silius. If his dialogue with us keeps him safe, so too does his reluctance to raise his head above the parapet; and thus, by implication (as so often in Jonsonian theatre) the metatheatrical game implicates us. Our admiration for Arruntius's insightful observations and ready wit is always likely to be tinged by the knowledge that we, too, are beneath Sejanus's contempt.

Sejanus's own relationship with the audience is equally complex. It has been suggested that *Sejanus* is Jonson's response to *Julius Caesar*; but the play can also be seen as situated within a developing tradition of plays featuring Machiavels: Richard III, for example, Barabas in *The Jew of Malta* and subsequently Edmund in *King Lear* and Flamineo in *The White Devil*. One of the surprising things about the twin Machiavels in Jonson's play is that neither Sejanus nor Tiberius make any effort to beguile the audience. In each of the other examples noted above, the Machiavel forges a charismatic relationship with the audience which simultaneously thrills and horrifies with amoral charm. *Sejanus* clearly eschews this means of unsettling its audience. Sejanus's challenge to the gods (to which I shall return later in this essay) may make us smile in knowing anticipation, but he does not attempt to make direct appeals to the theatre audience. He addresses the audience boldly, directly, but makes no attempt to get us 'on side'. This should alert us to the unusual role that Arruntius plays in this most experimental of tragedies.

Let us return, then, to considering specific ways in which the play is theatrically difficult and problematic. It certainly presents a number of major theatrical challenges. It is a play whose scope is enormous. Anyone wanting to produce it theatrically is confronted by the task of casting 34 named characters and groups of lictors, heralds, attendants and musicians. And yet, for a play with such a very large cast, it feels remarkably like a chamber piece for much of its length, with the action shifting constantly between public and private spaces. Scenes are juxtaposed in almost cinematic montage (the action shifts between state rooms, the Senate House, private houses and gardens, the street, and the Temple of Apollo; and includes several major temporal ellipses). Some of these scenes are remarkably short; others comprise lengthy allusive argument. One of the effects of this structural form is to destabilise an audience's perspective on events. The play is not 'about' the fall of Sejanus in the way that *King Lear* is about Lear's; but rather about the circumstances of Sejanus's fall; and the impact that corruption and favouritism has on the wider social group. Although there are aspects of the *Sejanus* experiment which make it very different from the majority of plays in the surviving Jonsonian canon, this multiple and shifting perspective is certainly a Jonsonian characteristic.

As Julie Sanders has noted in her essay on Jonson's Caroline Drama (Chapter 5), the late plays confirm a developing interest in social community. That interest may not be immediately evident in *Volpone* and *The Devil is an Ass* but it is certainly present in *Bartholomew Fair* and even in *Epicæne*. Although the Ladies Collegiate may be highly competitive, and Jonson's depiction of their 'community' may be acerbic, one of the purposes of the satire in *Epicæne* is to show by omission what the College lacks as a social community. Similarly, in *The Alchemist* Doll, Subtle and Face only thrive when they work together as a 'venture tripartite'. In this sense, just as *Sejanus* actively dramatises Arruntius's inaction, so too it also dramatises the failure of the community to resist Sejanus and Tiberius. Jonson does not give us even a glimpse of the Plebeians, but the 'popular rage' is immensely powerful. In the final horrific moments of the last act of the play, Terentius describes Sejanus's death at the hands of the mob:

> The eager multitude, who never yet
> Knew why to love, or hate, but only pleased
> To express their rage of power ...
>   ...with violent rage
> Have rent (Sejanus' body) ... limb from limb. A thousand heads,
> A thousand hands, ten thousand tongues and voices
> Employed at once in several acts of malice! ...
> The whole, and all of what was great Sejanus,
> And next to Caesar did possess the world,
> Now torn and scattered, as he needs no grave;
> Each little dust covers a little part.
> So lies he nowhere, and yet often buried.
>
> (5.769–71; 820–3; 838–41)

The collective 'eager multitude' is comprised of a 'thousand heads', but 'ten thousand tongues and voices'. Even here, where their rage is uncontrollable, Jonson characterises the populace as more vocal than active. Ten times as many express their rage vocally as through acts of physical destruction. And the nature of their rage? The syntax creates ambiguity: 'their rage of power' implies both a forceful, unstoppable rage *given power* by their new found ability to express themselves, but also a sense that they have long been harbouring deep-seated rage against those *in power*. This is the rage that has never been tapped into by those who have for so long resented Sejanus's elevation to power.

Terentius's shocked and shocking account of the behaviour of the 'rude multitude' (reinforced by Arruntius, who characterises them as 'rogues' (5.891) implies that Jonson is most certainly not advocating this kind of violent overthrow of those who abuse power, but it demonstrates that the play is intensely alert to the possibility of imminent popular violence. The imagery of Sejanus torn in pieces and scattered also acts as a potent metaphor for Tiberius's divide and rule strategies. Sejanus's physical dismemberment is equated in the terms of the play with his political destruction.[17] He has to be torn into pieces to be rendered powerless. Earlier in the play we have seen all political resistance to Tiberius and Sejanus dismembered, faction set against faction. Collective resistance, seen as so powerful (albeit brutish, mindless and horrific) in the final moments is precisely what Tiberius and Sejanus most fear. Jonson's self-proclaimed authenticity in his use of classical sources is more radically experimental than he himself seems to acknowledge. His desire to create 'truth of argument',[18] to present a literal version of what he perceived to be historical truth, may have driven him inadvertently to a multi-vocal history; but that is what the play presents us with, and if that creates theatrical problems, it also offers theatrical riches.

Characterisation

It has been noted that the play not only denies us spectacle, but also appears to refuse some of its own potential for dramatic action. In the hands of one of Jonson's contemporaries, the seduction of Livia, for example, might be far more sexualised. In effect, Livia's seduction is undertaken by Eudemus on Sejanus's behalf. The real seduction scenes are between Sejanus and Eudemus and subsequently between Eudemus and Livia. When Sejanus meets Livia (in the opening scene of Act Two) he professes his love and admiration for her:

> ... Royal lady,
> Though I have loved you long, and with that height
> Of zeal and duty (like the fire, which more
> It mounts, it trembles), ...
>   ... I protest
> Myself through-rarefied, and turned all flame
> In your affection. ...   (2.24–33)

His account of his own ardour is, however, more closely related to 'zeal and duty' than it is to sexual desire. What he offers her moves rapidly from the passion to the division of political spoils. He plans to 'share the sov'reignty of all the world' (2.37). There is very little evidence that he is excited by the sexual conquest of Livia. And whilst this is indeed a strategic and structural characteristic of the play (Sejanus enlisting Eudemus to undertake the seduction of Livia is a fine example of the way in which the form of the play echoes the various forms of corruption by proxy that it examines) it also offers a key to the characterisation of Sejanus himself, who seems to be sexually aroused by power itself rather than by the trappings of power. He has no interest in the 'new found lusts' attributed to Tiberius; gaining power is presented as a kind of sexual conquest in itself. In the only exchange he has with Livia (the only woman he speaks to in the course of the play) he talks of Drusus, Caesar, Augusta, Agrippina and Tiberius. His promise to Livia is not that he will offer her passion and sexual satisfaction, but that together they will eclipse Caesar and Augusta:

> Then Livia triumphs in her proper sphere,
> When she and her Sejanus shall divide
> The name of Caesar, and Augusta's star
> Be dimmed with glory of a brighter beam. ...
>
> (2.38–41)

Now it might be argued that this apparent lack of sexual interest in Livia relates to his sexual orientation. After all, Arruntius claims:

> I knew him at Caius' trencher, when for hire
> He prostituted his abusèd body
> To that great gourmand, fat Apicius,
> And was the noted pathic of the time.
>
> (1.213–16)

But there is no indication in the play that Sejanus has any greater sexual interest in men or boys than he does in Livia. The self-abusive sexual submissiveness referred to by Arruntius is significant because, as DiGangi has argued, it is indicative of the way he treats all bodies as flesh to be manipulated as a means to power (DiGangi, 1997: 121). In that he shows no sexual interest in other characters (although he is reported as having a wife and children, he takes no interest in them), Sejanus is presented as desexualised; but there is a way in which the character can be seen as sexually driven. The key to this comes late in the play in the extraordinary moment at the ritual that Sejanus has organised in honour of Fortune when the statue of the goddess 'stirs', 'turns away' and 'averts her face' (5.185–6). This incident is strange in itself, but it is given added significance because in this play it is a moment of such rare spectacle and also because it draws attention to the rigorous materialism that seems to be such a significant Jonsonian characteristic. This is a pivotal moment for Sejanus: it is effectively rejection by his one true love. In an exchange with Terentius near the beginning of Act Five, he proudly boasts that Fortune is the only deity he respects: 'Fortune. ... Her I indeed adore ...' (5.84). He sees himself in a personalised union with Fortune; the relationship is almost erotic in its intensity. Given Jonson's tendency to avoid the metaphysical in his plays for the theatre, what are we to make of this? Jonson's marginalia at this point are particularly revealing. He claims that in researching the sacred rite of propitiating the goddess Fortune he had consulted Virgil, Martial, Rosinus, Tibullus, Ovid, Giraldus, Suetonius and Seneca (amongst others).[19] There is something about these notes which 'doth protest too much'. As elsewhere in *Sejanus*, it is too easy to take Jonson's insistence upon authenticity at face value and to ignore the significance of the editorial decision that gives the moment such prominence. Sejanus's adoration of Fortune seems more than a compulsion to push risk-taking to extremes; it is risk-taking as a manifestation of a death wish. In the extraordinary speech which opens Act Five, Sejanus challenges the gods themselves:

> Great, and high,
> The world knows only two, that's Rome, and I.
> My roof receives me not; 'tis air I tread –
> And, at each step, I feel my advancèd head
> Knock out a star in heav'n! ...
> Is there not something more than to be Caesar?
> Must we rest there? ...
> It is our grief, and will be our loss, to know
> Our power shall want opposites; unless
> The gods, by mixing in the cause, would bless
> Our fortune with their conquest.
>
> (5.5–23)

This challenge to the gods is more than hubris. He is willing his own destruction; a destruction that will result not only in his own dismemberment, but in annihilation:

> The whole, and all of what was great Sejanus, ...
> Now torn and scattered, as he needs no grave;

Each little dust covers a little part.
So lies he nowhere, and yet often buried.

(5.838–42)

Georges Bataille[20] has written at length about such desire for self-annihilation, arguing that eroticism itself represents a desire to lose oneself. A Freudian analysis might argue that Sejanus's libido is channelled into a relentless, ruthless pursuit of power, but the play does not really examine this. Bataille's equation of eroticism (which he distinguishes from sexuality) and self-annihilation is quite different from the Freudian death wish. His analysis of eroticism ultimately takes him to the position where he declares 'Death is that putrefaction, that stench ... which is at once the source and the repulsive condition of life' (1991: 80–81). For Bataille, eroticism is inseparable from decay. This equation of death and desire, dissolution and annihilation leads to an illuminating reading of *Sejanus*, and one which is particularly useful when considering the characterisation of Sejanus. In *The Accursed Share*, Bataille writes of looking down from a great height: 'The view may cause us to step back, but the image of the possible fall, which is connected with it, may also suggest that we jump, in spite of or because of the death we will find there. ... What is certain is that the lure of the void and of ruination does not in any way correspond to diminished vitality' (1991: 108). Although Bataille is writing of a literal fall, this analysis bears a remarkable resemblance to Sejanus's own metaphoric fall. In imperial Rome, Fortune may have been revered as a god, but in Jonson's play the image of the goddess turning away from Sejanus is surely a figurative way of expressing that he is not only transfixed by the possibility of self-annihilation, but actively seeking it. Macro's sudden elevation also can be seen in the terms of Bataille's theories of eroticism; his rise representing a kind of hideous regeneration. Arruntius prophesies:

> ... out of this Senate's flattery,
> That this new fellow, Macro, will become
> A greater prodigy in Rome, than he
> That now is fallen.

(5.759–63)

Sejanus's erotically charged relationship with Fortune, his ambivalent desire for self-annihilation at her hands, can be seen as the driving force behind the final act of this extraordinary tragedy; but is that peculiar to *Sejanus* or might it be useful in considering other plays in the Jonsonian canon? Although such extreme manifestations of the urge to self-annihilation may not be seen elsewhere, the fascination with characters who seek obsessive degrees of control whilst pushing themselves to the very limits of excess most certainly is. Indeed, Volpone, Mosca, Morose, Sir Epicure Mammon, Zeal-of-the-Land Busy, Fitzdotterel and Polish can all be seen in a similar light. Although we may be encouraged to laugh at them, each is in the grip of an obsession that blinds them to the thoughts and feelings of others. Encountering Sejanus reminds us that each of these characters is a would-be tyrant. Volpone's compulsive determination to over-reach himself; Fitzdotterel's obsession with his own appearance; Morose's desire to control every aspect of his social environment; Mammon, with his unbounded appetites, seeking limitless multiplication in his own influence over all things: these may be trivial tyrannies when compared with Sejanus, but each is demonstrably in the grip of a kind of self-destructive madness.

Language and power

I want to conclude by briefly considering the use of language in *Sejanus*. Jonson has often been accused by his detractors of verbosity and over-embellishment. In the case of *Sejanus*, the tendency to refuse spectacle contributes to the sense of the play as 'bookish' and somewhat burdened by dense linguistic argument and verbal accounts of dramatic action rather than action itself. Although there is a self-imposed austerity at work here, it is again possible to see this as theatrically meaningful rather than as an example of self-conscious classicism. As Julie Sanders argues convincingly in her chapter on *The New Inn* and *The Magnetic Lady*, Jonson's off-stage spaces are highly significant. In *Sejanus*, this Jonsonian tendency manifests itself through the creation of powerful relationships between on- and off-stage spaces. We may not see Tiberius's Capri on the stage nor witness Sejanus's dismemberment; but I suggest that an audience at an intelligent production of *Sejanus* would see them in its mind's eye. Jonson constructs the workings of the Senate for us in great detail; we collaborate with him in creating our own images of the horrors that result from the decisions and failures of the Senate. Jonson repeatedly focuses our attention on the causes of the horrors rather than the horrors themselves. Arruntius and Cordus clearly identify flattery, deceit, false accusation and bribery as the standard currency of the Senate. Language in the Senate has become unstable in its meanings. Consider the following exchange between them:

Arruntius	Let me be gone...
Cordus	Stay.
Arruntius	What? To hear more cunning, and fine words,
	With their sound flattered, ere their sense be meant?

(1.505–7)

Language itself has become corrupt and corrupting. Throughout the play, language is used to articulate partial perspectives. And, whereas in *The Alchemist* language is used as an agent of transformation, in *Sejanus* language itself becomes the prime agent of power; and in doing so problematises its own logocentricity. Tiberius's Rome is a world in which moral insight and power are prised apart. Arruntius may be highly insightful in diagnosing the corruption that surrounds him but he is incapable of action; he 'only talks'. Tiberius does not even need to talk for his words to damn Sejanus.

In his own introduction to the play Jonson expressed the hope that 'in truth of argument, dignity of persons, gravity and height of elocution, fullness and frequency of sentence' he had 'discharged ... the offices of the tragic writer'. 'Frequency of sentence' refers to the use of *sententiae* or aphorisms. If that is indeed one of the offices of the tragic writer, then Jonson discharged his duties very well, for the play contains far more quotable aphorisms than any Dictionary of Quotations acknowledges. If, as he seems to imply in this introduction, they are included in the play as a means of creating gravitas, as another way of securing classical authority, they might add to our sense of the play as 'bookish'. I would argue, however, that Jonson does himself no credit in his own introduction and that (as so often seems to be the case) there has been a tendency to confuse these stated intentions (and we will never know whether they were or were not his actual intentions) with the meanings of the plays themselves. Close examination of the *sententiae* in *Sejanus* reveals them as both provocative and unstable in their meanings. A surprising number of them are spoken by Sejanus himself. How, for example, are we to read: ''Twas only fear first in the world made gods' (2.162).

Are we to consider Sejanus damned for his cynical materialism (to which we, in a more secular age, may well subscribe)? Or to recognise that in overthrowing tyrants such as Tiberius and Sejanus there can be no appeal to supernatural agencies?

Does Arruntius cry at night? In the face of such appalling abuse of monolithic power, such self-serving centralised authority, and such an insidious and brutally corrupt political regime, probably. As Brecht would doubtless have observed, however, the danger of such a conclusion is that it renders its audience as powerless as Arruntius, that we watch and are disempowered, feeling that Silius was right: an honourable death is the best we can hope for when confronted with tyranny. In spite of Jonson's determined classicism, this is most definitely not a play which offers catharsis. The elevation of Macro and the survival of Tiberius ensures that we are not provided with a resolution that leaves us with any sense of better times to come, nor even with any notion that we have been in some way purged by our encounter with these events. It has been widely assumed that Jonson wrote the play not as an allusive indictment of James, but, rather as a warning of how appallingly difficult it is to resist such a system of self-perpetuating corruption once it has been installed; and, by implication, a means of ensuring vigilance against such a prospect. Act now, or you may find yourselves as impotent as Arruntius. If the central concern of this terrifyingly bleak play is how we, an audience, respond to the contingency of corruption, the wake-up call that it offers may be more timely and relevant today than we would like to think.

Notes

[1] A series of workshops over a period of about 7 weeks culminated in a presentation of extracts from the play in December 2001 in a studio theatre at Bulmershe Court, University of Reading. These workshops explored issues of casting, staging, cutting and performance style. I am very grateful to the student cast of that production and to my colleagues in the Department of Film & Drama for their stimulating contributions to the lively seminar discussion which followed the presentation.

[2] Arruntius was played by James Madge.

[3] The fragment of *Mortimer his Fall* does not really qualify for inclusion in this group; and no text of *Richard Crookback* has survived. *The Magnetic Lady* is a more difficult case – in that the 'Magnetic Lady' may be the 'centre of attraction' but she is not the protagonist in any conventional sense.

[4] I have found the following particularly stimulating in this respect: Richard Cave's essay *Sejanus his Fall* in *Ben Jonson* (Macmillan 1991); Mario DiGangi's discussion of the play in *The Homoerotics of Early Modern Drama* (Cambridge University Press, 1997, pp. 119–24); Julie Sanders' essay *Roman Frames of Mind* in *Ben Jonson's Theatrical Republics* (Macmillan, 1998a).

[5] The relevant volumes are as follows: Volume II (1925), pp. 3–27, offers a commentary on the play; Volume IX (1950), pp. 191–92 gives a stage history; and, pp. 585–635 detailed analysis of Jonson's use of his sources.

[6] Ben Jonson's introduction *To the Readers*, l.40. This line reference, and all subsequent references to the text, refers to Philip J. Ayres's edition of the play for The Revels Plays (1990): Manchester University Press, Manchester and New York.

[7] Arguments have been made for Shakespeare as Jonson's collaborator; but the prevailing view is that it was George Chapman. See Ayers (1990) p. 52 n. 40, *H & S* II 3–5, IX, 592–3.

8. Herford and the Simpsons give details of this in *Stage History of the Plays*, Volume 9, pp. 190–92.
9. This rehearsed reading was prepared and co-ordinated by Richard Cottrell. The excellent cast included Timothy West as Tiberius, Richard Garnett as Sejanus, Jack Klaff as Silius and Frank Middlemass as Arruntius.
10. Although Poel's production was staged for one night only (12 February 1928), it seems to have been well received. In a letter to William Poel, written the day after seeing the production, Percy Simpson stated that he had never before 'seen an Elizabethan play done with so serene, effortless and pure beauty, and with such a sense of quiet, spacious grandeur.' (Cited in Speaight, 1954: 248). Robert Speaight, who played Arruntius, thought it 'a very effective version... swift in movement and elaborate in design, (giving)... a rich, satiric portrait of Roman decadence'. (Speaight: 247–8).
11. In the Folio edition of the play a list of actors, in two columns, follows the text of the play. Richard Burbage heads the left hand column, with William Shakespeare heading the other. Herford and the Simpsons deduce that Burbage played Sejanus and Shakespeare Tiberius.
12. The suicide occurs at the mid-point (lines 339–41) of the third act.
13. I have argued elsewhere that the active use of silence as a theatrical signifier is also an important and underestimated characteristic of Jonsonian theatre. *The Gift of Silence*, Woolland, in Cave, Schafer, and Woolland *Ben Jonson and Theatre* (1999) Routledge, London and New York, pp. 125–36.
14. Particularly useful in this respect are essays by Richard Cave (1991), 'Sejanus his Fall', in *Ben Jonson*; and Julie Sanders (1998a), 'Roman Frames of Mind', in *Ben Jonson's Theatrical Republics*.
15. The argument is developed in Chapter 3, 'Sejanus his Fall', in Richard Cave (1991), *Ben Jonson*.
16. Samuel Beckett (1958), *Endgame*, pp. 39–40 in paperback edition (1964), Faber and Faber, London.
17. In this context it is worth drawing attention to Mario DiGangi's brief but brilliant study of the play, in which he argues that in '... no Renaissance play are sodomy and parasitism so constitutive of national politics as in Jonson's *Sejanus*'. (DiGangi. 119–20).
18. To the Readers, 25.
19. For this short scene of 40 lines - from the entrance of the Flamen (the priest) and Ministri to the entrance of Pomponius and Minutius – Jonson offered no less than 16 marginal notes, each of them proclaiming his sources.
20. Georges Bataille (1897–1962), a French essayist and novelist whose wide-ranging work (including erotic novels and lengthy essays on cave painting, surrealism, religion, political economy and eroticism) has been seen as influential on Foucault, Lacan, Derrida and Barthes. His writing explores and embraces dualities and contradictions inherent in relations between eroticism and the desire for self-annihilation, sex and death, the individual and the social. One of Bataille's central concerns was to place eroticism at the centre of life, arguing not only that 'Eroticism is the most problematic part of ourselves' (1962: 273) but that there is a strong 'connection between the promise of life implicit in eroticism and the sensuous aspect of death' (1962: 59).

Chapter 4

Bartholomew Fair:
All the Fun of the Fair

Peter Barnes

Ben Jonson is the explosive creator of grand carnivals, giant belches, flowing lavatorial humour, strict classical learning, sublime lyrics, surreal rhetoric and mighty verse. He, therefore, has a problem in a theatre like ours, devoted to the small, neat and safe, which is one reason why his plays still anger and frighten so many.

At the heart of his work is *Bartholomew Fair*, a massive fresco, packed with thirty-two characters, all shouting for attention, plus some six competing storylines. There are no leading characters. Or rather, there are thirty-two leading characters; no one dominates and everyone uses their time and space on stage to maximum effect. This is surely democracy in action.

There are Puritans, middle-class idiots, fat ladies selling pork, ballad singers, gingerbread women, hobby-horse sellers, pickpockets, con-men, prostitutes, puppeteers, roving magistrates, madmen, policemen, seducers and drunks. All these extraordinary characters are kept in motion, dancing and spinning in a perpetual whirligig of silliness, cupidity, greed and delight. In some ways *Bartholomew Fair* is a reconstructed comic documentary on the condition of society at a given moment. Fairs haven't changed that much during the intervening centuries so it is still relevant.

Jonson's panoramic view of one day at a rumbustious fair is always on the point of exploding into a hundred fragments, but never does. Everything holds until the final mellow fade-out. *Bartholomew Fair*, like Robert Altman's *Nashville*[1], or even better, Jean Renoir's *La Règle du Jeu*[2], gives us a cross section of contemporary life, top and bottom; mostly bottom because that is where most human beings live, so that is where life is. He observes human frailty with irony and compassion without ever losing his sense of humour. Jonson believed in absolute human qualities, virtues as well as vices – generosity for instance. *Bartholomew Fair* is perhaps his best work because it shows this generosity in abundance.

It has a totally different start from the bomb-shell opening of *The Alchemist* which is slap-bang in the middle of a blazing row between two crooks and a prostitute. This tells us the whole plot of the play if we listen and is an astounding theatrical tour-de-force. But it would be wrong for *Bartholomew Fair*, where the theatrical pyrotechnics are reserved for later. Here the opening is a leisurely, sardonic induction, in which the Stage Keeper or Manager, talks to the audience and laments the fact that Jonson is too pig-headed to listen to sound advice about how to write a successful drama.

The play proper begins with a Puritan, John Littlewit, a type of solicitor, and his vivacious wife, Win, persuading Win's widowed mother, Dame Purecraft, who holds the purse-strings, to go to the fair. Other characters are introduced, Zeal-of-the-Land Busy, a fanatical Puritan, and the prize simpleton, Bartholomew Cokes, who is determined to go to the fair because he is named after it, and because it actually is St. Bartholomew Day.

All of Jonson's characters, unlike Shakespeare's, work for a living. That is the thing to remember when the play moves into the fair itself. At first it looks as though the fairground folk are all obsessive eccentrics: Ursula, the Pig-Woman, and her assistant, Mooncalf; the cut-purse Ezekial Edgeworth; and Lantern Leatherhead, the hobby-horse seller. But they are only ordinary people in extraordinary jobs, trying to make ends meet. It is the visitors to the fair that are the true eccentrics and obsessives, like Justice Overdo, who prowls around, disguised as Mad Arthur of Bradley, sniffing out sin and corruption. There is plenty of both but Overdo doesn't find any and ends up in the stocks. Jonson is sometimes accused of judging his characters. No one in *Bartholomew Fair* is judged except those who sit in judgement on their fellow men.

One of the many ironies of the play is that whilst Justice Overdo pretends to be a madman, a real madman, Trouble-All, zigzags through the fair like a demented ferret. I have directed two productions of *Bartholomew Fair*. In the first at the Roundhouse (1978) Trouble-All was played by David Claridge (the creator of *Roland Rat*). In the second at the Regent's Park Open Air Theatre (1983) it was Chris Ryan (one of the gang in the TV series *The Young Ones*). Each time he was played differently, yet each time he gained the most laughs and was one of the major characters, though his dialogue was sparse and consisted mainly of the phrase 'Have you a warrant for this?' Trouble-All proves, if it needed proving, that you can never judge a character's importance by the size of their part or the amount of dialogue they have to say.

Jonson's passionate attempt to express himself in language which shuns banality is an attempt, however desperate, to distance experience from its most deadly enemy – oblivion. He makes it so vivid it bites deep and hopefully stays in the memory of his audience.

With a writer of Jonson's power, it is tempting to just quote and leave out the commentary. Ford Madox Ford believed 'If you are a decently civilised man, you can tell a whole book from the turn of one phrase as often as not'.[3] Picking phrases at random from *Bartholomew Fair* can indeed tell you the quality of the whole play:

> Take a good heart, 'tis but a blister, as big as a windgall; I'll take it away with the white of an egg, a little honey and hog's grease.
>
> (2.5.173–5)[4]

> Now pig, it is a meat and a meat that is nourishing, and may be long'd for, and so consequently eaten; it may be eaten; very exceedingly well eaten.
>
> (1.6.49–51)

> O, they [coaches] are as common as wheelbarrows where there are great dunghills. Every pettifogger's wife has 'em, for first he buys a coach that he may marry and then he marries that he may be made a cuckold in 't.
>
> (4.5.96–99)

> Buy any pears, very fine pears, pears fine.
>
> (2.2.32)

> Buy a mousetrap, a mousetrap, or a tormentor for a flea.
>
> (2.4.7)

> Ballads, ballads! fine new ballads. Hear for your love and buy for your money!
>
> (2.4.9–10)

These phrases are the work of a master dramatist. That means, for them to fully come to life, they are meant to be spoken, made flesh, coloured, 'bent', speared through the outer ear, transmitted by actors; and reacted to. Just as every idea contains an image of the world, so does every word. The better the word, the better the image.

One of Jonson's strengths as a playwright is his mastery of invective, always a distinguishing mark of a good dramatist. It helps to be a healthy hater. When Jonson's characters quarrel most violently, they reveal themselves most fully. In his plays he uses bad temper like other dramatists use alcohol to loosen his characters' tongues. For when social restraints are momentarily dropped, we forget ourselves and show our true faces.

Bartholomew Fair shows Jonson at his insulting best. Ursula, the seller of roast pork, is never more herself than when she is in the middle of a slanging match. 'Out you rogue, you hedge-bird, you pimp, you pannier-man's bastard, you! ... Do you sneer, you dog's head, you trendle-tail! You look as if you were begotten a'top of a cart in harvest-time, when the whelp was hot and eager. ...' (2.5.112–17).

Compare this to the exquisite lyric in *The Devil is an Ass*, and we glimpse the full range of Jonson's genius:

That since love hath the honour to approach
These sister-swelling breasts, and touch this soft,
And rosy hand; he hath the skill to draw
Their nectar forth, with kissing; and could make
More wanton salts from this brave promontory
Down to this valley, than the nimble roe;
Could play the hopping sparrow 'bout these nets,
And sporting squirrel in these crisped groves... .

$(2.6.71-78)^5$

With Jonson, character revelations are always shown in dynamic action, not in static introspection. His characters are up and doing. Jonson never writes about kings and queens or any of the moth-eaten hierarchy of privilege and incompetence, but of people like us who work to live. And the people in *Bartholomew Fair* never stop working. They have one day to earn enough money, legally or illegally, (it makes no difference) to tide them over to the next fair in another town. They work to survive and if it means cheating, lying, and stealing then so be it. The visitors to the fair are no better, as a young woman is prepared to marry a rich idiot she does not even like and a widow is fought over by two yobbish layabouts for her dowry.

Jonson would be as dead as most books about him, without the one essential quality a dramatist must have. On stage his seemingly heavy, clotted verse and prose unfolds like beautiful Japanese paper flowers in water. Justice Overdo rails against strong drink:

Thirst not after that frothy liquor, ale: for who knows, when he openeth the stopple, what may be in the bottle? Hath not a snail, a spider, yea, a newt been found there? Thirst not after it, youth; thirst not after it.

(2.6.10–13)

On stage it is at once realistic and magnificent; never merely rhetorical. Such flowering is a wonder and a mystery but it works in the theatre. Ingredient 'X'. In the end that is the one thing that matters. Despite his tin ear, O'Neill has it, so does dusty Ibsen and half-buried Lope de Vega. Seneca does not.

This is why some academic studies of Jonson can be beside the point. Of course, they have their insights but they are often purely literary insights. They miss the heartbeat because they contain little knowledge of the medium Jonson wrote for: the theatre. It is helpful when writing about Jonson if you have worked in some capacity on an actual Jonson production, in a theatre, in front of an audience. Then you soon realise those seeming failures of characterisation are not failures when his words are spoken and his characters given flesh by actors.

Jonson always wrote speeches to be acted. No more so than in *Bartholomew Fair*, where characters come on in mid-flight; there is no pausing to deliberate as the men and women involved are too busy to pause for anything. I have personal experience of this frenzied business activity. My parents worked in amusement arcades and then owned a café in Clacton-on-Sea, a down-market seaside resort on the East Coast. Money earned had to be earned during the packed Summer Season, May–October. Open at 8am, close at 8pm, weekends included. No rest; ever energised to make money while the customers were there.

How much more energy is needed if it is a fair, where the opportunity to make money is crammed into one or a few days at most: the fairground folk must be on their toes to grab and loosen the tight pockets of the customers and suckers as quickly as they can. I can testify to the accuracy of Jonson's picture of such professionals. Their world has not changed that much.

In *Bartholomew Fair*, all is forward movement and every second counts. The colour and spectacle and energy is part of the game. Without it, the fair would not be performing its function of giving its visitors what they have come for: a day out, something different. And while they are dazzled and delighted, their pockets are picked. It's a two-way street, both parties get something out of it. The visitors get to be entertained, and the fairground hustlers get their money.

The songs, fights, dances, comic routines and puppet shows are part of Jonson's 'streaky bacon' technique – Dickens called mixed forms 'streaky bacon' and always used it. It is part of the essential fabric of his work. To criticise Jonson from the text alone is like criticising an opera from the libretto without hearing the music. To do Jonson justice you have to hear the music. Jonson is above all a comic playwright and to talk about Jonson's humour, it is better to go outside the drama or beyond critical studies and look to music-hall, vaudeville, comic novels and movies, particularly silent movies and screwball comedies.

Two comics, W.C. Fields and Jack Benny, are essentially Jonsonian characters, each one embodying a comic passion: booze and money respectively. *Bartholomew Fair* has countless examples. Cokes's valet-cum-tutor, Wasp, is Donald Duck or Yosemite Sam, a fierce, red-bearded, gun-toting outlaw from Bugs Bunny cartoons, forever in a temper and spoiling for a fight. ('I'm Yosemite Sam, the toughest desperado in the West') and forever being outwitted. Cokes himself has all the childish stupidity and innocence of Stan Laurel, whilst the madman Trouble-All has the demented energy of Jerry Lewis or Jim Carey and the blockheadedness of Spike Milligan's Eccles. Justice Overdo is Leslie Neilson's Captain Drebin, a figure of authority, always wrong and always ludicrous. Ursula has the irrepressible vulgarity and life-force of Martha Raye from *Monsieur Verdoux*;[6] the Littlewit's, John and Win have wandered hand in hand, out of a Woodhouse comic novel. These modern comparisons are important because they point to the continual relevance of the play. They still speak to us because they are our contemporaries.

Unlike Shakespeare, Jonson did not give his nobles verse to speak and his common folk prose. There are thankfully few, if any, nobles in Jonson, yet whilst *The Alchemist*, a tale about three crooks, is in verse, the great fresco of *Bartholomew Fair* is in prose. The division is probably because *The Alchemist* is about peoples' dreams and aspirations, whilst the even more down-to-earth *Bartholomew Fair* is about how they live.

The literary style, as befits a dramatist, is not uniform. Each of the multitudinous characters has a special way of speaking and each character is as closely observed as in a Brueghel canvas. There is no attempt at psychoanalysing. Such attempts are a debilitating weakness for a playwright, especially a comic playwright. We can see more clearly from the outside, looking in, than from the inside, looking out. What they do, how they interact, how they speak – the very words they use – defines and characterises them as accurately as in a Chekhov play or Dickens novel.

You notice at once how frequently the Littlewits use their Christian names, John and Win. It makes their conversations both tender and playful. They are still in love. Wasp, on the other hand, splutters in fury. His speeches are broken up and his sentences are mostly short and stabbing; 'To seek me? Why, did you all think I was lost? Or run way with your fourteen shillings worth of small ware here? ...' (1.5.8–10), or his truly memorable insult 'A turd in your teeth' (3.4.40). There are Zeal-of-the-Land's high biblical rantings 'The whole fair is the shop of Satan' (3.2.39–40) whilst Overdo stuffs his speeches with sententious quotations and Latin tags ... 'The husbandman ought not, for one unthankful year, to forsake the plough ... nor the piper o' the parish (*ut*

parvis componere magna solebam) put up his pipes, for one rainy Sunday.'
(3.3.26–35). Contrast this with Cokes's excited exclamations, usually of
pleasure: 'O' Numps! are you here, Numps? Look where I am, Numps!
And Mistress Grace too! Nay, do not look angerly, Numps: my sister is
here, and all, I do not come without her.' (1.5.1–4).

Bartholomew Fair is a fast-moving comedy full of jokes, verbal and
visual, like the clear stage direction when the smell of roast pork causes
Busy to '*scent after it like a hound*', (3.2.79). This is a Warner Brothers
cartoon carrying the image of Busy even rising into the air and following
the invisible scent above the crowded fair. There are the set comic routines
when Wasp escapes from the stocks by substituting his hand for his foot
and when Busy curses the wooden puppet for obscenity and the puppets lift
up their skirts to reveal they have no genitals in a marvellous 'pay-off' gag.

The carefully constructed anarchy of the play, its scope and dramatic
form – in this case an intimate panorama, as intricately constructed as a
Swiss watch, yet ragged as life at the edges – is unique in dramatic
literature. There is certainly nothing like it in European drama. You have to
go to the novels like Rabelais *Gargantua and Pantagruel* and Gogol's
Dead Souls.

Its tough, humorous vulgarity and loose morals makes this the warmest
of Jonson's plays. It lets its fools, knaves, liars and cheats remain
stubbornly themselves. Its true, bracing moral is that men and women are
not changed by experience. Cokes will remain gullible, Justice Overdo will
still be blind to what is really going on around him, Wasp will be angry
with everything. Moral reform, if at all, will have to come in other ways,
and it will have to start when we are young and susceptible to goodness.

It is specific acts that tell us so much, not just words. The sociologist
Max Horkheimer described an office New Year's Eve party in America,
where the classes mingled freely, where the differences between rich and
poor, high and low seemed meaningless. Then a young secretary spilled
some wine over her new dress. While she still laughed and talked, like
everyone else, her hands tried desperately to wipe away the stain. Those
hands betrayed the whole festive spirit of camaraderie.

Such significant moments are always occurring in Jonson's works. One
happens at the end of *Bartholomew Fair* when Justice Overdo discovers his
drunken wife in compromising circumstances and she is sick all over him.
But it is what happens afterwards that is significant. Streaked with his
wife's vomit, Justice Overdo, in a gesture of true magnanimity, invites
everyone to supper to talk over the adventures and misadventures of a
crowded day and to laugh at themselves.

Justice Overdo ignores the comment that his wife's drunkenness implies. For the moment, he accepts life's imperfections and grossness, gives up trying to root out vice and settles for a good dinner and good company. He will cause less misery that way. As in all good plays, our 'hero' has learned something; in this case a little tolerance. All in all, it is a good moral for a comedy.

It is a sign of the greatness of *Bartholomew Fair* that the play continues after the curtain has come down. For it is not only what happens during the play but after that is important. The audience should be able to speculate on the fate of the characters left standing. This gift of imagining is perhaps the most precious playwrights can give their audiences. With *Bartholomew Fair* these imaginings are of the best, for the play leaves us, above all, with good thoughts and good feelings.

Notes

[1] *Nashville*. Dir. Robert Altman. 1975. ABC / Paramount.
[2] *La Règle du Jeu*. Dir. Jean Renoir. 1939. Nouvelle édition française.
[3] Ford Madox Ford, *Critical Essays*, eds Max Saunders and Richard Stang (2002), Carcanet, Manchester.
[4] Ben Jonson, *Bartholomew Fair*, ed. E.A. Horsman, (1960), The Revels Plays, Manchester University Press, Manchester and New York. All references in the text are to this edition.
[5] Ben Jonson, *The Devil is an Ass*, ed. Peter Happé (1994), The Revels Plays, Manchester University Press, Manchester and New York.
[6] *Monsieur Verdoux*. Dir. Charles Chaplin. 1947. United Artists.

Chapter 5

The New Inn and *The Magnetic Lady*: Jonson's Dramaturgy in the Caroline Context

Julie Sanders

John Dryden's posthumous dismissal of Jonson's late plays as 'dotages' has been much cited in scholarly considerations of the playwright's Caroline drama.[1] More recent historicized readings of those same plays – *The Staple of News* (1626), *The New Inn* (1629), *The Magnetic Lady* (1632), *A Tale of a Tub* (1633) and the unfinished *The Sad Shepherd* (c.1637) – have effectively challenged that easy dismissal and drawn our attention back to their rich possibilities, both in critical and performance terms.[2] The biographical misnomer of a Jonson, bed-ridden in his Westminster home by a stroke during much of the Caroline reign, writing out his days in a haze of sentimentality and sub-Shakespearean romance, has in turn been queried by the intellectual control evidenced by a poem such as the Cary–Morison Ode (*Underwood*, LXX),[3] written in the same year that *The New Inn* was reputedly hissed from the stage, as well as the political and social engagement identified in the plays themselves (Barton, 1984: 203). It remains, however, to try to establish what is particular about Jonson's Caroline dramatic canon as well as the ways in which its themes, dramatic strategies and methodologies remain resonant in the theatre of the twentieth and twenty-first centuries. This chapter will deploy *The New Inn* and *The Magnetic Lady* as case studies for that exploration.

Anne Barton's influential studies of Jonson's Caroline canon established a reading of these plays as essentially retrospective in spirit: harking back in their social and political nostalgia, as well as in their manifest interest in the conventions of Shakespearean romantic comedy, to the age of Elizabeth (itself a mythologised construct). Barton's 1984 monograph on Jonson and related articles undoubtedly set the tone for both readings and performances of the plays in the 1980s.[4] *The New Inn* was a particular focus for this influence, not least because in that same decade it witnessed both a major new scholarly edition (Michael Hattaway's 1984 Revels edition of the play)[5] and a performance by a national company (the RSC's 1987 production at the Swan theatre, Stratford-upon-Avon which was directed by John Caird). The 'Shakespearean' inflection of the Caroline plays still holds sway in some quarters: a recent article by John Creaser has argued for the 'loveless, satiric' content of Jonson's middle drama by contrast with 'the more Shakespearean work of his later years'.[6] It would require another volume to explore in detail the denigrating and debilitating effect the Shakespearean comparison has often had on readings of Jonsonian drama, but Creaser's definition of what the middle comedies lack – 'Jonson celebrates the values of a supportive community only by their absence' – releases, by comparison, those aspects of the Caroline late plays which will inform our discussion here. For, by default, Creaser acknowledges that it is in the Caroline section of the Jonson portfolio that we find the clearest interest in heroines and, in a wider sense, in the potentials and possibilities of community.

These sensitive and sensitised depictions are achieved at a spatial, topographical, and representational level in the Caroline plays. This observation provides a key to the relevance of the dramaturgy of these play-texts to the work of contemporary writers discussed in detail elsewhere in this volume. Playwrights such as John Arden and Alan Ayckbourn (as well as screenwriters such as David Mamet) have obvious affinities with Jonson, not least in their sociological form of drama. But it is also important to note that a reading of these contemporary figures can in turn inform our understanding of Jonson. It is not a simple matter of tracing influences upon the modern writers, then, but of acknowledging how awareness of the function or operation of dramaturgic features such as spatial or temporal manipulation in Ayckbourn's social comedies or the civic drive of explorations of community or language in Arden can release readings and performances, repressed or otherwise, from Jonson's Caroline play-texts. Lois Potter has observed that productions of late Jonson, such as Caird's aforementioned version of *The New Inn*, are often charged with sentimentality if they represent a 'sympathetic side' to Jonson, as if that was somehow inaccurate. To make such charges, she stresses, presumes that there is only one 'Jonson' and that he is necessarily a satirical, unsympathetic dramatist, uninterested in community or communal values.[7] The aforementioned work by John Creaser opens up the possibility of different 'Jonsons' at different stages in his writing career. In truth, I am convinced that community concerned Jonson throughout his theatrical and poetic writing career and that future research will continue to find new means of reading and expressing this. Essays elsewhere in this volume on

Sejanus and *Poetaster* are indications of this fact. However, it does seem to me that plays such as *The New Inn* and *The Magnetic Lady* offer us particularly rich means of exploring such topics as Jonson's interest in the position of women, public and civic responsibility, and the sheer affirmative power of drama. His politics can be read on a practical, spatial and performative level.

Jonson's representation of women in his drama has been under critical review for some time and his later plays, including his 1616 *The Devil is an Ass*, have provided a pertinent focus for those discussions.[8] It is not that sensitive portrayals of women were absent from his plays prior to this date – Grace Wellborn in *Bartholomew Fair*, for example, provides a poignant articulation of the fate of the young woman commodified by the early modern marriage market, describing her uncle's wardship in these terms: 'he bought me, sir; and now he will marry me to his wife's brother . . . or else I must pay value o' my land' (3.5.317–20) – but there is something new about the decisive presence of women on Jonson's Caroline stages. In *The New Inn*, we have, for example, the hot-tempered Lady Frances Frampul and the erudite and sensitive servant Prudence whose actions as the carnival queen for the 'day's sports i'the inn' (1.6.44) drive the plot-line of the play, as well as the extravagant figure of Pinnacia Stuff, the tailor's wife who indulges in fetishistic sex dressed in clothes belonging to her aristocratic female superiors, and the 'feigned' Laetitia, who turns out to be the real Laetitia by the fantastic close of the play. In *The Magnetic Lady*, we have the midwives' conspiracy and the cradle-swapped daughters, which not only enables several exclusively female scenes but also a revealing treatment of the professional activity of women in society at this time.[9] At the very heart of the same play stands the Lady Loadstone, whose house, as her nomenclature implies, provides the 'magnetic centre' which Creaser has identified as a recurring trope of Jonsonian drama (2002: 86). *A Tale of a Tub* provides comparable variation in its portraiture of the female community of a Finsbury village: from the élite Lady Tub, obsessing over her son's romantic liaisons, and the High Constable's wife Sybil Turf, who has her own consuming anxieties over the poor display her husband's parsimony will make of their daughter's Valentine's Day wedding, to the various local village girls who long to serve as bridal attendants. Finally, there is the bride herself, freezing in the February air as she dreams of hats and velvets while the men of the village compete for her hand. Variations of age, rank and social function are carefully acknowledged in the dramatic register.[10]

Such details of representation do not necessarily make the case for Jonson as a proto-feminist. Rather, his nuanced female portrayals are to be understood as part of a wider social and civic drive that is detectable in these Caroline plays. The 'busy' Jonsonian stage, as we have seen in other essays in this volume, characterised his dramatic work from early on – the intricate choreographies of time and place in the Paul's Walk scene of *Every Man out of His Humour* are testimony to this fact[11]– but there is something indigenous to the late plays in terms of the spatial complexities of their depictions and the wider sympathies they seem to encourage from the audience in response. The geographical relocation of a number of these plays, away from the metropolis which had become something of a given in Jonson's commercial playhouse drama, is indicative of a more general shift in tonality and concern. The Barnet inn-house setting of *The New Inn*, the North Midlands pastoral of *The Sad Shepherd*, or the Finsbury hundred which provides the locale to *A Tale of a Tub* are alternative spaces to those which dominated Jonson's city comedies. In parallel with the geographical shift, we register an alteration in perspective. Even in *The Magnetic Lady* where the setting is one of Jonson's more familiar London house interiors – the feminocentric environment of Lady Loadstone's house – the men are, in the main, invited dinner guests, there only with female permission; this creates its own social alternatives.

What the dramatic structure of *The Magnetic Lady* confirms as a recurrent Jonsonian theatrical strategy is his adherence to the dramatic unities of place and time. The events in this play take place on a single day: we commence the first act in a street outside the Lady Loadstone's house and subsequently witness a dinner party, and its aftermath, from the house's interior. That dinner party, which is never seen onstage but which is described in intimate detail by several characters, culminates in a physical fight between the hot-tempered soldier Captain Ironside and the foppish courtier Sir Diaphanous Silkworm. This fracas in turn causes one of the women present, Placentia, to fall into premature labour. Following on from these events, a complicated plot-line of cradle-swapped children, concealed pregnancies, and family greed unfolds. By the fifth act, one character observes that the day has grown dark in the course of the proceedings: 'since six o'clock/ All stars were retrograde' (5.10.13–14).[12] The audience has shared the progress and eventual waning of this day in considerable detail. The aforementioned 'day's sports' at the Light Heart in *The New Inn* observe a similar unity of time and place, occurring as they do on a single day at Goodstock the Host's Barnet inn-house. The play's individual acts and scenes record the comings and goings of guests, as well as the quotidian practices of the professionals employed by the hostelry.

This concentrated focus has a particular effect on the audiences for these plays: there is increased identification and engagement with the spaces and places of the drama, a vivid sense of the locale(s) in which they occur.[13] When in *The Magnetic Lady*, Compass's new wife Pleasance has been hidden from him, to prevent her claiming her true inheritance – the Loadstone family fortune – the spaces in which, the audience is told, she is sought, seem vividly real to the imagination. This is predominantly because the creation of the Loadstone house throughout the play has been so intense and fully realised, despite the essentially bare stage typical of early modern drama.[14] We hear of Pleasance that:

> she is not to be found i'the house
> With all the hue and cry is made for her
> Through every room; the larders ha' been searched,
> The bakehouse and boulting tub, the ovens,
> Washhouse, and brewhouse, nay the very furnace
> And yet she is not heard of.

> (5.8.34–9)

The backroom spaces of an early modern urban household are vividly conjured up for audience imaginations here, from the sites of food production to the laundry.[15] Elsewhere in the play, of course, we are also made all too aware of that other unseen, 'private' space of the birthing room, where Placentia gives birth to her illegitimate son. In a striking moment, the midwife Mother Chair draws a direct analogy between this space and that of the theatre tiring-house or dressing room:

> Come, come, be friends, and keep these women-matters
> Smock secrets to ourselves, in our own verge.
> We shall mar all, if once we ope the mysteries
> O'the tiring-house. ...

> (4.7.40–43)

In its most literal sense, of course, the birthing room *is* the tiring house in the Blackfriars theatre where the play was first performed. The women characters, or the boy actors playing them, have retired to this off-stage arena in order to suggest a physical removal within the plot-line of the play to the conspiratorial space of the child-bed: it is one of Jonson's many masterful moments of metatheatricality.

This kind of intensity of spatial imagining on the part of the audience enables Jonson as creating dramatist to harness the potential of spaces other than the stage itself for the purposes of the performance. Off-stage spaces are invested and imbued with significance in these carefully orchestrated play-texts. In *The New Inn*, audiences never see Lovel's lodgings in the inn, where he has been practising the amateur science so beloved of aristocrats of the day and where he retires in a state of emotional turbulence following what he assumes is Lady Frampul's mockery of his love in the midst of the 'court' proceedings, and yet this space is vividly suggested to them. This solipsistic off-stage area signifies Lovel's isolation from the Platonic games of Lady Frampul and her numerous suitors as well as from the boisterous community of the inn-workers and drinkers. It separates him off from the onstage community as much as his melancholic's costume (a *Hamlet*-esque suit of sober black which serves to isolate him visually). Other off-stage spaces which are given vivid verbal portrayal onstage in *The New Inn* include the stables where Peck the ostler indulges in numerous petty criminal acts at the expense of the inn-guests who have stabled their horses in his care, as well as being kicked by his equine charges. The stables are given their most vivid realisation in the descriptions provided by Peck of his activities in Act 3 Scene 1, but later they also provide the site for the clandestine marriage of Lord Beaufort and Laetitia, made public in 5.1. The cellars and 'downstairs' service rooms such as the buttery, from which Pierce the tapster and the other inn professionals frequently appear with sustenance for the guests, are other suggestive off-stage spaces that inform our understanding of the stage tableaux. The audience's spatial awareness of these off-stage rooms was enhanced in the 1987 RSC production by an inventive deployment of trapdoors and alternative sites of entry.

In *The Magnetic Lady*, the most obviously influential off-stage space is the dining room. According to the spatial dynamics of the drama, this is a chamber just adjoining the main stage area. In the third act, it is that room in which the fractious dinner party occurs, an explosive event that causes various guests to burst into the adjoining room with their variant accounts and responses. Jonson has nurtured the audience's sense of that room by having characters peep off-stage and describe in detail the seating arrangements around the table:

> **KEEP**   How are they set?
> **NEEDLE**   At the board's end, my lady –
> **KEEP**   And my young mistress by her?
> **NEEDLE**   Yes, the parson
> On the right hand (as he'll not lose his place
> For thrusting) and 'gainst him, Mistress Polish:
> Next, Sir Diaphanous against Sir Moth;
> Knights, one again another: then the soldier,
> The man of war, and man of peace, the lawyer:
> Then the pert doctor, and the politic Bias
> And Master Compass circumscribeth all.

Following this, the audience hears various 'noises off' and then Compass, Ironside, Silkworm and the Lady Loadstone reacting onstage to the quarrel. Audiences also witness the dramatic sight of Placentia being carried away in what will prove to be the first stages of labour. Characters exit the stage into equally resonant off-stage spaces: Compass's nearby house; the closet to which the socially wounded hostess retires; and the birthing chamber to which Placentia is rushed and the midwife summoned in secrecy.

The comic and dramatic potential of the off-stage scene of the dinner party is exploited to the full by Jonson. The dramatic placement of the scene in the third act, at what Peter Holland has described as the 'central plateau' of early modern five-act drama, is only part of its resonance and centrality to audience experience.[16] In many respects we are dealing here with the enclosed spaces and ever-opening doors of the genre of dramatic farce; Jonson was a master at creating these restricted, yet suggestive arenas, as the intensely realised indoors settings of both *Volpone* and *The Alchemist* indicate.[17] *The Alchemist* is another play dependent on audience imagination of the off-stage area: the potential to believe in Subtle and Face's fabricated alchemical laboratory must exist so that audiences are shocked by Lovewit's description of what he finds on entering his house in the fifth act:

> Here I find
> The empty walls, worse than I left 'em, smoked,
> A few cracked pots, and glasses, and a furnace,
> The ceiling filled with poesies o'the candle:
> And 'Madam with a dildo', writ o'the walls.
>
> (5.5.38–42)

This picture of degradation scarcely fits the vivid theatrical performance audiences have been witnessing for the previous four acts. Jonson wants them to register the huge discrepancy: it is as if they share Sir Epicure Mammon's sense of shock: 'What! In a dream?' (5.5.83).

This manipulation of stage space and of the spaces just beyond the audience's gaze is a technique and strategy familiar in modern drama from the plays of Alan Ayckbourn. The carefully contrived architectonic structure of dramas such as the three play-texts which make up the trilogy of *The Norman Conquests* (1975) or the paired *House* and *Garden* (1999) is equally dependent on the audience's power on the night of the performance of any single play in the groupings to imagine what is going on in the other rooms of the house, or in the garden, just off-stage. Similarly, in Ayckbourn's *Absurd Person Singular*, set on successive Christmas Eves, the familiar rituals of eating, drinking and storytelling are displaced, as in *The Magnetic Lady*, to the space just off-stage and the audience is privy instead to the tensions expressed when characters 'exit' the party onto the stage.

Richard Cave explores the instructive affinities between Ayckbourn's *oeuvre* and the Jonsonian dramatic canon in detail in chapter 13 of this volume, but, as these brief invocations indicate, Ayckbourn's interest in social gatherings or festive rituals – his plays frequently occur on festive dates such as Christmas or birthdays, or focus around social and familial gathering points such as parties and funerals – have their own Jonsonian suggestiveness.[18] If, as Stephen Lacey's chapter indicates, the broad social canvas of a playwright like John Arden has its creative roots in the self-consciously festive drama of *Bartholomew Fair* (and by extension, I would argue, in the village environment of *A Tale of a Tub* and the unfinished pastoral *The Sad Shepherd*), the more specific and restricted stage communities of plays such as *The New Inn* and *The Magnetic Lady* find insightful echoes or parallels in much of Ayckbourn's work. In a manner directly akin to *The Magnetic Lady*'s temporal progress, the events of *House* and *Garden*, which take place on the day of a summer fête, another social ritual which Ayckbourn savagely dissects, are carefully timed to stretch from early morning to encroaching darkness (of course, in a manner which Jonson would surely have admired, they are also carefully timed to allow the actors to move between the auditoria in which the paired plays are staged on the same night). Michael Billington has observed Ayckbourn's own rigid adherence to the Aristotelian unities in his later dramatic works (1990: 20). Related manipulation of audience involvement and empathy is at stake in Ayckbourn's work. The historical line from Jonson's intricately depicted High Constable Toby Turf in *A Tale of a Tub*, clinging to the responsibilities and presumed status of his local office despite the near-collapse of his own daughter's wedding day, to the petty officials and committee-men of Ayckbourn plays such as *Ten Times Table* or the social pretence of Teddy, the prospective parliamentary candidate in *House* and *Garden*, seems remarkably clear, despite Ayckbourn's suggestion that any relationship with the Jonsonian style or aesthetic is happy coincidence.[19] In this way, the Valentine's day setting of *A Tale of a Tub* with all its attendant resonance of the lottery of love that was the early modern tradition on this occasion seems positively prescient of Ayckbourn's festive comedies.

A further recognisable trait of Ayckbourn's drama that seems to offer us a route back into considering the spatialities and significances of Jonson's Caroline drama is his interest in social rank, status and class. The contrast between the exchanges in the juxtaposed spaces of *House* and *Garden* are revealing in terms of demonstrating the deep pervasiveness of class distinctions in contemporary British society. In *House*, the full story of Pearl the cook, her daughter Izzie, and the gardener Warn, and their complex *ménage-à-trois*, is only heard in snippets through the door leading to the kitchen. This is another of those resonant off-stage spaces where pots seem to get thrown and tempers flare in a manner akin to the dinner party of *The Magnetic Lady*. These 'servants' – for it is clear that this is their assigned role in the modern country house that the play concerns itself with – are held just off-stage, offering moments of exquisite tension when they do accidentally stumble across the stage threshold and into the complex emotional and sexual worlds of their masters. Of course, Ayckbourn intends a levelling effect in some respects: why are the sexual complications of Warn's liaisons with both Izzie and her daughter any worse or better than the paedophilic tendencies of Gavin or Teddy's infidelities? Interestingly, Izzie's class-led veneration of Trish the 'lady of the house' and Admiral's daughter is exposed as equally false accounting as the paired plays unfold: the Trish who confronts Joanna about her affair with Teddy in *Garden* is scarcely the refined figure Izzie has constructed in her imagination. Jonson would have appreciated, I think, all the undoings and uncasings, social and sexual, of Ayckbourn's drama. The festive gathering of *House* and *Garden*, set as it is on the day of the annual country fête, seems self-consciously resonant of a play such as *Bartholomew Fair* which allowed for intermingling of a social and sexual nature within the Smithfield booths. Warn, deliberately confusing the guests by switching all the signs and revelling in the resultant misunderstanding, seems an almost Jonsonian creation: an agent of chaos and a catalyst for encounters and revelations held just in check as the play opens. Trouble-All of *Bartholomew Fair* provides an obvious comparison.[20]

The space of the public house in *The New Inn* offers an equally redolent site of cross-class and cross-gender liaison, parallel to, if also distinct from, the Smithfield fair of Jonson's 1614 play.[21] Levelling effects similar to those delineated in Ayckbourn's festive comedies are achieved in Jonson's innhouse play, since the environment of the Light Heart encourages encounters between ostlers and ladies, lords and tapsters. Early exchanges between Lord Lovel and the Host of the Light Heart, Goodstock, reveal the importance of social stratification in the society of the play: Lovel is surprised that someone of the Host's profession is so articulate. Of course, any claim to Jonson's sociological radicalism here is limited by the fact that the fifth act confirms Goodstock as Lord Frampul and therefore a member of the educated élite, but it remains a fact that the swift social judgements made by the likes of Sir Glorious Tiptoe according to a person's dress or profession are implicitly questioned. Prudence is never revealed to be anything other than of the servant class and she is, as her name suggests, in essence, the moral centre of Jonson's play. As with Ayckbourn's *House* and *Garden*, however, the spatial dynamics of *The New Inn* also encourage a consideration of class and rank and their operations in society. The inn itself offers a picture, as does the fair of *Bartholomew Fair*, of guests and workers, juxtaposing the leisured class with that of artisans and professionals. There are strict demarcations within the encounters and conversations of the play between the 'upstairs' and 'downstairs' worlds of the inn-house. Whilst Lady Frances is clearly of the élite 'upstairs' environs and so is Lovel, her liveried coach-driver Trundle associates with the inn-workers and the drunken underworld of the Light Heart's downstairs or cellar environment. Ironically, Tiptoe, in his egotistical desire to command this 'citizen militia', finds himself consigned for the majority of the play to this underworld, unable to operate at any effective level in the élite space of the mock-court. Richard McCabe, who played Tiptoe in the 1987 RSC production, was constantly pushed to the edge of the dominant stage space, consigned to the margins of a world in which his ego had perceived he was central. Prudence, of course, like Goodstock, is a transitional character in the play and on the stage; she can move between the two worlds, and understand the benefits and limitations of both. In any performance, these spatial dynamics are paramount to a successful staging of *The New Inn*. In the 1987 production, Sue Blane's inspired set design (shown in figure 1, p. 61) made much of the significance and symbolism of levels and stages. It mattered where a character was positioned when they presented a particular speech or remark. Many of the play's central speeches, such Lovel's expositions on love and valour, delivered as part of the neo-Platonic Court of Love, were delivered from an additional raised dais placed on the already raised space of the inn's central drinking space. The 'lower' characters were very much restricted to the below stage space accessed by traps and side doors in a spatial declaration of their social function. Like Warn the gardener in Ayckbourn's *Garden*, they seemingly 'know their place', though this should not cause audiences to underestimate such characters' capacity for mischief as the onstage 'battle of the centaurs' in Act 4 indicates.

Plate 1:   The stage set for *The New Inn* (Swan Theatre, 1987)
Designer: Sue Blane, Photograph © Geoff Lockyer

Reproduced by kind permission of Ronnie Mulryne, Margaret Shewring and Geoff Lockyer. This image first appeared in Mulryne, Ronnie and Shewring, Margaret (1989), *This Golden Round*, Mulryne and Shewring Ltd, Stratford-upon-Avon.

Sue Blane's stage setting of *The New Inn* also reveals the complex and suggestive blurring that was achieved between the theatre space of the Swan theatre and the 'stage proper' in the 1987 production. Lois Potter notes of this metatheatrical set:

> Made of the same golden wood as the theatre itself, it created a continuum between stage and audience, while at the same time the stairs and landings of which it was composed allowed the actors easily to become, and to see themselves as, performers on a stage.
>
> (Potter, 1999: 200)

The use of levels and stairs allowed upstairs/downstairs divisions to be maintained or collapsed as suited the purpose of each individual scene or exchange. It is a strategy Ayckbourn is adept at deploying in plays such as *A Small Family Business*. The metatheatrical continuum between playing space and play is something Jonson had earlier deployed to great effect in metropolitan plays such as *The Alchemist* and *Bartholomew Fair* which represented onstage the world that existed just outside the theatre doors, a little distorted and exaggerated for comic effect perhaps, but instantly recognisable nonetheless. Ayckbourn has inherited this gift for capturing the essence of the contemporary.

What Sue Blane's *New Inn* set also captured in a spatial and intellectual sense is the implicit metatheatricality of Jonson's play. Both the Host and the woman revealed by the close to be his eldest daughter, Lady Frances Frampul, espouse the commonplace of *theatrum mundi*: that all the world is a stage and all the men and women merely players. While Lady Frampul comforts her servant at the prospect of seeing her elegant dresses handed on to a company of players with the thought that 'Tut, all are players and but serve the scene, Pru;' (2.1.39), the Host says that the Light Heart is a space:

> Where I imagine all the world's a play:
> The state and men's affairs, all passages
> Of life, to spring new scenes, come in, go out,
> And shift and vanish;
>
> (1.3.128–31)

To emphasise these theatre/inn analogies in the 1987 production, when Joseph Connor as the Host made the observation that he enjoyed 'A seat to sit at ease here, i'mine inn,/ To see the comedy' (1.4.132–3), he descended a further flight of steps which lead off the main stage towards a seat reserved for him in the audience. He then momentarily watched the play with the audience, from their perspective, seeing in a very literal way their point of view. In this way, the levelling properties of stages and steps proved to have implications indirectly for the audience as well as directly for the characters: it is a trick of identification that early modern drama recognised well.

Adherence to the unities of place and space in early modern and modern drama alike encourages an awareness of blurrings and continuums on the part of audiences. In this way, Jonson ensured an audience as aware of its responses, and as tested by them, as any imagined by Bertolt Brecht in the early part of the twentieth century. Jonson's conscious and careful adherence to the dramatic unity of time, like Ayckbourn's in several of his dramas, also fostered a heightened awareness in the audience of the temporal and temporary nature of what is being witnessed onstage. In Ayckbourn's *House* and *Garden*, the day of the fête is always rushing headlong to its close and the climax of the day's revelations (Trish's Ibsenesque departure from her life with the slamming of the front door); in his *A Chorus of Disapproval*, the rehearsals for the production of John Gay's *The Beggar's Opera* are always destined to end in the performance itself (to emphasise this, Ayckbourn opens that play with this climactic moment, only then to move backwards in time to the production's embryonic stages). The puppet play of *Bartholomew Fair* or the fading light of *The Magnetic Lady* find their counterparts here. In the RSC *New Inn*, the time-limited aspect of the play's events were stressed via the deployment of simple yet effective stage properties: in order to emphasise the temporary nature of the Court of Love, called into session for two hours in the course of the day's theatricals, Prudence, the servant allowed to be Queen over her mistress during that carnivalesque moment, sat with an oversize hourglass alongside her on the stage. Unlike Jonson, however, John Caird as director chose to allow the downstairs community back onstage to share in the final song: an image of harmony resisted in Jonson's text. Perhaps though in Lord Frampul's bequest of the inn to Fly at the close of the text, the future of the downstairs workers is assured. The social concerns of Jonson are sounded in his Caroline drama not fainter as has sometimes been claimed, but possibly louder and stronger than ever. These concerns are realised in the characterisations, the stage communities, and the spatial dynamics of these rich and rewarding texts.

In his 1984 edition of *The New Inn*, Michael Hattaway drew a comparison between Shakespeare and Jonson and their relevant relationship to both literary criticism and contemporary performance:

> Every critic of Jonson is left with the disconcerting feeling that he has uncovered no more and no less in a poem or play than Jonson put into it. ... When it comes to the production of Jonson's plays, the best productions will

confine themselves within the hard outlines of Jonson's vision, whereas a good Shakespearean production may realise meanings that are merely latent in the text or which may be applied to it in the light of a modern director's own experience.

(Hattaway, 1984: 38)

This brief foray into the complexities of Jonsonian dramaturgy in the Caroline plays offers, I hope, a clear refutation of Hattaway's limiting account of Jonson. In the connections we find between these long-ignored dramas and the experiments of Brecht and Meyerhold, to the obvious affinities with the communal emphases of Arden and Ayckbourn (among others), we find instead of hard outlines and fixed meanings, the multiple possibilities of interpretation and performance: possibilities in part only revealed by close attention to these twentieth and twenty-first-century theatrical practitioners. This is happy proof that not only does Jonson give us a means to read modern play-texts, but that reading and staging his plays alongside those of his modern counterparts can release meanings, repressed or otherwise, from both. The relationship between Jonson and contemporary theatre is a two-way and ongoing process.

Notes

The research for this article has been generously assisted by a grant from the Arts and Humanities Research Board. The author would also like to thank The Shakespeare Centre Library in Stratford-upon-Avon for access to research materials on the 1987 RSC production of *The New Inn*. Ronnie Mulryne and Geoff Locker gave kind permission to reproduce the image of Sue Blane's set for that production. Further thanks are due to the participants in the University of Reading 'Jonsonians' symposium for their stimulating thoughts and ideas, with special mention going to Stephen Lacey who introduced me to the work of John Arden for which I shall be endlessly grateful.

[1] See, for example, C.H. Herford and Percy and Evelyn Simpson (eds) (1925–52), *The Complete Works of Ben Jonson*, Clarendon Press, Oxford, 11 vols., 1: 278–9 and Anne Barton (1984), *Ben Jonson, Dramatist*, Cambridge University Press, Cambridge. p. 263.
[2] The work of Martin Butler is seminal in this respect. See, for example, his (1992) 'Late Jonson', in Gordon McMullan and Jonathan Hope (eds), *The Politics of Tragicomedy: Shakespeare and After*, Routledge, London, pp. 166–88.
[3] 'To the immortall memorie, and friendship of that noble paire, Sir Lucius Cary and Sir H. Morison', in *The Underwood* in Herford and the Simpsons (1925–52), 8: 242–7.
[4] See Barton, 1984, and also her (1979), '*The New Inn* and the problem of Jonson's late style', *ELR* 9: 395–418.

[5] Ben Jonson, *The New Inn*, ed. Michael Hattaway (1984), Manchester University Press, Manchester. This is the edition of *The New Inn* cited throughout.

[6] John Creaser, (2002) 'Forms of Confusion', in Alexander Leggatt (ed.), *The Cambridge Companion to Shakespearean Comedy*, Cambridge University Press, Cambridge, pp. 81–101 (83).

[7] Lois Potter (1999), 'The Swan Song of the Stage Historian', in Martin Butler (ed.), *Representing Ben Jonson*, Macmillan, London, pp. 193–209 (204).

[8] The work of Helen Ostovich has been influential here. See in particular her (1997b) 'Mistress and Maid: Women and Friendship in *The New Inn*', *Ben Jonson Journal* 4: 1–26 and (1998) 'Hell for Lovers: Shades of Adultery in *The Devil is an Ass*', in Julie Sanders, with Kate Chedgzoy and Susan Wiseman (eds), *Refashioning Ben Jonson: Gender, Politics and the Jonsonian Canon*, Macmillan, London. pp. 155–82.

[9] For a more detailed discussion of this aspect of the play, see my (1999b), 'Midwifery and the New Science in the Seventeenth Century: Language, Print and Theatre', in Erica Fudge, Ruth Gilbert and Susan Wiseman (eds), *At the Borders of the Human: Beasts, Bodies and Natural Philosophy in the early modern period*, Macmillan, London, pp. 74–90.

[10] Barton has further noted that the portrayal of the Robin Hood-Maid Marian relationship in *The Sad Shepherd* is that of a 'mature, settled but passionate love' (1984: 346), not usually a subtlety with which Jonson is credited in accounts of his representations of women. That same play evidences a sensitive understanding of the witch-hunt phenomenon in its depiction of the social contribution to the demonisation and marginalisation of the sorceress Maudlin. See my (1999a) 'Jonson, *The Sad Shepherd* and the North Midlands', *Ben Jonson Journal* 6: 49–68.

[11] This scene is brilliantly analysed by Helen Ostovich in her Revels edition of the play: Ben Jonson (2001), *Every Man out of His Humour*, Manchester University Press, Manchester.

[12] The edition cited throughout is that edited by Peter Happé for the Revels series: Ben Jonson (2000), *The Magnetic Lady*, Manchester University Press, Manchester.

[13] There is a related argument to be made about the extent to which the private theatre location for these plays encouraged this more intimate engagement; certainly, Shakespeare's *The Tempest* (1611), rare in his canon in terms of its adherence to the dramatic unities, was a Blackfriars theatre play, as are *The New Inn* and *The Magnetic Lady*.

[14] For a brilliant description of Jonson's deployment of off-stage spaces in this play, see Peter Happé's introduction to his Revels edition (2000: 11).

[15] Something similar is achieved in Jonson's 1618 Masque, *Pleasure Reconciled to Virtue* when the 'downstairs' spaces of production for the feast that would have accompanied the Masque are made explicit in the antimasque's opening 'hymn', ll. 10–21 (Stephen Orgel (ed.) (1969), *Ben Jonson: The Complete Masques*, Yale University Press, Newhaven, Connecticut.

[16] Peter Holland (1997), *English Shakespeares: Shakespeare on the English Stage in the 1990s*, Cambridge University Press, Cambridge, p. 4.

[17] For a vivid exploration of the onstage and off-stage places of these plays, see Ian Donaldson (1997), *Jonson's Magic Houses: Essays in Interpretation*, Clarendon Press, Oxford, pp. 66–88.

[18] On Ayckbourn's propensity for these ritual and ritualised settings, see Michael Billington (1990), *Alan Ayckbourn*, 2nd edn., Macmillan, London, p. 52.

[19] In his 1995 *Plays One*, Faber, London, Ayckbourn recounts that when Peter Hall saw *A Small Family Business*, he 'described the piece as a modern morality play. He said it reminded him of Ben Jonson. I later read some Ben Jonson but I must confess I didn't understand much of it. Still, I was very flattered' (ix). See also p. 178, chapter 13 of this volume.

[20] It is interesting too to recall Bartholomew Cokes's vulnerability to the signs, literal and figurative, of the London metropolis in Jonson's carnivalesque drama. As Wasp recounts in the opening act:

> We ha' been but a day and a half in town . . . but before I will endure another half day with him, I'll be drawn with a good gibcat through the great pond at home . . . Why, we could not meet that heathen thing all day but stayed him: he would name you all the signs over, as he went, aloud: and where he spied a parrot, or a monkey, there he was pitched, with all the little long-coats about him, male and female; no getting him away!'   (1.4.121–32).

[21] Rebecca Ann Bach makes fruitful comparisons between the two texts in her (2000), *Colonial Transformations: The Cultural Production of the New Atlantic World 1580–1640*, Palgrave, London, pp. 113–48.

Part II

Sons and Daughters of Ben

Chapter 6

The Playwriting Sons of Ben:
Nathan Field and Richard Brome

Richard Allen Cave

Some problematic terms

Attempting to determine degrees and kinds of influence is not an easy
matter, particularly in the present critical climate where postmodernism and
intertextuality have considerably extended the sphere of activities which
may be defined as 'influence'. The task is easier with post-Romantic
authors, since memoirs, diaries, correspondence make it possible to gauge
either the extent to which one writer may have advised another over the
creating of a given work or the way in which one artist may be consciously
imitating aspects of the style, structure or thematic content of a peer or
predecessor. With Renaissance authors this kind of guide is generally non-
existent. With dramatists engaging in the practice of performing or
mounting plays (as was the case with many Renaissance playwrights) the
possibilities for both deliberate and unconscious influence are legion. There
is always too the pressure to imitate currently popular conventions to
achieve a like success, which is another (culturally determined) kind of
influence.

Intertextuality has alerted us to the degree to which authors may 'quote'
from others' work, the better to define their own difference in method of
handling, value-system, aesthetic principle and so on. (The technique in
Western drama can be traced back at least as far as Euripides and
Aristophanes.) But this too argues a kind of influence, at least a knowledge
of the work cited as the groundbase against which the new variations are
being worked. Can we think of influence when the context, as here, reveals
an intention to define an independent line of artistic development or
enquiry? The answer would seem to be in the affirmative, since the
outcome for the reader or spectator is to be invited to participate in a
dialogue between two modes of expression and the social, psychological,
emotional and aesthetic principles that are bound up in each of them.

Postmodernism takes this technique to an extreme, flaunting references to the past, often with prodigal abandon, to define a freedom from all determining forms of closure, aesthetic, moral, structural. But that conscious rejection of the past (recent or remote) is an acknowledgement of familiarity with what is being rejected; and even that degree of 'knowing' is, arguably a form of influence. What that line of argument supposes is that 'influence' may be subtly pervasive and not simply a matter of detecting precise correspondences between one author's work and another's.

Mention of 'correspondences' raises another pertinent issue. Discussion of 'influence' generally tends to suppose a one-way activity: that an established, mature artist helps guide and shape the budding talent of a younger disciple, until the junior finds her or his own 'voice'. This was the popular mode of interpreting influence by late nineteenth-century and early twentieth-century critics. But an alert mentor can learn much from a bright pupil; and so influence again becomes problematised. This is particularly the case in the context of Renaissance theatre, where most writers, even Shakespeare and Jonson, at various stages of their careers were involved in collaborative ventures. Indeed the processes involved in staging a performance encompass an intricate web of collaborations, especially in the Renaissance theatre, between dramatist and actor. Does shared creative endeavour amount to influence? The insight gained in the process may subsequently be put to positive or critical use by all the contributors involved. The *potential* for influence was extensive and extensively varied where Jonson and his contemporaries were concerned; and this must be borne in mind when assessing Jonson's relations with his playwriting 'sons'.

'Sons' is a second problematic term. Jonson himself deployed the word in respect of a number of younger men who imitated his style of poetry (Herrick, Suckling, Sir Kenelm Digby and Lord Falkland) rather than his work as dramatist. That there was a two-way flow of influence as consequence of his collaborations with the likes of Marston and Chapman (on *Eastward Ho!*) or in the creating of the Masques with Inigo Jones is evident, but these, like his playwright friends (Shakespeare, Beaumont and Fletcher), are all too senior as peers to be designated 'sons'. Caroline dramatists, Shirley particularly, could not but be aware of the aged Jonson's lingering presence and authority. But though there are traces and resonances of Jonson's plays in Shirley's first comedy, *Love Tricks* of 1625 (later re-titled, *The School of Compliment*), the influence of *As You Like It* appears much stronger and one can detect echoes of Fletcher and Massinger too. Jonson was no major tutelary spirit, for all that Shirley was named in the period as Jonson's literary successor, except in the devising of Shirley's

Masques, where he cultivates a light, elegant and diverse fancy in the framing of the spoken and sung lyrics which show a decided debt to his senior.

The two dramatists who best qualify for the denomination of 'sons' would appear to be Nathan Field (1587–1619) and Richard Brome (d.c.1652). Both dramatists are named in Jonson's works (*Bartholomew Fair* refers to Field along with Burbage as the acme of actors, while Brome is described there as 'his [Jonson's] man' in a context which makes him less a servant than his assistant in the tiring house behind the stage).[1] Field was one of the stars amongst the boy players after 1600; he specialised initially in playing female roles and then excelled in a range of young romantic *male* leads. It has variously been estimated that he played in the following Jonsonian comedies: *Cynthia's Revels*, *Poetaster*, the 1608 revival of Jonson's early work *The Case Is Altered*, and *Epicœne*. His leading role in *Eastward Ho!* may have led to his imprisonment along with Jonson and Chapman, when the king expressed his displeasure at the play and the company of the Queen's Revels. Jonson informed Drummond fondly of their reading Latin authors together. Theirs was a working relationship, lasting over a decade, focused on the practicalities of staging comedies. Clearly from the reference in *Bartholomew Fair* Jonson thought highly of Field's gifts as an actor and (on the evidence) as a female impersonator. Brome's relationship with Jonson lasted far longer: though nothing is known for certain about the date in which Brome entered the dramatist's household, he survived Jonson and cared for him in his final years, seemingly having the responsibility for supervising the staging of Jonson's later Caroline comedies after the poet became bedridden. It too, then, was a relationship centred for much of its time on the practice of theatre. Field authored two plays in his own right; Brome at least fifteen; both were involved in collaborations, though not ostensibly with Jonson. The prefatory material to Brome's plays frequently admits to his creative debts to Jonson, while Jonson in the poems congratulating Brome on the publication of *The Northern Lass* (1632) praised him as 'my old Faithful Servant and (by his continu'd Vertue) my loving Friend'[2] and admired Brome's tenacity in undertaking a proper apprenticeship to the craft of playwright 'which few do now adays'. It may seem presumptuous or foolhardy to refer to Brome and Field as 'sons of Ben', since nowhere does Jonson explicitly refer to either in that fashion (while, to complicate matters, in his complimentary verses accompanying the publication of Field's first comedy, *A Woman Is A Weathercock* (1612) Chapman claims the young actor-dramatist as his 'loved son').[3] But when one approaches their work with the complex issues surrounding the nature of influence in mind, then Field and Brome would seem to merit the designation as properly and fully as any of the poets Jonson himself chose so to honour. Both sustained a creative relationship with Jonson which was productive for all three writers. It is characteristic of Jonson that he valued his poetic imitators more highly than his younger associates in the writing and staging of drama, since it is to poetry that he invariably awarded the supreme accolade amongst the literary arts. But that his particular (and fiercely guarded) independent genius had a fertile effect on these two dramatists is notable, because it is difficult to think of any other writer of comedies in the period of whom the same might be claimed. Perhaps after the Poetamachia and the public bruising of Marston, Dekker and Jonson that resulted, playwrights were careful to avoid imitating Jonson's dramaturgy, lest he chastise them for their arrogance. Field, however, had won Jonson's respect as a practitioner; Brome as a steadfast and loyal amanuensis and as a diligent apprentice; neither needed to fear risking his scorn.

Jonson and Field

A remarkable fact is that Jonson's *Epicœne* in which Field acted[4] and Field's *A Woman Is A Weathercock* were first played within weeks or even days of each other at the start of the 1609–10 season. Since plague delayed public performances that season till early December, Beaurline dates the staging of *Epicœne* 'to a period between December 7, 1609 and early February 1610'.[5] Perry opines, with impressive scholarly support, that 'it seems probable that the original Whitefriars production of *A Woman Is A Weathercock* occurred between 1 December 1609 and the performance at Court that Christmas' (p. 58). Both comedies take as their subject an investigation of the nature of gender; the way social pressures have determined stereotypical patterns of behaviour which are judged as properly masculine or feminine; and the battling between the sexes that is the likely consequence of this (a situation clearly aggravated by the strongly patriarchal social and political context that obtains). These are sensitive issues requiring sensitive handling and it is not surprising that Jonson has been accused of misogyny in his play. Much, however, depends on the manner of the playing (particularly in the original production when all the roles would have been played by boys or young men, which might have led to a satirising of one sex more predominantly than the other); but it is possible to read *Epicœne* and stage it as equally critical of male and female behaviour, when it becomes at first deeply disturbing for its lack of any balancing corrective stance and later, at least to a modern view, liberating in its suggestion that gender characteristics are fluid.[6] The play is more an attack on the processes of stereotyping than on either gender. That Field may have faced similar charges of misogyny may be deduced from the published quarto of 1612, where the author promises in the prefatory matter addressed to any woman vexed by seeing or reading his depiction of her sex in his comedy that his next play will make ample amends (p. 68). And indeed it bears the title *Amends for Ladies*. But it can be argued that *A Woman Is A Weathercock* also examines the way stereotypical gender assumptions, especially by men of women, can dangerously control and affect judgement, leading to the discomfiture of both sexes. Though not as dark a comedy as *Epicœne*, it contains some sharp-edged scenes where a man's harassing of a woman's reputation or her psyche has a force that leaves one more critical of him than of her.[7]

Given the proximity of the dates of performance, it is not possible to determine whether one play directly influenced the other or whether, as seems more likely, they exist creatively in a kind of symbiotic relationship.[8] Field's has the appearance of rather hasty composition (while much of the action focuses on two of Worldly's three daughters, the third, Lucida, who affects to renounce men and their amatory pursuits, is hardly developed beyond an emblematic cipher, sporting her willow garland;[9] and the ending is not well paced if the resolutions of the various strands of plot are to be readily grasped); Jonson's play exhibits signs of longer planning and drafting to achieve what to Dryden was its perfect structure. It is significant that Jonson gave his new comedy to the Children of Her Majesty's Revels rather than to a company of adult professionals: it is markedly different in tone and content with its emphasis on life in fashionable London society from the earlier *Every Man in His Humour* (staged by the Lord Chamberlain's Men) which, though it interrogates styles of masculinity, does so in a less caustic vein. The boy-players had a reputation for playing comedies and tragedies with a marked sexual content. Jonson, knowing the expected audience, seems initially to be catering to their taste before he begins systematically to hold that taste up to question. Field's comedy sustains a similar strategy, giving voice to a misogyny which is then deconstructed. Considering that all the historical evidence proves the men at the time were working regularly together and for a specific company with a particular repertoire, it is not surprising that their two plays should bear marked resemblances.

Both plays withhold the first appearance of the leading female roles (Epicœne and Bellafront) till some way into the action, building up expectation by a variety of means. When finally we see Epicœne (2.3.1), she says little and that in decorously suppressed tones, and scarcely moves except when instructed to do so. She is in every respect the model wife that Morose has fantasised over possessing. Her doll-like *presence* is the focus of the stage picture, since her appearance, vocal timbre, manner of address, conduct and deportment are the continuing topics of the dialogue. It is a calculated strategy to make the character's transformation into the married Epiccene, wilful, commanding, intransigent and feisty, all the funnier. Bellafront does not physically appear till the marriage procession (2.1.116–21), though the striking up of an offstage band with appropriate wedding music (1.2.393) which causes her father to assure her would-be groom that 'Your Bride is readie', might have led spectators to expect to see her sooner. However her presence and her 'voice' are potently felt throughout Act One, since by a brilliant creative stroke the play opens with the reading of a letter from her to her (former) suitor, Scudmore. Because it seems to flatter his fondest hopes of marrying her, it sends him into ecstasies of delight; but he is soon pitched into the nadir of despair when his friend Neuill casually informs him that he is in haste to go to a wedding which is Bellafront's with Count Frederick. That despair unleashes a fierce misogyny in Scudmore, who rails against the inconstancy of women. But the fluctuating of his emotional extremes and the violence of his language cause one to ponder retrospectively whether her meaning in the letter might have been different from how Scudmore has interpreted it. She had dismissed his worries about the differences in their class and background, rehearsed her sense of his excellence, and promised herself as constant *'through the world, and to the end of Time'* (1.1.24). Beside Scudmore's passionate outburst which ensues, the tone of her letter is remarkably controlled in its rhetoric and extended syntactical periods. It could be a stoical farewell, pledging like Penthea in Ford's *The Broken Heart*, a spiritual fidelity even though the body may have been forced by circumstance to give itself reluctantly elsewhere (the mention of social difference at the start of the letter might hint at patriarchal pressures to conform to parental will, as proves to be the case). So: we have Bellafront's 'voice' and Scudmore's interpretation of it, followed by her prolonged abstention from appearing to anyone's gaze, even when the music would seemingly announce her approach. Field has built the construction of Bellafront as an enigma.

She says little to Scudmore when he confronts her on her way to church, urging the procession 'forward a Gods name there' (2.1.145); when he persists, she is coldly dismissive: 'You are insolent, nay strangely sawcie Sir, / To wrong me in this publicke fashion' (2.1.162–3). Scudmore, left alone when the procession enters the church, vows to find a time to shame her, threatening to 'looke her dead, speak her to hell' (2.1.218). But when the bridal party returns, the action changes its focus to the fortunes of Bellafront's sister, Kate, to which she remains onstage a silent witness. It is not until Act Three Scene Two that Scudmore seizes his moment when, disguised, he enters the private room to which significantly Bellafront has withdrawn away from the marriage celebrations where she chooses to have no part. What follows is a curious sequence: curious, because of the resonances which the dialogue carries of Hamlet's scene with Gertrude in her closet (*Hamlet*, 3.4.) Perry refers to these carefully in his Introduction to the play as 'suggestions' (60), which implies unconscious borrowing or casual echoes.[10] Initially Scudmore watches over a sleeping Bellafront, much as Hamlet broods over the praying Claudius, trying to reconcile her appearance of innocence with his sense of her falsehood to him: '...could Nature make / So faire a superficies, to enclose / So false a heart...' (3.2.81–3), yet he cannot but admit '*Pallas* so sat (methinkes) in *Hectors* Tent' (3.2.86). The sense of her likeness to the majestic Athene is lost the moment he wakes her, when all his scorn and injured dignity pours forth in a torrent that allows her little space within which to frame a defence: 'Oh peace, for you speake sharpnesse to my soule' (3.2.125). When she contrives to define her social predicament that has forced an unwanted marriage on her ('the threats / Of a seuere Father, that in his hand / Did gripe my fortunes'), he will have none of it. Chiefly, one suspects, because she intimates that a further motive in her leaving him was his misogyny:

> ...next to that, the fame
> Of your neglect, and liberall talking tongue,
> Which bred my honour an eternall wrong.

> (3.2.135–9)

Scudmore does not listen: he dismisses her words as 'painted causes' (3.2.140) and sees her as wearing a 'Diuels Vizard / That did deforme this face, and blinde my soule' (3.2.176–7). He refuses the pity she begs of him and remains 'implacable'. Though she urges him to find the means to prevent her entering the marriage bed and threatens to commit suicide if he fails her in this, he races out with the cruel riposte: 'Pish do, the world will haue one mischiefe lesse' (3.2.230).

We have been presented as spectators largely with Scudmore's view of Bellafront: we too have heard the letter, since he read it aloud; we have seen her near-silent progress to the church; but we have also noted her marked absence from the wedding festivities. Are we to interpret the echoes of Hamlet's interview with Gertrude as borrowings or as a deliberate intertextual strategy? Gertrude, though touched with a degree of guilt, does not merit Hamlet's savage critique, to stem which requires the

Ghost's re-appearance. How are the audience, as distinct from Scudmore, to interpret and judge Bellafront and the seriousness of her final bid for freedom or vow to seek her own means of death? Field, when younger, excelled in female roles. Is it not possible that he has constructed a complex test of acting skill with the role of Bellafront who, despite the evidence seemingly against her, may be trapped between the demands of her private desire and her father's autocratic will? The challenge in playing the role in this interpretation is that it becomes a study in suppressed feeling, a woman whose father, groom and would-be lover allow her no space to express herself and define her integrity. The dialogue of the closet scene certainly indicates the pain Scudmore's outbursts give her: she may like Gertrude be awakening to a moral conscience; but with this alternative reading she may be seen as suffering from the insensitivity of men to view her actions in a manner that would allow her even a modicum of integrity. Her suffering, largely silent figure, is the focus of Scudmore's abuse; but a performer in the role with the right degree of *presence* could deflect the critique back on him. Misogyny is voiced but not necessarily endorsed. By the end of the scene it is Scudmore who, protesting too much, stands condemned.[11] The strategy somewhat resembles Jonson's in *Epicœne*, where Dauphine ruthlessly exposes the failure of everyone else in the drama to live up to the demands of their gender but in his final unfrocking of Epicœne and derision of his uncle, Morose, scarcely qualifies for the title of gentleman, even though he has secured the financial means to parade himself as such in future. Again the moral complexion of a character is deliberately withheld from our knowledge the better to sharpen spectators' powers of discrimination. With Dauphine the tactic reveals the cunning that hides his amoral duplicity (his is a game with masks); with Bellafront the tactic reveals the pain of being misprized, of being accused wrongly of sporting a mask of deceit. One can detect parallels in theme and dramaturgy between Field's comedy and Jonson's, but one cannot push the issue of influence much further. Field's second comedy, *Amends for Ladies*, raises the possibility of a more significant kind of influence altogether.

Perry's research leads him to date the initial performance of Field's play as early October 1611 (144) in a year when Jonson had turned from comedy to writing his second tragedy, *Catiline*. In *Amends for Ladies* Field again uses a multiple-stranded plot structure but carries it off with considerably more flair in pacing of events and the matching of the strands to illuminate an organising theme, which centres as in the earlier comedy on the integrity of women. The most noticeable difference is in the greater extent of the dialogue given to the female roles and the quality and tone of statement with which they are invested. The play begins with a Maid, Wife and Widow debating and contrasting their lifestyles and contending which has the preferable status. We then see each in her relations with a man. The Maid decides to test the steadfastness of her lover, Ingen's affections by teasing him much as Rosalind-as-Ganymede teased Orlando, except here it goes horribly wrong and the pair end up estranged and with him later announcing he has married elsewhere. There are the usual complications we find in romantic comedy from Shakespeare through to Beaumont and Fletcher with disguisings, the averting of a death-threatening duel between Ingen and the Maid's vengeful brother, and an inevitable reconciliation. The Wife finds herself subject to the amorous attentions of her husband's best friend, Subtle, unaware that the Husband has set Subtle up to test his wife and prove whether or not his fears of being a cuckold have any grounds. She resists, despite the indignities her husband subjects her to, to add 'authenticity' to his games with her honour and she proves her point that she respects her status even if he does not. The Widow, who enjoys her established independence, accepts into her service a waiting woman of mature years, who turns out when they lie abed together to be a young man (Bould) in disguise who has passionate designs on her, clearly suspecting she is a widow of the 'merry' sort. She thwarts his schemes, despite an attraction to him, until he matures into learning the difference between sex and love. A fourth plot-strand shows a citizen shopkeeper's wife, Grace Seldome, who enjoys her husband's complete trust, refusing the advances of two titled men who assume they have a right to her favours in return for patronising her husband's business. (This is the world of Middleton and Dekker's *The Roaring Girl* and, as if to point up the comparison, Moll Cutpurse makes a brief appearance in Grace's first scene (2.1.16–56) but is harshly repelled as 'lewd, impudent' and 'without a sexe').

We have here various tropes common to romance and to city comedy, but none is developed true to type, since in each the central female figure resists being so stereotyped. Maid, Wife and Widow, as they are generally addressed within the dialogue, are revealed eventually to bear the names Honor, Perfect and Bright respectively. This is again a comedy about the ways men misprize women by reducing them to functional caricatures of their complex selves. Field is destabilising the tropes that underpinned many of the comedies he played in and is doing so by giving his female figures resonant (but decidedly not strident or scolding) voices to speak out their resistance. It is as if the characters resent deeply the plots into which they have been immersed. Or, to put it another way, Field is challenging and deconstructing the whole impulse to create stereotypes in drama and to continue deploying them because they have with time become established conventions. The Wife on discovering how her husband is investigating her, aptly observes:

> Oh men! What are you? Why is our poore sexe
> Still made the disgrac't subiects, in these plaies?

> (2.2.106–7)

The metatheatrical reference extends the criticism out of the immediate situation to challenge audience expectation generally as a mode of cultural conditioning. (Jonson works a like process of deconstruction of sexual and gender stereotyping in *Epicœne*, while many of his comedies directly or indirectly cite specific plays before interrogating their ideological and moral constructions.)

What is remarkable even off the page at a reading is the *power* that resides in the voices with which Field endows Maid, Wife and Widow. Each has a scene in which the expected dramatic development in line with a given convention is disrupted by her refusing to serve the prescribed functions of the plot. Each has affection for the man who wishes to circumscribe in her in this way and so the refusal is not voiced as railing (the tone that promptly invites the chauvinist put-down of being overly emotional, and so unreasonable, beyond all reason, *mad*). Field finds a tone that is firm, controlled, self-assured and even passionate in its sonority. Whatever light-hearted disagreement may exist between the three central women in the opening exchange about the relative merits of their states, they have a common bond in this mode of asserting a fierce integrity. Consider the Widow who arrives from her bedchamber with drawn sword holding at bay the near-naked Bould:

> Pish, I regard not (at a straw) the world:
> Fame from the tongues of men doth iniury
> Oftener then Iustice: and as conscience
> Onely makes guilty persons, not report:
> (For shew we cleare as springs vnto the world,
> If our owne knowledge doe not make vs so,
> That is no satisfaction to our selues.)
> So stand wee ne're so leprous to mens eye,
> It cannot hurt hart-knowne integritie.
> You have trusted to that fond opinion,
> This is the way to haue a widdow-hood,
> By getting to her bed: Ahlas young man,
> Should'st thou thy selfe tell thy companions
> Thou hadst dishonour'd mee (as you men haue tongues
> Forked and venom'd 'gainst our subiect sexe)

It should not moue me, that know 'tis not so:
Therefore depart, Truth be my vertuous shield.

(4.1.23–39)

Here is a sharp intelligence at work (she later parries his every attempt to find his way back into her bed and her good graces with sound reasoning which continually points out his lack of direct knowledge of a woman's mind). She dismisses the power of public opinion in preference for private self-knowledge. It is men like Bould who stand condemned as superficial for trusting so much to appearances, but she implies rather than states that criticism of him. The control of the syntax over extended periods of seven and later eight lines (offsetting the aphoristic force of a nearly-rhyming couplet at the heart of the speech) brings an authority to the utterance which will brook no denial. When the verse flowers into imagery, it is to enliven and endorse a moral discrimination. This is no naïve voice; it carries a due weight of worldly knowledge but refuses to let that insight undermine personal intent. Throughout there is the awareness that still she is a member of a 'subject sexe', which renders the assumption of command and a measured tone the more impressive. Destabilising a stereotype even while acknowledging its ongoing power is what ultimately wins conviction for the speech, since it embraces a recognition that this is an isolated episode which may affect one man (Bould) but is unlikely to re-shape inherited cultural modes of expression. But that is the point at which the speech extends beyond the theatrical situation to embrace the spectator in its implications. The Wife with similarly quiet confidence (5.1.) disarms Subtle's efforts to traduce her on her Husband's behalf. In doing so she finds both men kneeling to her, repentant; at which point her response is to urge them to 'Embrace and loue, henceforth *more really*, / Not so like worldlings' (5.1.142–3. My italics). The choice of 'really' challenges the whole game of illusions which is theatre on the grounds of its questionable need for conventions.

So what has this to do with Jonson? In *The Devil Is An Ass* (1616) we find a pair of caricatured women (the ladies Eitherside and Tailbush) obsessed with their 'place' at court, with perfumes and make-up and prepared practically to undress a male servant (Pug) as their predatory sexual inclinations are roused. Into their company is forced the younger Frances Fitzdottrel by her husband and instructed to learn civility at their hands. Worse she finds her husband paying court to a third woman who arrives (the Spanish lady), so enamoured is he with her punctilious attention to questions concerning good breeding and self-presentation. To Frances alone is it revealed that the Spanish lady is a man's projected fantasy of a woman, since 'she' is in fact the disguised Wittipol, her would-be suitor, who has dressed as a woman to gain private access to her. So taken are Eitherside and Tailbush with the Spaniard's superficial display, that they have no means of detecting the fabrication that Wittipol is perpetrating. Fitzdottrel actively encourages his wife to go into a room apart with the Spanish lady for some private tuition in upper-class manners. Alone together, Wittipol urges Frances to make of him a 'most true friend'. It is a tempting moment for her and for spectators, since, being married to a total dolt, the whole pressure of romantic convention within drama encourages one to hope that the dramatist will find some means of bringing the pair into a relationship. But Jonson is always the realist: for that to happen, he must needs find some means of killing off the character of Fitzdottrel or allow Frances and Wittipol to become adulterous lovers. The tension is at a pitch. What is not expected is the speech with which Jonson endows Frances at this instant. She has till now been largely a cipher on stage, a beautiful woman, marked out as another of Fitzdottrel's possessions for him to use and abuse at will. When she speaks (like Field's Bellafront she has been something of an enigma for audiences till now), it is with a voice of total self-command in which she confesses to her liking for him and wish to take advantage of the situation offered them, but not for the ends he supposes. She admires his wit and skill in devising ways to present himself to her and now hopes he will deploy that intelligence in the only fitting way possible to them: to protect her future security from the depredations Fitzdottrel is making of her one-time dowry:

> ...I am a woman
> That cannot speak more wretchedness of myself
> Than you can read; matched to a mass of folly,
> That every day makes haste to his own ruin;
> The wealthy portion that I bought him, spent;
> And, through my friends' neglect, no jointure made me.
> My fortunes standing in this precipice,
> 'Tis council that I want, and honest aids:
> And in this name I need you for a friend!
> Never in any other; for his ill
> Must not make me, sir, worse.
>
> (4.6.18–28)[12]

Till now the women's roles in Jonson's plays have been minimally characterised or caricatured. Doll Common is an exception but her complexity is achieved partly through role-play along with Face and Subtle's endless shape-shifting and partly as indicative of her street-wise background. The women in *Bartholomew Fair* are all defined by their particular appetites as they become enmeshed in the underworld of carnival. Frances is in every way an original creation in Jonson's comedies and the originality is offset by the deliberate contrasting of her with the other female roles in the play. It has been supposed that Jonson's working with aristocratic women as actresses on the Masques at court for over a decade by 1616 is the likely explanation for this sudden emergence of more powerfully characterised female roles. Perhaps that was the case (though the women in question were at this date chiefly engaged in the dancing rather than the acting content of the entertainments).[13] But Frances's *tone*, the passionate sense of selfhood that motivates her refusal to be swallowed up in a mad world of her husband's making and her equal determination not to lose her own self-respect, exactly matches the moral stance and eloquence of Field's Wife and Widow. When after a long period away from the public stage Jonson returned to playwriting, it was to shape plays where women possess voices independent of men's control, quick intelligences and boisterous wits (this is particularly the case in *The New Inn* and *The Magnetic Lady*). Is the shaping of Frances Fitzdottrel an instance where a pupil has influenced his master? Field's championing of the roles of women in drama, building up not only the size of their roles but their status within the hierarchy of the playworld is not surprising given his earlier career as a female impersonator. Did his attack on the moral and social dangers of stereotyping hit at Jonson even as it hit several of his contemporaries (Middleton especially)? The difficulty with tracing influence is the complex inter-relation of the possible with the inability to determine proof. But that Frances gains a voice in the precise circumstances in which she is impelled to speak and that that voice sustains a particular tone of self-derived authority such as we find summoned in adversity by Field's female characters is remarkable. If it was initially an experiment on Jonson's part, it was one to which he properly returned and to good effect in his Caroline comedies.

Jonson and Brome

Brome is more overtly a Jonsonian than Field; he regularly signals his creative allegiances, since his characters often mention figures from Jonson's comedies in their dialogue. In *The City Wit*, for example, when Crasy, Tryman and Crack join forces together they agree they must 'be linckt in Covenant together…By Indenture Tripartite, and't please you, like *Subtle, Doll*, and *Face*' (3.1, Vol.1, p. 318); and in *The Weeding of the Covent Garden*, Cockbraine claims Adam Overdo as his 'reverend ancestor' (1.1, Vol.2, p. 2) as he sets about weeding the new piazza of iniquity. It would be wrong to imply that Brome is copying Jonson; this is not plagiarism, nor is it pastiche. Brome gives a glancing reference that admits to influence, to a similar interest in a particular type of character or situation to indicate traditions within which he considers himself to be writing. This again is different from Jonson's intertextual strategy whereby he often reminds spectators of other plays the better to highlight his own different treatment or thematic purpose. Brome's intertextual referencing is both a gesture of respect for his mentor and a way of drawing attention to his working a variation on a proven comic device. Though it is not as strong as in Jonson's plays, Brome's works do carry a similar pedagogic imperative. Jonson's plays repeatedly demonstrate his desire to teach through entertainment; Brome's referencing of Jonson before offering his own individualised handling of Jonsonian material alerts spectators to the degree to which the objects of Jonson's satire are still current in society, and in need of eradicating. If Jonson disturbs audiences to make them question their relation to the play and their attraction to the art of performance, Brome disturbs them with his metatheatrical referencing into questioning how much they have paid serious attention to Jonson's artistry. This is subtly to question the value of drama as a cultural enterprise. What has been the *point* of Jonson's satire, as it were, if it still needs repeating? This is to approach the issue of audience reception from a somewhat different perspective from Jonson's. And it is in the space created by that difference that Brome situates his own originality. Brome at a first reading might appear to possess a gentler, more genial and modest writing personality than Jonson: but this is misleading, as Martin Butler has memorably shown.[14] Brome's later works grow increasingly critical of the prevailing social and political situation under Charles's autocratic rule and, while his comic invention can appear warm in its treatment of human folly, that surface tone often masks an acerbic undertow to the drama.[15] Equally impressive is the brilliance of Brome's structural experimentation, which again often shows him developing Jonsonian techniques into new possibilities. Brome is both Jonson's and his own man.

It is not certain when precisely Brome became Jonson's 'man', but a date c.1610 would seem likely since, though there are echoes of earlier Jonsonian plays in his work, it is to *The Alchemist, Bartholomew Fair* and *The Devil Is An Ass* that the referencing is most frequently addressed. The Jonsonian character who might be seen as the most creative influence on Brome is Trouble-all, the man who lost the office he held under Justice Overdo and now, virtually naked and maddened by his loss of status in the community, roams Bartholomew Fair demanding to know of everyone he meets whether they have a warrant for what they are doing. He weaves in and out of the action, always arriving unexpectedly and often destabilising momentarily whichever individual he accosts. That his pleas become ever-more searching is an indication within the play of the degree to which all forms of licence are being subverted or overthrown. Trouble-all, though memorable within the vast cast that make up the *dramatis personae* of *Bartholomew Fair*, never gave rise to a line of troublesome beggars in Jonson's work. If he might be said to have a favourite type to which he returns repeatedly with curiosity and creative insight it would be the con-man on the make: Jonson found ever new depths and darkly comic potential within such masters of the art of gulling as Tucca, Mosca and Volpone, Face and Subtle, Quarlous, Meercraft and Everill. Con-men abound in Brome's comedies too; however, his favoured type is the beggar, the outsider who reflects the actual condition of a society beneath its carefully maintained façade.

Brome's beggars are beggars with a difference, as is implicit in the title of one of his plays: *The Court Beggar* (1640). Brome's line in satire can be appreciated from a comment in one of his earlier plays, *The City Wit* (?1629): when Bridget, the maid, informs her mistress that a gentleman is at her door craving admittance, Josina asks 'But are you sure he is a true Gentleman? Does he weare clean Linnen and lack Money?' (2.2., Vol. 1, p. 300). Lack of money might be termed the groundbase to all the King Charles's policies at large in England; and lack of money and the need for imbursement by any means is what motivates most of the upper-class characters in Brome's later plays. There is in this a notable difference from Jonsonian con-men and their scams: Jonson endowed the likes of Face or Meercraft with dynamism, a power of invention in living by their wits, which challenges spectators' moral scruples even as it captures their imagination. Brome's courtly beggars are drier, more urgent and altogether less attractive on the whole, and so are more easily placed morally. Mendicant, the court beggar of the title, who makes his money by acting as go-between, helping lower-class figures gain access to courtiers, who will help them pursue business at court, is a kind of financial pimp. He gains further profit by selling patents and arranging gifts and sales of land and estates which have fallen through bankruptcy into the administration of the crown. Mendicant is a parasite whose dealings affect the legal processes and the ownership of land throughout the kingdom by begging for either office or justice for himself or his clients. To further the process of establishing himself as a necessary presence at court, Medicant has sold a sizeable estate, as his daughter, Charissa reminds him in the opening scene of the play. Given freedom of speech by her father, she deconstructs his lifestyle with precise insight:

> Your ayme has bin to raise
> Your state by Court-suits, begging as some call it,
> And for that end you left your Countrey life,
> And Lands too ever since my Mother dy'd,
> Who while shee liv'd with best of womans judgement
> Which held you from that course of selling faire
> Possessions to enable you with money
> To purchase *wit* at Court.

(1.1.,Vol.1, p. 187)

Where Jonson's comedies show us a world depending on the art of the scam, Brome's reveal a world given over to the arts of scrounging. The less cash, power or influence there is in circulation, the more people want ever larger shares the more pressingly in what is going. The courtiers of these plays have fine, assiduously observed manners, but their affairs are corrupt and draining on the common wealth and they require the likes of Mendicant to undertake the actual dirty details of business for them. Brome's is less a moral anger than a political anger at the systematic erosion of the country's human and natural resources.

Significantly Brome ends his play with a truncated version of a Court Masque to celebrate the union of Charissa and her own preferred suitor, Frederick; but there are notable differences from Jonson's usual structuring of the material. Masques throughout Charles's reign were a substantial drain on the economy in the mounting of their elegant artifice. What is of note is how Brome continually reminds spectators that such spectacle is a feeble form of illusion. Cupid and Venus open the ceremonies, but the goddess is portrayed by a woman the audience know to be a whore, while the woman's bastard plays the goddess's son. However grand their appearance, the illusion is shattered by the Boy's continually forgetting his lines and his continually repeating the few words of his speech he can remember ('*Venus* and *Cupid*, my Mother and I – / Helpe me –') serves to draw attention to the incongruous juxtaposition of the actors and their roles (5.2., Vol.1, p. 265). Further incongruities follow. Jonson's Masques were generally preceded by an anti-masque so that a grand rhetorical display of concord would displace from the stage images of anarchy and misrule. But in Brome's Masque this ordering is reversed: there is a display of actors impersonating chivalric qualities sent from Mars, Apollo, Mercury, Jupiter and Diana as Moon; but again appearances are deceptive for it is the darker, somewhat malign aspects of these godheads that the actors mostly portray

(Mercury's slyness is celebrated, while the cloud-covered Moon is revered as symbolising spying). Before their dance is well established, they are disrupted by the arrival of a crowd of projectors (Mendicant's one-time 'beagles' who sought out gulls for him to asset-strip) and Medicant himself, *'attir'd all in Patents; A Windmill on his head'* (5.2., Vol. 1, p. 267). He is literally stript of all he possesses and then danced out of his madness. While this makes for a seemingly happy ending, its basis (like many a Jonsonian ending) leaves one highly unsettled. Can a man so wholly committed to the quest for wealth at any cost really be so readily converted to better ways?[16] There is also the impact of the inversion of the conventional form of the Masque, which here declines into an anti-masque of whirling figures around a man crowned with a windmill (image of inconstancy, of one who turns every which way depending on a given stimulus). This has a powerful visual iconic symbolism which is profoundly disturbing both within the world of the play and that of the intended audience. Anarchy and madness are too powerfully represented in the episode for there to be any firm sense of closure. The tension between content and form opens up a debate which has ramifications outside the theatricalised context, as king and court are judged by the very means (Masque and anti-masque) to which they regularly turned to promote belief in their own excellence. For Jonson the Masque was designed to intimate to beholders what ideally authority should be;[17] Brome deploys the form that Jonson devised for the genre to show how far short of the ideal the reality of court life falls.

Inversion is a favoured strategy in Brome's many plays. Immediately before the episode just analysed, an outsider wanders into the room where most of the minor characters in *The Court Beggar* are rehearsing the Masque. He tries to speak with each of the participants in turn but all are too bound up in their practice to respond to his urgent questioning. Whether they are jigging up and down, reciting grandiloquent speeches, indulging operatic flights of singing, or flourishing their bizarre costumes, these actors appear to Sir Raphael as 'all lunatick' or 'heathenish' (5.2., Vol. 1, pp. 261 ff.). The audience knows what in fact is taking place but they are also made party to an outsider's view, which challenges spectators by questioning the extent to which they have been conditioned to interpret the Masque in specific ways. Brome exploits this shifting of perspectives to brilliant effect in his finest comedy, *The Antipodes* (1638) and to do this he again takes up a device that Jonson returned to repeatedly throughout his dramatic career: the use of an onstage audience. Cordatus and Mitis watch their friend, Asper's play and his performance of the central role (*Every Man out of His Humour*), the four Gossips observe the development of the plot (*The Staple of News*), and, more subtly integrated into the body of the action, Arruntius and his friends study the machinations in Tiberius's court (*Sejanus*): in all these cases Jonson deploys a framing device involving spectators who give voice to their perceptions and to the need they have to make judgements about what they are seeing. This is directly to challenge how the theatre audience chooses to perceive and interpret what is played before them. Jonson's strategy continually requires audiences to be self-reflexive, to interrogate their responses to the drama.

Brome deploys this strategy in *The Antipodes* but for rather different ends. A bizarre but philanthropic lord, Letoy, and his doctor endeavour to cure the young Perigrine of the melancholy that renders him impotent in his marriage to Martha and they do this by staging a play in which Perigrine becomes increasingly involved as actor. Letoy and Perigrine's family (who have their own problems to solve too) watch and comment on the proceedings, which have a positive outcome. On the level of plotting, that is the sum of the action. The play that this plot frames involves a fantastic journey to the Antipodes, an upside-down version of Caroline London, where inversion is the controlling principle of existence. It is a wonderful conceit that Brome works through in meticulous detail. The comments of the onstage spectators are narrow and trite (chiefly because they are taken up with their own private preoccupations: Joylesse, Perigrine's father, suspects his wife Diana of adultery and Letoy's treatment of her and her responsiveness fuels the old man's suspicions); the sheer inadequacy of their responses invites deeper consideration of what they are watching from the theatre audience.

Like many journey plays, the form is picaresque: numerous short scenes present us with glimpses of life in the Antipodes. Initially the inversions, though pointed, are simple enough: lawyers refuse to take fees, the swans there are black, usurers are beggars' benefactors, women love fencing and getting bloody faces; but steadily the sheer accumulation of reversals comes to undermine our amusement. For example, we watch a *man* being ducked for scolding who in tears laments how he is forbidden

> To use the naturall members I was borne with,
> And of them all, the chiefe that man takes pleasure in:
> The tongue...
>
> (4.4., Vol. 3, p. 301)

Meanwhile a woman bystander hopes someone will enrage the scold, since she longs for a second ducking so there will be 'more holiday sport of him' (Ibid., p. 302). The stage picture of a weeping, expostulating man and a jeering woman opens up complex possibilities of interpretation. It challenges the very basis of gender definition within a patriarchal society like that current in Caroline London in a manner that is far from straightforwardly comic. If this image is to be considered an inversion of a norm, what does that suggest about the construction of the norm? Does the picture not leave both norm and inversion open to moral questioning? The inversion emphasises the brutality of the practice of ducking, which the victim finds unmanning (the *double-entendre* involved in the play on 'members' makes that clear); so is the situation any less brutish if the victim is female? Any laughter that the scene promotes must be decidedly uneasy, particularly given Perigrine's response to observing the couple:

Can men and women be so contrary
In all that we hold proper to each sex?

(4.4., Vol. 3, p. 302)

This is one of several disturbing episodes which begin to elide the Antipodes with the actual London of the audience, making it difficult to interpret the one as simply a reversal of the other. The Antipodes becomes increasingly akin to a mirror-image which partially distorts only to highlight what is being reflected. This becomes decidedly the case when Perigrine ransacks the actors' dressing room and property cupboard and re-appears clad with all the tinsel finery and accoutrements of a stage king, intent on reforming the wrongs, as he sees them, in this society:

Call you these Courtiers? They are rude sillken Clowns;
As course within, as water-men or Car-men.

(4.6., Vol. 3, p. 304)

Again the satire is challenging, asking us to view a contrast but exchange the terms of reference; such an exchange reduces both terms to the level of sameness. Given the number of plays in which Brome shows how on certain terms it is well nigh impossible to discriminate between courtier and beggar,[18] this collapsing of distinctions is a signal for anarchy to prevail. Peregrine sees he 'shall have much to doe in reformation' (4.8., Vol. 3, p. 307). He wishes to put to rights the topsy-turvy world, but his intention in doing so is described by Letoy's chief servant and actor, Byplay, as beginning 'to governe / With purpose to reduce the manners / Of this country to his owne' (3.6., Vol. 3, p. 286). Brome's choice of diction is always precise; so what are we to read into this usage of *reduce*? Is London a *reductio ad absurdum* of the Antipodes? If Perigrine is to be considered mad with melancholy, as his family believe, how are we to interpret his antics as king? Or, to phrase it differently: how are we to respond to this image of a king attempting to resolve the absurdities of an alien world by making it conform to his conception of an ideal kingdom, given our awareness of the futility of Charles's propagandist ambitions, which ideologically shaped his much-loved masques and his own and his queen's performances within them? It is as if Brome is testing Charles's rule by the standards that his mentor, Jonson, originally built into the Masque form; and the result is stinging satire, remarkable for its fearless and clever invention. Marvell may have chosen to see the dying Charles some years later as a 'Royal actor born',[19] but Brome stages him as a sad and motley clown.

Brome is a dramatist in need of re-discovery. In terms of influence, he is deservedly to be depicted as a 'son' of Ben; his plays show him to be deeply versed in his mentor's work, its ideological and cultural strategies and dramaturgical artistry. But Brome was more than an imitator, he chose to take Jonson's satire and extend its interrogative force to conceive dramas of a highly radical and subversive nature. One might observe that such invention is a mark of a developed and original wit, except a study of Brome's work shows how he held the very term under considerable suspicion. Jonson's rogues live by their wits which have the quicksilver brilliance that is the mark of genius. But that wit is directed at crime. When Brome took up the term in his early and most overtly Jonsonian comedy, *The City Wit* (?1629), it was to define a man, Crasy, akin to Timon of Athens, who discovers his generosity lays him open to cynical manipulation by the people he thinks he is helping. He recovers his lost fortune only by being a 'wit', that is by robbing his former 'friends' of the wealth they stole from him and doing so by complex and devious practices involving disguise and impersonations. Crasy (so aptly named) is the first exercise by Brome in strategic inversion, where generosity is equated with folly and wit with sly cunning as a commentary on the worldly ways of early Caroline London. What began as an interrogation of terms had evolved by the time of Brome's writing of *The Antipodes* into the complete organising principle on which the comedy is structured so that, even at his most different and original, Brome still can be seen as honouring Jonson's artistry. And this creative affinity was not lost on Brome's contemporaries. 'C.G.', whose poem 'To censuring Criticks, on the approved Comedy, *The Antipodes*' was offered as preface to the published text, frames the conceit that 'Jonson's ghost' is no longer 'a Tenant i'the Elizian Coast'; after extolling Jonson's work as the enduring repository of his genius, he ends:

> But stay, and let me tell you, where he is,
> He sojournes in his Brome's *Antipodes*.

(Vol. 3, p. 229)

Notes

[1] See Ben Jonson, *The Alchemist*, F.H Mares (ed.) (1966), The Revels Plays, Manchester University Press, Manchester. Field is referred to V. iii. 82 and Brome in the Induction l. 8. The reference to Field is particularly interesting, since he was at this date (1614) lead actor with the Lady Elizabeth's Servants who were actually staging *Bartholomew Fair*.

[2] Richard Brome, *The Dramatic Works* (1873), John Pearson, London. Volume 3, p. ix. Throughout the following essay all references to Brome's plays will be to this three volume edition, which is relatively accessible. There have been some few modern editions of individual plays but these vary in the degree of their scholarly apparatus and it seemed best to use this edition which offers closely transcribed copies of all the original seventeenth-century publications. In bibliographical terms it is not an easy edition to reference since regular pagination is followed only in volumes one and three; in volume two fresh pagination is begun with the third play in the collection and with each subsequent play. While act and scene numbers follow the original editions, no line numbering is proffered. Consequently references in the text here will give details of act and scene followed by volume and page numbers. The major plays are contained within Volume 3.

[3] William Perry (ed.) (1950), *The Plays of Nathan Field*, The University of Texas Press, Austin, p. 70. All subsequent references in the text to either of Field's comedies will be to this edition. The one modern production of Field's *A Woman Is A Weathercock* was staged by Patrick Kirwan's company at the Shakespeare Memorial Theatre, Stratford-upon-Avon, during the Festival Season of 1914. To judge by published reviews, the play clearly took critics by surprise for its remarkable actability. The reviewer for *The Stratford-upon-Avon Herald* (10 April 1914) opined that, from first to last, 'it is drama all the time. It is a marvel to me how such an excellent dramatic play could have lain unnoticed for over three hundred years'. More importantly, the reviewers invariably drew comparisons (favourably) with Jonson. The critic for *The Times* (28 April 1914) commented: 'There are other characters too [the Ninny family, Wagtail and Pouts] mainly conceived *in the manner of Field's master, Ben Jonson*' *(*my emphasis). Crucially, from the experience of a performance, informed spectators were perceiving creative links between the two dramatists.

[4] Field's name appears first in the list of performers appended to the text published in the 1616 Folio.

[5] Ben Jonson, *Epicœne or The Silent Woman*, edited by L.A. Beaurline (1966), Regents Renaissance Drama Series, Arnold, London, p. xx. The divided date refers to the old calendar where the new year began on Lady Day (March 25).

[6] For a fuller discussion of this line of argument, see Richard Allen Cave (1991), *Ben Jonson*, Macmillan, Basingstoke and London, pp. 62–75, where there is reference to the handling of stereotypes in Danny Boyle's production for the RSC (Swan Theatre, 1989).

[7] Reading these plays while recalling the criticism that especially Jonson is profoundly misogynist, calls to mind the controversially mixed responses that greeted the London production of David Mamet's *Oleanna* (Royal Court and Duke of York's Theatre, 1993). Treating a fraught teacher-pupil relationship (of an older man with a younger woman) within a patriarchal context, performances gave rise to diametrically opposed reactions (often loudly and aggressively vociferous) from spectators. Some spectators actually cheered when the teacher lost his control and hit the student; others audibly expressed profound shock at the moment. The production occasioned lengthy correspondence to newspapers.

[8] We know from the papers of the Venetian ambassador (8 February 1610) that *Epicœne* was banned because of an unfortunate allusion to Lady Arabella Stuart. It seems that the plays staged at the Whitefriars Theatre throughout December 1609 were likely to be the ones to be offered at court during the Christmas festivities of 1609–10. Records show that some five plays were staged then by the boys' company before the King and Prince Henry. Had *Epicœne* been originally chosen for staging at court? And had it then to be replaced after the ban? If so, did Field hastily prepare *Weathercock* to fill the gap? That would to some extent explain the similarity in thematic content.

[9] The willow garland, as in Desdemona's song, signifies loss of love and pain at rejection (Lucida has been rejected by her former suitor, who now is to marry her elder sister, Bellafront). The ever-present garland is all Field does to develop in her a distinctive character, though as a contrast to her sisters whose relations with men bear near-tragic consequences, she would have merited fuller treatment.

[10] Perry lists and comments on three echoes of Shakespeare's scene. *Epicœne* also for the alert spectator (and audiences at performances by boy actors could readily be assumed to be theatrically aware) carries subtle hints of an intertextual strategy at work in a more pervasive manner. Classical and Italian renaissance drama afforded Jonson precedents for his plot structure: the plot of the seemingly modest woman who becomes a virago after marriage and the plot of the man who is tricked into marrying a boy dressed up as a girl. But previously they were not linked as Jonson handles them and in the case of the second plot the audience was invariably let in on the trick from the start. Jonson allows audiences to suppose they are being treated to a London updating of the first plot-line, which intensifies the surprise when it is revealed in Dauphine's uncasing of Epicœne that we have actually been watching a cunning deployment of the second to which we as spectators have not been party. The device stresses the coldly calculating quality of Dauphine who has tricked everyone, including his supposed friends *and* the audience. The 'tragic' references in Field's scene allow him subtly to direct audience response to judge the inflated self-importance of Scudmore, who is 'playing' a Hamlet persona here.

[11] The patterning of the play into three plot structures strengthens this interpretation. Kate, Bellafront's sister, also suffers public humiliation at her marriage when a rival of her husband's accuses her of lying with him often. Her husband, Strange, neither leaps to her immediate defence nor assures her that he doubts the charge. Instead he leaves her and pursues ingenious ways to trick his rival, Captain Powts, into admitting his guilt and then repeating his admission before the wedding party. The misogyny here is not overt as with Scudmore, but Strange has to satisfy himself and then the public at large that his wife is the virgin he took her for. Again as with Scudmore and Bellafront, it is Strange (not Kate) who is found wanting in generosity and trust, the fundamentals of a decent integrity. He does not judge Kate but his silence is disturbing for spectators and cruel for Kate. In the third plot, an innocent, Sir Abraham Ninny, is tricked into wedding his mother's waiting woman who, being pregnant, is in hasty need of a husband. Sir Abraham knows her condition, and knows he is not responsible but is happy to comply. No hint of accusation or misogyny passes his lips. Three diverse and unrelated plots cohere in *A Woman Is A Weathercock* around a thematic preoccupation with misogyny rather than with the changeability of women's affections, despite the play's title. Both Bellafront and Kate have to wait while their would-be spouses find comfortable grounds for believing the women worthy of their trust; it is not the women who are wanting in integrity, but rather Scudmore and Strange (so aptly if subtly named) who, wayward in the strength of their affections, are found wanting in manliness, courtesy and insight.

However, it must be noted that, when the play was revived at Stratford in 1914, reviewers registered no criticism of Scudmore's misogyny (despite the increasing social presence at that date of New Women and the suffragette movement), instead they commented on the character's eloquence and the actor's tonal range. The critic for *The Times* (28 April 1914), for example, commented: 'For all the fury with which Scudmore rails at women and at his folly in trusting a weathercock, he rails with a fine poetic intensity and music – bright, loud and keen.' It is clear from the reviews that Patrick Kirwan, who directed the revival, did so in a manner that wholly endorsed Scudmore's perspective on events.

12 Ben Jonson, *The Devil is an Ass*, Peter Happé (ed.) (1994), Revels Plays, Manchester University Press, Manchester.

13 See, for example, Elizabeth Schafer, 'Women act Jonson', in Cave, Schafer and Woolland (eds) (1999), *Ben Jonson and Theatre: Performance, Practice and Theory*, Routledge, London, pp. 172 ff.

14 Martin Butler (1984), *Theatre and Crisis: 1632–42*, Cambridge University Press, Cambridge. This volume attempts a complete revaluation of Brome's plays and is noteworthy for Butler's meticulous linking of theatrical motifs with contemporary political events to show how remarkably forthright Brome was in his social and political criticism.

15 Repeatedly the plays make specific references to Charles I which are far from flattering. The projectors, for example, who try to wheedle Mendicant into their schemes in *The Court Beggar* assume it will convince him of the worth of what they are trying to do when they offer him as assurance:

    ... then the certainty o' th' propounded profits
    Both to the King and us   (1.1., Vol. 1, p. 192)

16 This questioning of an all too rapid conversion hangs over the resolution of Kitely's fears of being cuckolded in *Every Man in His Humour* and of Macilente's renunciation of his envy in *Every Man out of His Humour*.

17 See the introduction to the printed text of Jonson's Masque, *Hymenaei* (1606): 'though their voice be taught to sound to present occasions, their sense or doth or should always lay hold on more removed mysteries' (ll. 16–18). The fullest edition of Jonson's masques where the lavish illustrations give admirable indications of the scenic and emblematic distinctions made in performance between Masque and anti-masque is Stephen Orgel and Roy Strong (1973) *Inigo Jones: The Theatre of the Stuart Court*, 2 vols., Sotheby Parke Bernet and the University of California Press, London and Berkeley / Los Angeles.

18 See especially *A Jovial Crew* (1641).

19 See Andrew Marvell, 'An Horatian Ode upon Cromwell's Return from Ireland', l. 53.

Chapter 7

'This Play will be mine A[rse]': Aphra Behn's Jonsonian Negotiations

Carolyn D. Williams

Aphra Behn (?1640–89), née Johnson, was auspiciously named. Thomas Colepeper (1626–97) pronounced her 'a most beautifull woman, & a most Excellent Poet', adding that 'she might be called Ben Jonson.'[1] One of the three most prolific writers for the professional Restoration stage, she could be regarded as an honorary Son of Ben. Many of the features which Restoration and later critics considered typical of Jonson appear in her works; as she grew older, she also began to adopt Jonson's advocacy of royalist politics. In *Poems upon Several Occasions* (1684), one 'F. N. W.' praises these qualities:

> Would you know what Wit doth mean,
> Pleasant wit yet not obscene,
> The Several garbs that Humours wear,
> The dull, the brisk, the jealous, the severe?
> Wou'd you the pattern see
> Of spotless and untainted Loyalty [?][2]

Behn's theoretical resentments and rebellions, however, appear better suited to Shakespeare's Sister. She engages with Jonson and his admirers in her prologues, prefaces and postscripts, where she expresses her views on theatre in general, and on her own unprecedented case: there had been woman dramatists in England before, but none had earned her living by the pen. Jonson's influence presides, explicitly or by implication, over her dialogue with her chief rivals: her friend John Dryden (1631–1700), who esteemed him highly, though not uncritically, and her enemy Thomas Shadwell (1642–92), who considered Jonson 'the man, of all the World, *I* most passionately admire for his Excellency in Drammatick-*Poetry*'.[3] An impression of unresolved conflict emerges: Behn owes much to Jonson, regarding him as a standard of dramatic excellence, but is often prevented by her turbulent career from acknowledging the full extent of her debt.

Schools of Virtue

Most early modern critics expressed deep concern with theatre's effect on society. Jonson's convictions on drama's ethical influence harmonise with the *Ars Poetica* of Horace (65–8 BC), whose admonition that poetry should mix '*utile dulci*' (instruction with delight) became a staple of neoclassical criticism (Fairclough, 1955: 478). Jonson declares, in the dedication of *Volpone*, that he has tried to deliver 'the doctrine, which is the principal end of poesie: to inform men in the best reason of living.'[4] Had he witnessed the civil wars which began in 1642, and left England under the control of theatre-hating Puritans, he would have deduced that his audience had not been paying attention. In 1660, the restoration of Charles II to the throne inaugurated an immoral backlash, as the cavaliers who had shared his exile came roistering home, eager to pay off old scores – and to reopen the theatres. Drama's didactic function was once more routinely proclaimed, however unconvincing the context. It appears, for instance, in a royal patent, drawn up on 25 April 1662, making the presence of actresses on stage not only permissible but compulsory, thus offering high-born spectators (including Charles II) unprecedented opportunities for spectacularly scandalous fornication:

> we do likewise permit and give leave that all the women's parts to be acted in either of the two said companies for the time to come may be performed by women so long as their recreations [. . .] may by such reformation be esteemed not only harmless delight, but useful and instructive representations of human life, to such of our good subjects as shall resort to the same.
>
> (Thomas and Hare, 1989: 18)

Dramatists who did not pay lip-service to this doctrine incurred accusations of irresponsibility and, worse still, ignorance of the classics. In his 'Defence of *An Essay of Dramatick Poesie*' (1668), Dryden tried to balance respectability with common sense by arguing that 'delight is the chief, if not the only end of poesy; instruction can be admitted but in the second place, for poesy only instructs as it delights.' (Swedenberg, 1956–89, IX, 5–6). Shadwell, who consistently struck a moralistic pose which the scandalous goings-on in his plays did little to support, observed that a poet with that attitude was 'of as little use to Mankind as a Fidler, or Dancing-Master, who delights the fancy only, without improving the Judgment', adding that '*Horace*, the best Judge of Poetry, found other business for a Poet.' (Summers, 1927: Vol. I, 183–4).

At first, Behn distanced herself from these views. In her preface to *The Dutch Lover* (1673), she dismisses all moralistic claims: as for 'the amending of mens Morals, or their Wit', she declares, 'sure I am, no Play was ever writ with that design.' (V, 161, 68–72).[5] A few years later, however, she used the theatre as a political arena in which to express her views on the Exclusion Crisis, when Charles II's right to leave his throne to his Roman Catholic brother James was disputed by many of his most influential subjects. She addresses the anti-Catholic party with mock deference in her prologue to *The Rover, Part II* (1681); they are so stupid that she has dumbed down her work to please them:

> The Rabble 'tis we court, those powerful things,
> Whose voices can impose even Laws on Kings.
> A Pox of Sense and Reason
>
> (20–22) (VI, 231)

She then abandons irony to make a straightforward claim for drama's political utility: in ancient Greece and Rome,

> Plays were so useful thought to Government,
> That Laws were made for their establishment
>
> (42–43) (VI, 232)

Even weightier appeals to ethical influence and classical precedents appear in her dedication of *The Luckey Chance* (1686) to Laurence Hyde, Earl of Rochester, Lord High Treasurer of England (1621–1711). She observes that

> Cardinal Richelieu, that great and wise Statesman, said, That there was no surer Testimony to be given of the flourishing Greatness of a State, than publick Pleasures and Divertisements – for they are, says he, – the Schools of Vertue, where Vice is always either punish't, or disdain'd. They are secret Instructions to the People, in things that 'tis impossible to insinuate into them any other Way.
>
> (9–13) (VII, 213)

Therefore 'The Phylosophy of Greece, and the Majesty and Wisdom of the Romans, did equally concern their Great Men in making them Venerable, Noble and Magnificent.' (VII, 213, ll. 20–22). Why did Behn now stress the political applications of her art? The forces that had won the civil wars and lost the peace were still formidable. Although Charles II was sufficiently proficient in kingcraft to avoid having to go on his travels again, James,

who had succeeded him in 1685, was not so clever: he was to be
manoeuvred off his throne in 1688. Behn's enemies strongly resembled
Jonson's.

'Practible by a Woman'

Could any female dramatist regard Jonson as a posthumous ally when his
attitude to women seemed so contemptuous? The Restoration theatre
presented Jonson at his most misogynistic. His dramatic output as a whole,
including the later work, contains 'a rich seam of empathetic roles for and
consideration of women.' (Sanders, 1999c: 179–90, 189). But Jonson's
later plays were not performed. Dryden, in his *Essay of Dramatick Poesie*
(1668), reflects contemporary opinion when he dismisses them as his
'dotages'. For Restoration theatre-goers, the Jonson experience consisted of
The Silent Woman, Volpone, The Alchemist, Bartholomew Fair, and some
highly prestigious but dramatically disastrous performances of *Catiline*:
plays in which the only interesting women are bad women, and clever
women a nasty joke.[6] It was not Jonson, however, but his over-zealous
admirers, who raised Behn's proto-feminist hackles. She pours scorn on the
'affectation' of 'a man the most severe of Johnson's Sect', presumably
Shadwell himself, who sat unmoved throughout *The Alchemist*, but laughed
so much at *Henry IV* that he 'very hardly kept his Doublet whole' (V.162.
ll. 131, 125–6, 128–9). This attitude is closely associated with the sexist
prejudice which, she claims, contributed to the demise of *The Dutch Lover*.
She begins her assault by recalling an unpleasant incident at the first
performance: 'there comes me into the Pit, a long, lither, phlegmatick,
white, ill-favour'd, wretched Fop. [. . .] This thing, I tell ye, opening that
which serves it for a mouth, out issued such a noise as this to those that sate
about it, that they were to expect a woful Play, God damn him, for it was a
womans.' (V, 162, ll. 100–108). She refuses to admit that women
dramatists are necessarily inferior to men: 'Plays have no great room for
that which is mens great advantage over women, that is Learning.' (V, 162,
ll. 118–19). Her ensuing observation is even more daring: 'We all well
know that the immortal Shakespears Playes (who was not guilty of much
more than often falls to womens share) have better pleas'd the World than
Johnsons works.' (V, 162, ll. 119–21).
   An underlying irony operates here: Behn takes to its logical conclusion
an idea about Shakespeare, derived from Jonson's own words, which is still
influential. What most people believe about Jonson's views on Shakespeare
is based on one remark in his ode, 'To the memory of my beloved, The

Author Mr. William Shakespeare: And what he hath left us', prefaced to Shakespeare's First Folio. Jonson has branded himself as a snobbish pedant by his observation that Shakespeare had '*small* Latine, *and lesse* Greeke' (l. 31). Yet this ill-fated sound-byte was intended to demolish the prejudice it allegedly upholds: Jonson invokes '*thund'ring* Æschylus, / Euripides, *and* Sophocles' (ll. 33–34) as suitable companions for Shakespeare, who, blessed with natural genius, excelled even the most learned of his compatriots, and matched the greatest of the ancient Greek tragedians. Shakespeare's indignant defenders ignored the fact that Jonson himself had provided the material for their ripostes. This happens in Dryden's *Essay on Dramatick Poesie* (1668): 'Those who accuse [Shakespeare] to have wanted learning, give him the greater commendation: he was naturally learn'd; he needed not the spectacles of Books to read Nature; he look'd inwards, and found her there.' (Swedenberg, 1956–89, IX, 55). The gender implications also demand attention: Dryden's words turn Shakespeare into a hermaphroditic figure, deprived of the cultural androgens provided by a classical education, and containing a feminine element, 'Nature', within himself. Shakespeare's feminisation is even more conspicuous in a 'Prologue to *Julius Caesar*' (1672), sometimes ascribed to Dryden:

> In Country Beauties as we often see,
> Something that takes in their simplicity,
> Yet while they charm, they know not they are fair,
> And take without their spreading of the snare;
> Such Artless beauty lies in *Shakespears* wit,
> 'Twas well in spight of him what ere he writ.
>
> (ll. 1– 6)[7]

The patronising simile sets Shakespeare, nature, inspiration, and femininity on one side of the creative divide, with Ben Jonson, art, reason, and masculinity on the other. The only wonder is that Behn did not consider Shakespeare too soppy to deserve the emulation of any self-respecting woman.

Yet this 'Nature' imagery was not really hospitable to women. Concepts of manliness were complex and varied: although learning facilitated the cultural enhancement of masculinity, nature was a source of rough, macho virility. Dryden aligns Shakespeare with a poet who, in this period, was frequently cited as the supreme exemplar of artistic potency: '*Shakespeare* was the *Homer*, or Father of our Dramatick Poets; *Johnson* was the *Virgil*, the pattern of elaborate writing.' (Swedenberg, 1956–89, IX, 58).[8] Jonson himself combines images of father and lance-wielding warrior, describing Shakespeare's works as the result of conscious, well-informed, effort:

           Look how the fathers face
      Lives in his issue, even so, the race
   Of Shakespeares minde, and manner brightly shines
      In his well torned, and true filed lines:
   In each of which he seems to shake a Lance,
      As brandish't at the eyes of Ignorance. [9]

The gendered language in which critical debates are conducted reveals a fundamentally masculist mindset, placing Jonson and Shakespeare on eminences inaccessible to women.

Behn responds in the preface to *The Dutch Lover* with a virtuoso display of linguistic female drag: her satirical approach 'allows her to denaturalise the superiority of male learning and question its pertinence to comedy.' (Runge, 1997: 134). Sometimes she assumes the pose of an ignorant woman, whose sheer common sense enables her to prove that the things she does not know are not worth knowing. She deplores the fate of those 'ignorant, unhappy souls' who waste their time 'for ten, twelve, twenty years in the University (who yet poor wretches think they are doing something all the while) as Logick, &c. and several other things (that shall be nameless, lest I should mispel them.' (V, 160, ll. 23–26). This mockery is sharpened by reference to a broader contemporary attack on classical learning and formal logic as the mainstays of education.[10] On other occasions she demolishes the mystique of 'manly' learning by demonstrating that she has already mastered its jargon. She ridicules the pointless obscurity of arcane terms like '"Indiscerptibility, and Essential Spissitude" (words, which though I am no competent Judge of, for want of Languages, ought to mean just nothing)' – as, of course, they do (V, 160, ll. 10–11). Both strategies unite in her remarks on ancient writers' views on plays: 'for their musty rules of Unity, and God knows what besides, if they meant any thing, they are enough intelligible, and practible by a woman' (V, 163, ll. 133–5). She might have been recalling the prologue to *Volpone*, where Jonson makes the proud claim that he has followed classical precepts to the letter:

   The laws of time, place, persons he observeth,
      From no needful rule he swerveth.

                                                      (ll. 31–32)

But Behn declares the only important rules for writing plays concern 'making them pleasant, and avoiding of scurrility' (V, 163, ll. 135–6). By the eighteenth century, 'Jonson was to lose his position as the centrepiece

of a proudly English classicism to a still more aboriginal Shakespeare.'
(Craig, 1990: 12). The preface to *The Dutch Lover* shows the process under
way, as Aphra Behn undermines Jonsonian influence with her own
despised femininity, and with arguments which Jonson had been one of the
first to provide.

'A way too cheap for men of wit'

Yet Jonson always meant more to Behn than a looming bastion of
patriarchy. In the prologue to *The Amorous Prince* (1671), Behn presents
him both as a critical icon whose conservative influence on theatre practice
should be rejected in the interests of amusement, and as a great dramatist
whose achievements she dare not emulate, for fear of displeasing her
audience. First, she expresses fears that the abundance of comic material
will displease 'grave Dons who love no Play / But what is regular, Great
Johnson's way' (ll. 13–14), 'whose judgments will admit, / No interludes of
fooling with your Wit' (ll. 17–18; V, 87). This is, of course, an effective
method of assuring the majority of the audience that they are going to enjoy
themselves. But she adds that she may also have alienated more frivolous
spectators, who will not find her humour sufficiently vulgar. At the cultural
nadir, she places the gags of the star comic actors, James Nokes (d. 1696)
and Edward Angel (d. 1673), and in the zenith, a Jonson tragedy:

> So! there's a party lost; now for the rest,
> Who swear they'd rather hear a smutty jest
> Spoken by Nokes or Angel, than a Scene
> Of the admir'd and well-penn'd Cataline [. . .]
> You too are quite undone, for here's no Farce,
> Damn me! you'l cry, this Play will be mine A—
>
> (ll. 21–24, 27–28) (V, 87)

The coarse language of her imagined speakers exposes their lack of taste.
Since *Catiline* aroused more admiration in the closet than in the theatre,
there may be a touch of sarcasm; on the whole, however, Jonson emerges
well from this encounter.

Behn's treatment of Jonson reflects ambivalence about her own position
as a professional playwright, torn between her public's coarse appetites and
the demands of her more austere muse. In the preface to *Sir Patient Fancy*
(1678), she responds to hostile comments by pointing out that she

is forced to write for Bread and not ashamed to owne it, and consequently ought to write to please (if she can) an Age which has given severall proofs it was by this way of writing to be obliged, though it is a way too cheap for men of wit to pursue, who write for Glory, and a way which even I despise as much below me.

(VI, 5, ll. 24–28)

Longing for unattainable 'Glory', and clinging almost defiantly to the honourable (and, in that era, overwhelmingly masculine) title of 'Authour', Behn expresses almost unbearable tension. By 1686, critical opposition provokes her to abandon compromise: in the preface to *The Luckey Chance*, she declares

All I ask, is the Priviledge for my Masculine Part the Poet in me, (if any such you will allow me) to tread in those successful Paths my Predecessors have so long thriv'd in, to take those Measures that both the Ancient and Modern Writers have set me, and by which they have pleas'd the World so well. [. . .] I value Fame as much as if I had been born a *Hero*; and if you rob me of that, I can retire from the ungrateful World, and scorn its fickle Favours.

(VII, 217, ll. 119–23, 127–9)

Does her invocation of 'Ancient' writers indicate new-found respect for classical standards, or merely a hope that their prestige will enhance her own? In any case, both passages, though not mentioning Jonson directly, raise aesthetic and personal issues important to both dramatists. Behn's mood recalls the hurt and rage, thinly veiled by contemptuous indifference, which drove Jonson to append an 'Ode (To Himself)' to *The New Inn*, after it had met with a hostile reception:

Say that thou pourst them wheat,
And they will acorns eat:
'Twere simple fury still thyself to waste
On such as have no taste[.]

(11–14)

Incidentally, another link between these protests is the fact that both authors have been involved in transgressively-gendered appropriations of masculine learning. Among the responses to this ode in Appendix I of the Revels edition is an 'Answer' by Owen Feltham (? 1602–68): he objects strongly to the climactic scene, a debate on love and valour, treating material from Plato according to the methods of scholastic logic, on the grounds that the umpire is a mere 'chambermaid' (l. 28). Although Behn may never have realised this, she was again adopting a Jonsonian position.

Intrigues and robberies

Turning from theory to practice, we can see that some of Aphra Behn's most frequently adopted techniques were associated with Jonson, both by her contemporaries and by modern critics. According Dryden's *Essay of Dramatick Poesie*, Jonson's chief contribution to English dramatic tradition was 'the copiousness and well-knitting of the intrigues' (Swedenberg, 1956–89, IX, 53). The complication of plots, with an attendant proliferation of characters, was also characteristic of Behn. Although her elaborations probably originated as attempts to enhance enjoyment, some contemporaries apparently found the experience bewildering: she attempts to disarm their criticism by claiming that the plot of *The Dutch Lover* was 'busie (though I think not intricate)' (V, 163, l. 145). Twentieth-century critics endeavour to account for her complexity in thematic, even political, terms. Thus, Derek Hughes interprets the love intrigues in *Rover II* as the dramatist's comment on the power of obsessive desire (for the beautiful courtesan La Nuche) and the omnipresence of masculine folly (embodied in Fetherfool):

> When Willmore eventually sleeps with La Nuche, her diary for the night is quadruply booked: of the three other prospective clients, Blunt's friend Fetherfool and the elderly Spaniard Carlo are put in bed with each other, and the disappointed Beaumond hopes to slake his unsatisfied lust for La Nuche on the unrecognised body of Ariadne. But there is another, overlapping, quadruple booking, in which two pairs of men (Blunt and Fetherfool, and the English tricksters Shift and Hunt) compete to marry the monsters [a female dwarf and giant]. Seven men thus form two quartets.
>
> (Hughes, 2001: 127)

Like Jonson, too, Behn is skilled in constructing scenes where characters watch each other. A typical Jonsonian masterpiece is the episode in *Bartholomew Fair*, Act III, where Winwife and Quarlous watch Wasp watching Cokes watching Nightingale, Overdo watching Edgworth, Edgworth and Nightingale co-operating to rob Cokes, and Overdo getting the blame. Susan Owen, apparently judging Behn's intention from her own response to a scene in *Rover II*, suggests that a type of alienation effect is in progress:

> we are distanced from the action in a way which encourages us to reflect upon the various sex plots, rather than to engage with the characters. Thus in Act I we watch Ariadne and Lucia watching Willmore watching La Nuche watching her bawd, Petronella, gull Fetherfool.
>
> (Owen, 1996: 11)

This scene matches Jonson's in its atmosphere of ubiquitous deception and its quadruple layering, if not in the complexity of the characters' interaction.

Restoration dramatists worked in a period when theories about the value of originality conflicted with ideas about the beneficial influence of tradition. Dryden regards Jonson as a magisterial exponent of creative imitation:

> there is scarce a Poet or Historian among the *Roman* Authours of those times whom he has not translated in *Sejanus* and *Catiline*. But he has done his Robberies so openly, that one may see he fears not to be taxed by any Law. He invades Authours like a Monarch, and what would be theft in other Poets, is onely Victory in him.
>
> (Swedenberg, 1956–89, IX, 57)

Behn, however, is equally unimpressed by Jonson and his admirers: ' I am inform'd his Learning was but Grammer high; (sufficient indeed to rob poor Salust of his best Orations) and it hath been observ'd, that they are apt to admire him most confoundedly, who have just such a scantling of it as he had.' (V, 162, ll. 122–5). Her indignation was probably sharpened by her awareness that a woman who reworked material by her contemporaries and immediate predecessors would not escape as lightly as a learned man who pillaged the classics. Perhaps any man would get off more lightly than a woman, whatever material he used. She suggests that this is the case in her postscript to *The Rover I*, where she refutes an accusation that her *Rover I* was merely 'Thomaso *alter'd*.' (V, 521, l. 2). Behn alludes to the massive two-part closet drama, *Thomaso: or, the Wanderer* (1664), by Thomas Killigrew (1612–83), cavalier, courtier, and, in his capacity as patentee of the Theatre Royal, 'the most powerful single individual' in 'the London theater world' (Rosenthal, 1996: 171-2). She declares, somewhat disingenuously, that her borrowings are limited to the misfortunes of Angellica, a courtesan who displays pictures of herself, setting an exorbitant price on her favours. Like Jonson, Behn commits her robbery openly: 'I, vainly proud of my Judgment, hang out the Sign of Angellica, (the only stoln Object) to give Notice where a great part of the Wit dwelt.' (V, 521, 8–10). She then cites *The Novella* (1632) by Richard Brome (c. 1590–1652), formerly Jonson's servant; here, too, a woman's self-advertisement drives the plot: 'if the Play of the Novella were as well worth remembering as Thomaso, they might (bating the Name) have as well said, I took it from thence.' (V, 521, ll. 10–12). This sets Killigrew beside her in the frame: both are plagiarists, or both should walk free. In either case, Jonson belongs with them.

The three mountebanks

The true strength of Behn's Jonsonian affiliations emerges from comparison of scenes in *Thomaso I* and *Rover II* which are based on *Volpone* (2.1), where the hero disguises himself as a mountebank, in order to see a beautiful woman. This affords an excellent opportunity for stylistic and dramatic comparisons, since eloquence and showmanship are a mountebank's most important stock-in-trade. Killigrew's mountebank, Lopus, is no impersonator, which reduces dramatic tension. An even greater contrast lies in the effectiveness of their respective wares. In Jonson's city comedies, magic is the impossible claim of confidence tricksters. Killigrew's comedy shares Jonson's realistic tone, but in his dramatic world love powders are effective, while enchanted baths can alter size, shape, and sex. (*Thomaso* would make most sense to modern audiences if that plot strand were regarded as science fiction.) Lopus must therefore be taken seriously when he describes his products' virtues, which he does in a speech of over a thousand words, largely based on *Volpone*, but lacking the interruptions which gave the performance of Jonson's rogue so much dramatic interest. Some sections, like the following, are verbatim imitations from *Volpone*; if Killigrew did not copy this from a book, his memory must have been morbidly retentive:

> It hath power to fortifie the most indigest and crude stomack in the world, though it be one that (through extreme weakness) vomits bloud. Applying onely a warm Napkin to the place, after the Unction and Fricace; for the Vertigo in the head, putting but a drop into your Nostrils, likewise behind your Ears, a most Sovereign and approved remedy. The Mal Caduco, Cramps, Convulsions, Paralysies, Epilepsies, Tremor Cordis, retired and shrunk Nerves, evil vapours of the Spleen, stoppings of the Liver, the Stone, the Strangury, Hermia ventosa, Iliaca passio, stops a Dysenteria, immediately easeth the Torsion of the small guts, and cures Melancholia Hypochondriaca, being taken and applied according to my printed Receipt;'
>
> (*Thomaso I*, 4, 2, p. 360)[11]

However, Killigrew seems to have lost either his memory or his nerve, when confronted with passages such as this:

> some other gallants say, 'O, there be divers that make profession to have as good, and as experimented receipts as yours!' Indeed, very many have assayed,

like apes, in imitation of that which is really and essentially in me, to make of
this oil; bestowed great cost in furnaces, stills, alembics, continual fires, and

preparation of the ingredients (as indeed there goes to it six hundred several
simples, besides some quantity of human fat, for the conglutination, which we
buy of the anatomists); but, when these practitioners come to the last
decoction, blow, blow, puff, puff – and all flies *in fumo*: ha, ha, ha! Poor
wretches! I rather pity their folly and indiscretion than their loss of time and
money; for those may be recovered by industry: but to be a fool born, is a
disease incurable.

(Volpone, 2.2.152–65)

Killigrew produces a tamer, more abstract effect:

And though divers have professed to have as good and experimented Receipts
as my self, and have assayed to make both of this Oyl and water; bestowed great
cost in Furnaces, Stills, Alembicks, continual fires, and preparation of
Ingredients (as indeed there goes to each of them six hundred several Simples,
at least,) yet they ever lost their labour and cost, for want of that large Talent of
knowledge, requisite to such a work.

(Thomaso I, 4.2.361)

Departing further from Jonson's words, Behn nevertheless restores
features which modern critics find distinctively Jonsonian: relentless
realism, dramatic energy, and vivid concrete detail. Her mountebank is
once more an imposter, selling potions that have no effect: the rakish
hero, Willmore, is amusing himself at the expense of his gullible
companions. Like Volpone, he also has a sexual agenda, stampeding the
fair La Nuche into bed with him by fraudulent fortune-telling. His patter
is constantly interrupted by asides from spectators, or business of his
own. Echoes of Jonson resound in new contexts when Willmore displays
an elixir which purportedly restores the dead to life: a 'little Vial, which
contains in its narrow bounds, what the whole Universe cannot purchase,
if sold to its true value: this admirable, this miraculous Elixer, drawn
from the Hearts of Mandrakes, Phenix Livers, and Tongues of
Maremaids, and distill'd by contracted Sun-Beams.' (*Rover II*, II, i, 192–
99) (VI, 248–9). This speech, combining hyperbolic invention with
ingenious precision, appears to be an adaptation of the outrageous menu
with which Volpone attempts to seduce Celia:

The heads of parrots, tongues of nightingales,
The brains of peacocks, and of ostriches,

Shall be our food, and, could we get the phoenix,
Though nature lost her kind, she were our dish.

(3.8.201–4)

An exciting demonstration follows when Willmore's servant fakes suicide and is revived by his master's remedy, accompanied by another flood of colourfully erudite verbiage:

Coffin him, Inter him, yet after four and twenty hours, as many drops of this divine Elixer gives him new life again; this will recover whole Fields of slain, and all the dead shall rise and fight again – 'twas this that made the *Roman* Legions numerous, and now makes *France* so formidable, and this alone – may be the occasion of the loss of *Germany*.

(Rover II, 2.1.216–20) (VI, 249)

Behn exploits the satirical potential of this device with truly Jonsonian vigour, exacerbated by a malicious woman's eye view of masculine exploitation and cowardice:

What Cully wou'd be Cuckolded? What foolish Heir undone by cheating Gamesters? What Lord wou'd be Lampoon'd? What Poet fear the malice of his Satyrical Brother, or Atheist fear to fight for fear of death. Come, buy my Cowards Comfort, quickly buy.

(Rover II, 2.1.227–30) (VI, 249)

Behn is most Jonsonian when she is most herself.

Notes

1 Thomas Colepeper (1690), 'Adversaria', British Library Harley MSS 7587–7605. 7595, f. 25

2 'To Madam A. Behn on the publication of her Poems', ll. 87–93. Summers, 1915: VI, 134–5.

3 Montague Summers (ed.) (1927), *Complete Works of Thomas Shadwell*, 5 vols., Fortune Press, London. Vol. I, p. 11.

4 The Epistle preceding *Volpone*. Lines 101–2. This, and all subsequent references to *Volpone*, will be to the Revels edition. Manchester University Press. Ed. R.B. Parker (1983).

5 This and all subsequent Aphra Behn references are taken from *Works*, ed. Janet Todd, 7 vols., London: William Pickering, 1992–96. References in the text will give volume, page and line numbers for prefaces, postscripts and dedications; line, volume and page numbers for prologues; and act, scene and line numbers followed by volume and page numbers for plays.

6   See Noyes (1935) and Lennep *et al* (1965–68).
7   Cited in Kinsley (ed.) (1958) I, 142.
8   See also Williams (1993), pp. 62–3.
9   From Jonson's poem, *To the Memory of My Beloved ... Mr. William Shakespeare*. Lines 65–70.
10 See Todd (1996), pp. 171–2.
11 Thomas Killigrew, *Comedies and Tragedies*, London: Henry Herringman, 1664. References in the text will give act, scene and page number.

Chapter 8

Daughters of Ben

Alison Findlay

> – *Most mighty* Ben! *Father of the Stage, and Parent of the*
> *whole* Dramatick *Generation*! *May it please thy venerable*
> *Shade to cast an Eye on the unhappy circumstances of thy*
> *Children*
>
> (Gildon, 1702: 43–4)

When Christopher Rich appealed to the spirit of Ben Jonson to help the United Theatre Company, recently deserted by Betterton and other leading players, Ben's children were not only male performers and dramatists. Jonson was the parent of a 'Dramatick *Generation*' which included daughters as well as sons.

I The Epicœne Effect

Women's entry to the professional theatres as actors and dramatists inaugurated a major groundshift in performance traditions. Jonson's *Epicœne or The Silent Woman* epitomised that change and, significantly, this was the first and most popular Jonsonian text to be performed in the years 1660–1710. Charles II saw it on 6 June 1660, and it was the first play performed at court in the Cockpit at Whitehall on 19 November 1660.[1] Edward Kynaston, the most accomplished female lead, played the title role. Pepys's diary for 7 January 1661 indicates how *Epicœne* captured the spirit of the age because of its witty exploration of sexual identity as fluid and unstable:

> Kinaston the boy had the good turn to appear in three shapes: I, as a poor woman in ordinary clothes to please Morose; then in fine clothes as a gallant, and in them was clearly the prettiest woman in the whole house – and lastly, as a man; and then likewise did appear the handsomest man in the house.
>
> (Pepys II: 7)

The epicene qualities of the role were given a new twist after May 1663 with the appearance of Mrs Knepp as the boy. Casting a female actor seems perverse since Jonson's *coup de theatre* in *Epicœne* depends on the audience's silent acceptance of the tradition of transvestite acting represented by Kynaston, and the ultimate exposure of Epicœne as a boy character. When a woman performed the boy's part, audiences must, of necessity, have read it differently to the breeches roles performed frequently by female actors in other plays. Nevertheless, it obviously had appeal since Mrs Knepp was still playing Epicœne in 1668, and was succeeded by Mrs Oldfield, who performed it frequently until 1722, with other performances by Mrs Knight, Mrs Porter, Mrs Garnet, and Mrs Thrummond (Noyes 1966: 189). One reason for the popularity and topicality of this perversely transvestite tradition is that *Epicœne* dramatises precisely the crisis of new female volubility as the daughters of Ben began to speak for themselves in the theatre. An early seventeenth-century production with a boy actor would have exposed all the 'women' on stage as explicitly male constructions. The 'Medusa' Mistress Otter, the Collegiates, and the outspoken 'Semiramis' (3.5.60) appear as caricatured projections of male fears and prejudice; the silent woman as a ridiculous male puppet. A female actor playing Epicœne inverts the usual effect of the final scene. Morose's lines 'I am no man, ladies' (5.4.48) now seem more appropriate to Epicœne, and when the audience are told this is 'a boy' (5.4.230), it is the boy actor rather than the woman who is absent. The early Stuart audience had to imagine 'woman' and were made critically aware of their own constructions of the sex, but post-Restoration spectators are asked to imagine or remember the tradition of boy actors instead. The woman's living flesh and moving tongue step out of the theatrical frame to discredit the male construction of woman as 'a statue, or a motion only, one of the French puppets with the eyes turned with a wire?' (3.4.40–41).

This shifts the play's emphasis: *Epicœne* becomes the story of the emerging female voice. Actresses were trained with particular attention to their vocal qualities, as Jane Milling shows, and contributed significantly to the development of an authorised feminine public speech (Milling, 1996). Jonson's play dramatises the presence of the actress as 'a manifest woman' (3.4.45), and the new cultural construction of women's voices. Its satiric preoccupation with woman's 'longings' (5.4.57), her appetites for fashions, sex and autonomy take on a new resonance in the context of women's struggles for greater self-determination in the late seventeenth century. By 1666, the role of Epicœne had become a model for assertive female behaviour as can be seen from the much-reprinted picaresque tale *The English Rogue*:

My Wife acted the silent Woman to the life, whilest in a single state, for before we were married all her answers were very short, comprehended within the two Monosyllables of I, and No; and those too must be forcibly extracted from her; But now her tongue wag'd in a perpetual motion, and her voice so shrill and loud, that it would be heard distinctly, though a piece of Ordnance were discharged near her at the same time, or standing in the *Bell*-room door whilest the Bells were ringing.

(Head 1666: 200)

The self-transforming figure of the silent woman functioned as a trope for the possibilities and the limitations to self-expression experienced by the wider female population. Within the many examples of female transvestism in plays produced between 1660 and 1700,[2] women dramatists adapt the 'Epicœne effect' set up by Jonson's text to offer a self-reflexive interrogation of the advantages and risks of their own entry onto the professional stage. Transvestite disguise is a sartorial register of the vocal possibilities for women within a male-dominated institution. What kinds of masculine or feminine voice could they employ in the commercial theatre? The commodified ambience of 'the Exchange' in *Epicœne* (1.3.36) is rewritten in the light of the new exchanges negotiated there.

Elizabeth Polwhele's *The Frolicks* (c.1670) uses the 'breeches role' to foreground the ambiguity of the actress's power to represent woman in the theatre.[3] The heroine Clarabell's 'frolic' to 'turn boy for an hour or two' (2.543–45) is not a complete disguise so much as a mask which gives the character and the actress licence to play. 'You may serve for a girl in boy's habit,' says her servant (2.547–8). The identity of the actress is visible through the boy's costume and signals the presence of woman. However, the female body is in danger of being constructed from a specifically masculine perspective. Rightwit finds Clarabell 'preetily metamorphos'd' (3.48), her legs and thighs a source of delight to the hero and probably to some spectators. The 'frolic' presents Clarabell and the actress as a spectacle of (male) pleasure. Nevertheless, the plot allows both to exploit the charismatic energies of theatrical spectacle and move from object to active subject. Within her 'boy's habit', Clarabell fashions her own comedy. She escapes the possibility of an arranged marriage and the danger of being over-mastered by the licentious Rightwit, the object of her desire. Perhaps more importantly, the cross-dressed heroine and actress makes full use of her seductive attractions to manipulate his, and the audience's, desires. Clarabell successfully manoeuvres Rightwit into arranging their marriage rather than simply seducing her. The comic resolution suggests a working marriage between an emerging female voice and masculine, commercially-driven theatrical conventions.

The Frolicks also uses a woman-centred perspective to glance retrospectively at the tradition of all-male performance which dominates *Epicœne*, and, inevitably, finds it wanting. Clarabell persuades her suitors Sir Gregory and Mr Zany (neither of whom recognise her), to 'disguise and act' the parts of women for a dance called 'The Frolics' (3.137–39). Pearson notes that female-authored plays often feature male-transvestism as a source of comedy, as Polwhele does here (1988: 106). Zany eagerly recalls how he 'personated Maid Marian in a country morris' (3.144), borrowing the tavern mistress's clothes, a detail which recalls parodic drag performances in inns or alehouses. The old men 'strive which shall woman it best' (3.156), but the effects are ridiculous. Clarabell masters the scene, dancing the male part to the cross-dressed Sir Gregory's lady, and leaving him and Zany with the tavern bill. The final condemnation of male transvestism comes when the suitors are arrested in their women's clothes as 'strange, old, moded gentlewomen' who are 'not worthy to be styl'd "women"' (4.41–5). The woman actor is now centre stage.

She Ventures and He Wins (1695) by '"Ariadne" (a young lady)' moves on to examine woman's performance of identities across the social scale.[4] Its class-based focus echoes Jonson's concerns with aristocratic identity in *New Inn* as well as *Epicœne*. In *Epicœne* Jonson dramatised the beginnings of London's fashionable West End. By the 1690s, the theatres were geographically and culturally central to that *beau monde* in which courtiers and actors performed in close proximity. *She Ventures and He Wins* is closely attuned to this context. Charlotte, a rich heiress, follows Clarabell's lead and as 'one of my mad frolicks' (p. 111) adopts male disguise to test whether her suitor's affections are for her person or her fortune. The play opens with Charlotte and her cousin Juliana, both cross-dressed, discussing the epicene effect. This intimate all-female conspiracy powerfully inverts the conventional male dramatic opening and the Jonsonian text where Clerimont and Truewit inaugurate the play and Dauphine controls the its central illusion.[5] In spite of Charlotte's claim that their male attire 'will give us greater liberty' than petticoats (p. 109), the play shows that male identity does not, in itself, equal power. It is Charlotte's ability to direct and 'enact various identities' which gives her authority as Jenn Fishmann observes (1996: 36). By performing herself as a boy, a masked woman and finally an unmasked woman, she wins Lovewell as a husband: 'I claim you as my own' (p. 131).

Juliana shrewdly points out that 'a woman once vested in authority, though 'tis by no other than her own making, does not willingly part with it' (p. 109). Charlotte continues to play the woman's part 'with most masculine, or rather hermaphroditical authority' (*Epicœne* 1.1.90–91). She alienates herself from her social identity by re-casting herself into two *dramatis personae*, enlisting the help of her cousin Bellasira to play the part of heiress. This ingenious device enacts the pleasures of doubleness which Terry Castle identifies with eighteenth-century masquerade: 'a fantasy of two bodies simultaneously and thrillingly present, self and other together, two in one.'(1986: 4–5). The paired roles of Bellasira-as-Charlotte and Charlotte-as-deceiver highlight the performativity of social identity, particularly when they appear one after the other to test Lovewell's affections. They dramatise an increasingly 'theatricalised' aristocratic self-awareness, born out of social insecurity, a crisis of the aristocracy dramatised by Jonson's *New Inn* in 1629 and current again by the 1690s as Michael McKeon has shown (1987: 169). Charlotte plays a typically aristocratic game, attempting to naturalise her nobility and attractions for Lovewell through elaborate performance. Lovewell, like Morose, is deceived by an illusion which is finally exposed as the real thing. The examples of Margaret Hughes, Nell Gwyn, and Moll Davis remind us of the overlap between the heiress and her theatrical equivalent, the successful actress. As Cynthia Lowenthal remarks, 'onstage and sometimes off, common women *enacted* the aristocratic imperatives supposedly denied them by their non-aristocratic status.'(1996: 229).

Freedom to play is, nevertheless, an exclusive privilege in *She Ventures and He Wins*. Its sub-plot, like many of Jonson's, satirises the attempts of those inferior in social status or theatrical wit to break into the fashionable *beau monde* represented on and off stage. Squire Wouldbe's pretensions to dress beyond his '*poor extraction*' depend on the pawn shop owned by Mrs Beldam, his mother-in-law. Her own unease when '*dressed in an old fashioned point coif, a laced Mazarine hood*' (p. 143) – the cast-off fashions of the nobility – point up the instability of the family's social and theatrical aspirations. Although 'Squire' Wouldbe longs to play the fine, seductive rake, he is inextricably bound in marriage to Mistress Dowdy. She and Mrs Beldam cannot plot like the risqué, witty heroine in St. James's Park, in spite of their borrowed clothes (p. 144). The presumption of trying to imitate their betters is severely punished. Drawing on the same social dynamics as *The New Inn*, the sub plot concludes with a 'farce' (p.156). Like Jonson's Master Snuff and 'Lady' Pinnacia, Wouldbe and Dowdy are stripped of their fine clothes and exposed '*wrapped in a blanket*' and '*in a nightgown*' (p.169). Not every actress could translate herself into a lady.

Women's increased confidence to take control of 'frolics', fashion and the Jonsonian text is shown in Susanna Centlivre's *The Beau's Duel* (1702).[6] Gender inversions and a preoccupation with costume inform this explicit rewriting of *Epicœne*. Clarinda's 'Frolick' (p. 98) is to turn soldier with 'a Bush of Hair... furz'd out' (p. 110). She vows to be 'my own Knight-Errant', her task to 'deliver the distress'd Damsel', that is herself, from the effeminate suitors Sir William Mode and Captain Ogle (p. 95). Centlivre remodels the duel between Daw and La Foole when these fops meet for a duel in Hyde Park *'with Files, Pumps and Night-caps'* (p. 98). It is no longer Dauphine and Truewit who taunt the cowards; Clarinda and Emilia's disguises as 'two pretty Volunteers' (p. 102) give them privileged control of the duel like the wits, and the so-called ladies enjoy kicking and pulling the ears of Mode and Ogle.

Clarinda's father, Careful, is anxious 'to have you in your feminine Capacity again' for marriage (p.103), but his attempts to match her are thwarted by a second, sartorial rewriting of the *Epicœne* plot. Careful is deceived into marrying Mrs Plotwell, who disguises herself as a Quaker, 'as averse to the Fashions as other women are fond of 'em' (p. 104). Plotwell claims that 'the very Idea of a Gallant is neauseous to me' (p. 85) and in that sense, *The Beau's Duel* is very different from the comedy of the young gallants celebrated by Jonson. As in *Epicœne*, however, the play turns when Plotwell reveals her true self with demands, ironically, for costume and make up: 'fetch me a *French* Night-gown, and *French* Head [Hood], set my Dressing-Table in order' and 'Let my Paint, Powder and Patches be ready' (p. 119). Instead of excess of noise, Careful must endure a house lined with looking glasses, cabinets and the maintenance of an expensive wardrobe, alongside the certainty of being cuckolded. The prospect of such a marriage horrifies Careful, and he is quickly persuaded to reinstate his fortune on Clarinda and her chosen husband Colonel Manley, 'a man of Sense and Honour' (p. 127), in return for the dissolution of his own vows. The witty tricksters are triumphant, as in *Epicœne*, but in this play they are female.

The framing of men is physicalised when a curtained picture is delivered as a present to Plotwell by 'Lady *Manlove*'. Toper emerges from the picture in the role of seducing rake, and Careful sees this as indisputable evidence of his imminent cuckoldry. Barry O'Connor (1995) argues that there is a correlation between heroic portraiture and the physical framing effects of the stage in the creation of Restoration heroes, but here the ostentatious frame deconstructs the gallant. Toper is nothing but a decorative tool in the women's plots: put on display briefly, only to be discarded. The picture acts as a counter-discourse to Plotwell's supposed fascination with her own appearance and the commodification of woman as the object of a male gaze. In this way, *The Beau's Duel* offers a critical response to the commercial ambience of *Epicœne*. Jonson's play presents the women Collegiates and Mistress Otter as shrewd manipulators of the world of fashion; Centlivre's extends their role from consumers to dismantlers. In opting for the plainness associated with soldiers or Quakers, her heroines uncover the performative nature of typically gendered behaviour. Plotwell asks Mr Careful to 'pardon the Frolic' and he concedes 'With all my heart. I'faith the Frolic was a pretty Frolic – Now 'tis over' (p. 127). Female authorship of plots and plays are sanctioned within the limits of the stage.

Centlivre's feminist rewriting of *Epicœne* is taken even further in *The Busybody* (1709) where the covetous Morose-figure and the young gallants are both outwitted by a heroine whose silence wittily conceals her plots.[7] Miranda recognises the dangers which her guardian, Sir Francis Gripe, and the rakish Sir George Airy pose to her freedom and happiness, and plays one off against the other. She confounds Gripe's plot to disinherit his son, make her his heir, and marry her, by tricking him into giving her 'an authentic paper' giving her leave to marry as she chooses (p. 327). 'Now will I have the act my own', she jokes (p. 327), usurping Dauphine's manipulative role by acquiring the necessary papers to secure Charles's inheritance.

Miranda manipulates Sir George Airy just as ruthlessly as her guardian, even though she finds the gallant attractive. When she discovers that Sir Gripe has sold him an hour's conversation with her for a hundred pounds, she shows her disgust at being bartered over as a commodity by making the title role of Jonson's play her own. She performs the silent woman to the letter and rejoices 'to think how damned mad he'll be when he finds he has given his money away for a dumbshow' (p. 308). Her performance of feminine modesty comically undercuts Sir George's egotistical protestations: 'View me well, am I not a proper handsome fellow, ha?' (p. 312). In addition, the failure of verbal courtship forces him to adopt a tactile approach; the subsequent touching and kissing is a source of pleasure for her but tortures her voyeuristic, possessive, guardian. Miranda entertains Sir George's affections, but keeps her higher status, hiding him behind the chimney board when Sir Francis returns. Her pretence that he is a pet monkey of which she is 'fond...to distraction' ironically speaks the truth about their relationship (p. 346).

Contrary to her performance as the silent woman, Miranda is in fact a mistress of language. In spite of the financial and physical power of the men, her vow 'I'll fit him for signs' (p. 313) proclaims a superior control. As Jaqueline Pearson observes, the heroine and former servant Patch 'reflect very directly the dilemma of the woman writer as she attempts to insert herself into a male-dominated culture' (1988: 222). Even the jokes in this play are woman-centred. Sir Jealous Traffick's threat to castrate Charles is to 'equip him for the Opera' (p. 325), which carries a positive charge rather than a sense of loss or lack. It is Miranda and Patch, a woman of 'prodigious brain' (p. 131) who are equipped to drive the play forward, and the play marks a clearly gendered contrast between their success and the blunders of the idiotic Marplot, whose interventions jeopardise the futures of both sets of lovers.

II   'A New Amalgama'[8]

The plays discussed thus far show how Jonson could be appropriated by female actors and dramatists to remodel theatrical tradition. As a distinctively masculine symbol of high *literary* culture Jonson also presented a challenge to female dramatists as authors, and they responded in different ways. A display of deference to Jonson's authority characterises Margaret Cavendish's preface to her 1662 *Playes*. However, this collection parallels Jonson's 1616 Folio and thus implicitly contradicts its author's protestations that her spectators should 'not think to see / Such Playes, that's like Ben. Johnsons *Alchymie*, / Nor *Fox*, nor *Silent Woman*'.[9] Cavendish's modest claim that her plays 'have not such store of wit' as Jonson's gives her licence to compose her own witty versions of the silent woman, in *The Presence* and *The Publick Wooing*, and, most notably in Sir Serious Dumb and Lady Bashful in *Love's Adventures I* and *II* (1662), as Gweno Williams has noted.[10] Julie Sanders points out that allusions to *The Alchemist* in Cavendish's prose fantasy *The Blazing World* (1666) suggest that Jonson offers her 'a paradigm and a model of authorship' (Sanders 1998b: 296).[11] Certainly her reworking of the beast-fable from *Volpone* in her 'Piece of a Play' hints at the attraction which Jonson's model of authorship might have held for her.

Cavendish stated '*the following Fragments are part of a Play which I did intend for my Blazing-World, and had been Printed with it, if I had finish'd it.*'[12] The fantastic population of *The Blazing World*, including louse-men, bird-men, fox-men, is ideally suited to a reworking of *Volpone*, and Cavendish's play script uses caricatures to mock the fashionable theatre world of London. Monsieur *Ass* leads the 'Company of Mode-Wits' (p. 2) who promote dramatic satirical portraits, while Madam Leverit, a rich widow, and Lady Monkey and her maid Dormouse play the stock female types of post-Restoration comedy. The ladies are courted by Lord *Bear-man*, the innocent Sir *Puppy Dog-man*, Monsieur *Satyr*, and the Volpone-figure *Sir Politick Fox*, aided by his Mosca, *Mr Worm-man*. Lady *Leverit's* eventual choice of Monsieur *Ass* as a husband allows Cavendish to vent her full scorn for the limited horizons of commercial drama. Monsieur *Ass* invites the ladies to see a play and Lady *Monkey* declares 'If you be the Author, Monsieur *Ass*, surely the Play is an excellent Play' (p. 20). Cavendish's plays were not performed in the professional theatre and in *The Blazing World*, her persona blames the short-sightedness of the 'Blinking World of Wit' which condemns her texts as unactable. She tells the Empress that plays approved 'according to the judgement of the age' are nothing more than a trivial 'nursery of whining lovers' (Cavendish 1994: 220). Such blatant criticism of the audience's taste recollects the impatience of Jonson, seen most blatantly in caustic comments like the 'Ode to Himself' (*The New Inn*, pp. 204–9).

Like Jonson, Cavendish self-consciously positions herself above the popular, common rate. She dramatises her transcendence to a more enlightened aesthetic realm through the figure of Lady Phoenix. The town ladies, all figured as birds, twitter with gossip about this mysterious figure, who seems to have stepped from a Jonsonian Masque 'clothed all with light' and attended by 'Blazing-Stars' (p. 4), in such incomparable splendour 'as will astonish all her Spectators' (p. 3). Although none of them have seen her they believe 'she is as proud as *Lucifer*' (p. 5), yet Dormouse, her former maid, gives a flattering picture which matches closely with Cavendish's accounts of herself:

> She is of a studious nature, in a retired life, ever retireing from much Company, and of a careless humour, not regarding what the World says or doth; in Company she is of a free Disposition, and an airy Conversation... She may chance to seem proud to an *Ass* and vain to a *Buzzard*; but otherwise, she is as one of her quality ought to be.
>
> (pp. 6–7)

Cavendish models herself as a person of 'quality', whose worth depends upon her retirement from the commercial rat (or *Ass*) race. The connections with Jonson become more pointed when we recall that, as Jonson's last patron, William Cavendish, Earl of Newcastle, was instrumental in maintaining the poet during his final years of retirement from court.

More radical attempts to break away from the Jonsonian legacy and establish a female dramatic tradition appear in commendatory prefaces to the plays of Delariviere Manley, Catherine Trotter and Mary Pix, who self-consciously styled themselves as a literary sisterhood and daughters of Behn rather than Ben. *The Female Wits*, premiered at Drury Lane in 1696, satirised the attempts of 'the Female Triumvirate' to supersede Jonson's eminent position as learned author (*Female Wits* 1704: 5). Jonson's self-styled authority within the theatre looks positively benign in contrast to the tyrannical presence of Marsilia, the Manley caricature, who arrogantly tries to dominate all aspects of the on-stage theatrical production. However, as the satire cruelly points out, her authorial presence is needed 'to enlighten the understanding of the Audience' (p. 44). Marsilia's presumption to Jonson's laurels is undercut in this joke on the incomprehensibility of female-authored scripts.

Marsilia's real audacity is not in presuming to direct the Company, but her 'Design to alter *Cateline's Conspiracy*', rewriting all of Jonson's tragedy except the first speech. Her creativity is satirised 'as a destruction of her precursor', as Rosenthal remarks (1996: 175). It is a form of literary parricide designed 'to let the World, that is so partial to those old Fellows, see the difference of a modern Genius' (p. 9). Even her suitor Mr Praiseall is shocked, exclaiming 'Poor *Ben*! Poor *Ben*!' and lamenting 'Your Ladyship has lay'd his Honour in the Dust. – Poor *Ben*! 'Tis well thou art dead; this News had broke thy Heart' (p. 10). The second female wit, Calista, based on Catherine Trotter, also tries to improve on Jonson. To display her superior scholarship and out-do Marsilia, she claims she has translated the first speech of *Catiline* into Latin. Her ignorance about Jonson's Latin sources confounds her own pretensions to learning. In contrast to her female rivals, Mrs Wellfed does not so much challenge Jonson as reincarnate him in female form. This caricature of Mary Pix is 'a fat, Female Author, a good sociable, well-natur'd Companion' (*dramatis personae*), embodying the popular myth of Jonson. The numerous jokes about Wellfed's size point to her success as a writer; while Jonson is father of the dramatic generation, she is 'big enough to be the Mother of the Muses' (p. 5). Pix's talent for writing sharp city comedy makes her a suitable heir to Jonson's satiric wit.

In contrast to Cavendish's use of *Volpone* to figure retreat, the Jonsonian city comedies of Mary Pix and Susanna Centlivre are embedded in the world of commercial theatre and the wider mercantile space that was London. The 1690s saw a financial revolution, with the creation of the Bank of England (1694), The New East India Company (1698), dozens of new corporations (some sounder than others), and an increase in stock transactions at the Royal Exchange, regulated in 1697 (De Krey 1985: 121–2). London's merchant investors, including Dutch, German, French, Italian, Polish, Jewish and Swiss traders made London just as cosmopolitan a city as Venice, so Jonson's *Volpone*, and the comic 'projections' of Sir Politic

Wouldbe, were equally apt in late seventeenth-century London as in its earlier counterpart (Gauci 2001: 38–42).

Pix's play *The Deceiver Deceived* (1698) appropriates the central trope of blindness and deception in *Volpone* and develops it from a specifically feminist perspective.[13] Jonson's Mosca carefully anoints Volpone's eyes to make them bleary, and tells Corvino that Volpone cannot see them 'No more than the blind harper. He knows no man, / Nor face of any friend' (1.5.39–40). In Pix's play, the Venetian merchant Bondi, whose 'Religion lies in filling [his] Bags' (p. 2), counterfeits blindness to avoid civic duties and scrutinise the behaviour of his wife Olivia and daughter Ariana. Part of the appeal of *Volpone* is, to quote Dryden, that the rogue 'has carried on a Cheat for three years together, with Cunning and with Success' (Noyes 1966: 52). Pix's play appeals in the opposite way, as Bondi immediately loses mastery of the situation to the superior cunning of Lady Temptyouth, who distracts him with financial bills while setting up assignations between Olivia and her lover Count Andrea. She thwarts Bondi's wish to match Ariana to the stupidly vain, but wealthy Count Insulls, promoting instead a love match with the poor Fidelio. Affection for the young lovers turns even the Steward Gervatio to an early Mosca-like betrayal of his master, and he and Lady Temptyouth are always one step ahead of Bondi. As he begins to glimpse the failure of patriarchal surveillance, he exclaims 'Are all blind men served thus?' (p. 18) and the play implicitly associates blindness with a view of women as possessions. In a highly symbolic climax, Bondi must 'make the best of a bad Market' (p. 42): he is tricked into signing bequests to his daughter as supposedly the only way to avoid losing all his material possessions. While signing a will is endlessly deferred in *Volpone*, in Pix, the deceiver is forced to account, and repossession of his property is granted only by his vow to trust in his wife's fidelity and accept his daughter's marriage.

The triumph of women's desires and ingenuity in this plot must surely have delighted female spectators, but the high level of risk also appeals more broadly to one of the key sensibilities of the age: a love of gambling. 'Gaming is an Estate to which all the World has a Pretence,' Thomas Brown observed in 1705, and indeed, it flourished beyond the profusion of gaming houses. In the City, a vast circulation of trading capital meant that speculation fuelled the stock exchange, early forms of insurance were sold, and in 1709 gambling was given a governmental stamp of approval in the first State Lottery (Ashton 1883: 82–3). The dangers of trade 'could ruin the individual within a very short space in time, particularly in a competitive business climate' (Gauci 2001: 57). Making a fortune instantly, by play rather than work, is, of course, the central magic in Jonson's *The*

Alchemist, revived in 1701–2. Dapper is easily gulled into believing that he will 'win up all the money i' the town' (1.2.67), and, blessed by the Queen of Faery in wider financial speculation, his 'gaming mouth' will 'draw you all the treasure of the realm' (1.2.102).

Doll Common's brief appearance as the Queen is an empty parody and hardly fulfils her wish for equality in the 'venture tripartite', in the form of a high-status role that will match Subtle's: 'Why, if your part exceed today, I hope / Ours may, tomorrow, match it' (1.1.146–7). Susannah Centlivre's remodelling of Jonson's theme in *The Gamester* (1705) responds to Doll's plea.[14] The play's ostensible protagonist is the hero Valere, who states 'there is an Air of Magnificence in't' – a Gamester's Hand is the Philosopher's Stone, that turns all it touches into Gold' (p. 163). This disciple of Subtle is not allowed to engineer the plot of Centlivre's play, which departs radically from *The Alchemist*. *The Gamester* still 'caters to audience interest in gaming' with its scenes of card play, as Nancy Cotton pertinently observes (1980: 131), but its heroine Angelica plays the gamester's part as actively as the hero. She cross-dresses as 'a pert young Bubble' (p.179) and outplays her male rivals at the table to win back the portrait she gave Valere in a final bet which he cannot resist. The love-token symbolises Angelica herself. She says 'whilst you keep safe this Picture, my Heart is yours' (p. 153), but giving it to Valere is, she knows, a gamble. Throughout the play, it remains unclear whether he is more attracted to her person or her dowry, a wonderful prize to play for, and perhaps with.

Winning back the picture is a form of self-possession and emotional self-control: not to lose her heart to a profligate who does not return her emotions, but to choose how and when to give it to a deserving partner. Angelica rigorously attacks his attempt to commodify her: 'Is it possible thou could'st be so base to expose my Picture at a common Board' (p. 189), and claims 'I have Liberty to give it to whom I please' (p. 190). Her control of the symbolic and material capital (her dowry) is short lived. Centlivre, like Jonson, is a hard-headed realist and the play shows that, in spite of this moment of triumph, Angelica is just as ideologically and emotionally trapped as Valere appears to be. She ends the play by venturing her heart again, promising to marry him with no guarantee that he will reform or love her for herself: 'Condemn'd good People, as you see, for Life, / To play that tedious, juggling Game, a Wife' (p. 196). Angelica's sister, Lady Wealthy, highlights the confines within which the women operate. She rejoices that 'being free, I'm free to chuse' (p.146), but by gambling for Valere's love, proves that her desires operate only within the limited competitive frame for male attention. In *The Gamester* Centlivre shows that

Doll Common's wish for an equal place at the gaming table is insufficient to change the rules of the game itself.

The Basset Table (1705), Centlivre's next play, emphasises the limitations of keeping within the man-made rules of the game and offers a radical escape route. Lady Reveller's freedom to play away her fortune and refuse her lover Worthy is cut short by a rape plot.[15] Like Mosca's direction of the seduction scene with Celia in *Volpone*, this is a male orchestration, offering the appearance of liberation. Lord Worthy is secreted to rescue Lady Reveller from the unwanted attentions of Sir James Lovely, who behaves as tyrannically as Corvino: locking her in, treating her as a prostitute, laying hold of her; and, Volpone-like, threatening to force her love. When she cries out 'Murder! Rape! Rape!', Lord Worthy comes to her rescue on cue like Bonario. He subdues her into a penitent who asks forgiveness 'for all my folly' and accepts his love (p. 284).

Lady Reveller's cousin, Valeria, symbolises a more active control of the Jonsonian legacy, seen in her delight to have 'a huge flesh-fly' (p. 251) – like Mosca – to dissect (though, significantly, it escapes). Valeria's interest in scientific experiment represents a radical way forward for women inside the theatre and beyond. Her rational approach is matched by the ability to control her lover, her father and her environment, and although eccentric she is not unsympathetic. She may well be an affectionate portrait of Margaret Cavendish (Rosenthal, 1996: 238). Valeria finds dissecting a dove more appealing than conventional romance, responding to Ensign Lovely's invitation to elope with the words 'What, and leave my microscope and all my things for my father to break in pieces?' (p. 261). When Sir Richard enters and begins to destroy her experiments, Lovely is forced to conceal himself under a tub as a specimen. As with Sir Politic Wouldbe's disastrous tortoise-shell disguise in *Volpone*, Lovely is humiliated, kicked, and finally uncased. Valeria comically shows greater distress for the loss of her fish and worms than fear for her beloved. While Lady Reveller and her maid exclaim that women's learning is ridiculous, Valeria is confidently determined that reform will succeed: 'Custom would bring them as much in fashion as furbelows, and practice would make us as valiant as e'er a hero of them all. The resolution is in the mind. Nothing can enslave that' (p. 251). In *The Alchemist*, the laboratory had functioned as a carnivalesque space in which new social relations between characters, and between actors and spectators could be played. Valeria's laboratory in *The Basset Table* serves as a metaphor for the experiments in female education, autonomy and self-expression promoted by pioneering figures like Margaret Cavendish and Mary Astell. By appropriating, imitating or rewriting Jonson's comedies in 'a new amalgama' (*The Alchemist* 2.3.80), the daughters of Ben, and later of Behn, were able to advertise these feminist futures within the public domain of the theatre.

Notes

[1] Noyes (1966), pp.173–6. Noyes lists 36 recorded performances of *Epicœne*, 26 performances of *Bartholomew Fair* and *Volpone*, 21 performances of *The Alchemist* in these years and notes that Langbaine records them as being acted in the theatres in 1691 (1966: 319–22).

[2] On transvestism in plays by men and women see Jacqueline Pearson (1988) pp.100–18.

[3] Elizabeth Polwhele, *The Frolicks*, ed. Judith Milhous and Robert D. Hume (1977), Cornell University Press, Ithaca and London. Quotations are from this edition.

[4] *She Ventures and He Wins*, in *Female Playwrights of the Restoration*, ed. Paddy Lyons and Fidelis Morgan (1991), J.M. Dent, London. pp. 103–59. References are to page numbers in this edition.

[5] See P.A. Skantze's 'The Lady Eve, or Who's on First?', *Women and Theatre*, 2 (1994), 73–87.

[6] Susanna Centlivre, *The Beau's Duel: Or, A Soldier for the Ladies* (1702), in *The Dramatic Works of the Celebrated Mrs Centlivre with A New Account of her Life*, 3 vols. (1872) John Pearson, London, Vol. 1, pp. 59–129. All references to the play are to page numbers in this edition.

[7] Susanna Centlivre, *The Busybody* (1709) in *Female Playwrights of the Restoration: Five Comedies*, ed. Paddy Lyons and Fidelis Morgan, Everyman (1991), J. M. Dent, London, pp. 293–363. References are to page numbers in this edition.

[8] *The Alchemist*, 2.3.80.

[9] Margaret Cavendish, *Playes* (London, 1662), A7r–A7v.

[10] See Alison Findlay and Stephanie Hodgson-Wright with Gweno Williams (2000), *Women and Dramatic Production 1550–1700*, Pearson, Basingstoke. Chapter 5.

[11] The reference to *The Alchemist* is found in Margaret Cavendish, *The Blazing World and Other Writings*, ed. Kate Lilley (1994) Penguin, Harmondsworth, p. 166.

[12] The 'Piece of a Play,' just short of two acts, is included at the end of Margaret Cavendish's *Playes Never Before Printed* (London, 1668), p.1. All page numbers are to this edition.

[13] Mary Pix, *The Deceiver Deceived* (London, 1698).

[14] *The Dramatic Works of Susanna Centlivre*, Vol. 1, pp. 131–87. References are to page numbers in this edition.

[15] Susanna Centlivre, *The Basset Table* in *Female Playwrights of the Restoration*, pp. 235–92. References are to page numbers in this edition.

Part III

Jonsonians in the Modern Period

Chapter 9

Embarrassments to the Tidy Mind: John Arden and Ben Jonson

Stephen Lacey

In much of this book, the idea of a Jonsonian tradition is deliberately and productively loose, as is the conception of influence: in the case of John Arden the connection to Jonson is much more direct. Arden declared an early interest in Jonson, the man and the playwright. This connection is particularly strong in Arden's early plays, but it is possible to argue that Jonson is a presence in all his work (though not evenly or in the same way). The plays themselves provide clear evidence of Arden's debt to the earlier writer, and, as we shall see, Jonson was a model for Arden at the beginning of his career as a dramatist. But this is not the full extent of the relationship between them, which emerges when the trajectory of Arden's career as a whole is considered. For the benefit of readers who may be unfamiliar with Arden's work, it is worth summarising that career here.

John Arden came to prominence in the late 1950s in the wake of the explosion of new theatrical activity, collectively known as the New Wave, triggered by John Osborne's *Look Back in Anger*. Like Osborne's, his plays were first produced at the Royal Court Theatre by the English Stage Company. In the 1960s, his work was produced in a variety of professional contexts, including the National Theatre at the Old Vic, *Armstrong's Last Goodnight* (1965), and the Chichester Festival Theatre, *The Workhouse Donkey* (1963). By the late 1960s, most of his work was written with his wife, Margaretta D'Arcy. After a much-publicised argument with the Royal Shakespeare Theatre over a production of their Arthurian epic *Island of the Mighty* in 1972, Arden and D'Arcy quit the professional English stage to live and work in Ireland. This led to a range of experimental and often highly political work, produced outside the constraints of the established professional theatre (for example, *The Non-Stop Connelly Show* [1975], a 24-hour epic on the Irish socialist James Connelly and the abortive Easter Rising of 1916). Since the late 1970s, Arden and D'Arcy have written for radio, *Pearl* (1979), written by Arden alone, and *Whose is the Kingdom?*

(1988). Arden has also written novels (*Silence Among the Weapons* was shortlisted for the Booker Prize in 1982) and short stories.

Even this brief summary indicates some of the many paradoxes of Arden's career. Although he was frequently allied with the New Wave, his work sits uneasily in a metropolitan theatre dominated by Naturalism, and although his plays were well regarded by some critics and many theatre professionals, they did not find an audience at the Court, or indeed on any metropolitan stage. Arden has always had a difficult relationship with mainstream theatre, and this was evident even before the debacle over *Island of the Mighty*. The reasons why are indicated by his comments on the first production of *Armstrong* at the Glasgow Citizen's Theatre in 1964: 'the production… was under-budgeted, unevenly cast, hastily-prepared, and yet there was a vigorous sharing of a lively experience with the audience.' (1977a: 6). This illustrates one of Arden's guiding theatrical principles, and brings us back to his relationship with Jonson: that the central objective of theatre is to connect to a broadly-based audience, to whom the issues of the play *mattered*. This connected Arden to the era as a whole; and the period of the late sixteenth and early seventeenth centuries, the period of both Jonson and Shakespeare, is a constant presence in his work, providing both subject matter – see *Pearl* and *Books of Bale* (1988), Arden's second novel – and a consistent point of reference. Arden saw this as a time when theatre drew its vitality from a popular audience, one which crossed class and educational barriers and which could be addressed in a shared language. Indeed, Arden has written throughout his career *as if* he were addressing that audience. As a result, he has spent great deal of time and effort, courageously, and often against the grain of the times, finding a working context, in which he could engage with the kind of spectator that Jonson could take for granted.

But why Jonson and not Shakespeare? In fact, at different times in his career, and for different reasons, Arden has been influenced by Shakespeare (there is even a family connection, and Arden is a direct descendent of Mary Arden, Shakespeare's mother). Michael Cohen has argued that the influence of Shakespeare and, before him, the pre-Elizabethan dramatists of the mid–sixteenth century, has been a more decisive influence[1]. But however one reviews the evidence, the influence of Jonson remains crucial – the more so for being acknowledged at an early stage (and it is the early plays, written by Arden alone, that I am most concerned with in this essay).

In one sense, it is a case of a maverick being drawn to a maverick. Arden recognised that, like Jonson, he did not fit easily in the neat boxes of traditional dramatic criticism: they were both, in the words that give this essay its title 'an embarrassment to the tidy mind'.[2]

Jonson's pattern book

Both Arden and Jonson were / are intellectuals, with a strong sense of the classical tradition, operating in theatrical contexts where such learning was not always valued. As Arden observed, somewhat ruefully, 'Jonson was able to invoke the great names of Tacitus, Juvenal, Horace, Sallus, Seutonius and heaven knows who, all read and comprehended in the original Latin and impeccably inserted – whole paragraphs at a time – into the matrices of his text' (1977b: 27). Arden himself is alone in his generation of new British dramatists that came to prominence in the late 1950s in having a very strong sense of theatrical tradition. He is familiar not only with the Elizabethan and Jacobean periods (a knowledge that extended a long way beyond Shakespeare and Jonson) but also with a great deal of European theatre and literature, classical and contemporary (few of his fellow dramatists in the 1950s have his complex awareness of the politics and theatricality of Brecht, for example). There are also few writers – of any period – with such a strong sense of popular traditions, from Aristophanes to the music-hall, about which he has written lucidly and persuasively (and to which we shall return). Arguably, it is the force of his enthusiasm for earlier forms of drama, and his ability to incorporate the theatrical values and conventions of those sometimes unfamiliar and unfashionable forms into his plays (to the evident incomprehension of many critics and some of his audiences), which has led to his marginalisation in British theatre.

There is also another connection between the two writers that, at first sight, seems arbitrary, but is not: both writers have connections to the building trade. Jonson was the stepson of a bricklayer and practised that trade as a young man. Arden was an architect by training and worked briefly in the profession. This gave them both a particular attitude to the craft of play*wrighting* (as well as play*writing*), for which the building trade provides both a metaphor and a discipline. The title of Arden's key essay on his mentor is 'Ben Jonson and the Plumb-Line' (1977b). In that piece he argued that 'bricklaying is very much the kind of early skill that one would deduce from the finished plays. A bricklayer needs to be patient and precise... every brick must be exactly laid...' (1977b: 29). It was Jonson's meticulous and intricate *craftsmanship* that led Arden, the architect, to adopt him, rather than Shakespeare, as an early model – a debt Arden has openly acknowledged:

> I determined, in short, that if I were to write social comedy, Jonson was the man to follow.... I could not find anything in Shakespeare in the nature of a craftsman's pattern book. I was very much in need of a pattern book, as I had already decided that no modern play was constructed in a way that I would care to imitate (I had not then discovered Brecht – who does in many ways resemble Jonson). Jonson, the bricklayer, could teach me how to lay the bricks in order. If I wanted to allow them to deviate now and then from the rule of the plumb-line, I would have to work that out for myself.
>
> (1977b: 33)

The Jonsonian pattern-book gave Arden a great deal. In particular, it gave him a way of conceiving dramatic action in terms of plot and situation, rather than character alone. All of Arden's plays have complex plots, rivalling at times the labyrinthine twists and turns of Jonson's. Arden's narratives are driven by action, incident and invention, and it is not dramatic situation that is determined by character, but rather characters that are defined by the situations in which they find themselves. Character development, therefore, is less important than the complexity (social, moral and political) of those situations. It is from the meaning of the *story* that the meaning of the play will be deduced, and the Naturalist habit of placing the authorial point of view in the mouth of a privileged character should be avoided. As Arden wrote of the ballad tradition, which resembled the drama in this respect, 'we are given the fable and we draw our own conclusions. If the poet intends us to make a judgement on his characters, this will be implied by the whole turn of the story, not by intellectualised comments as it proceeds. The tale stands and it exists in its own right'(1970: 126).

This makes Arden's plots, like Jonson's, notoriously difficult to summarise, as these brief attempts will demonstrate. *The Waters of Babylon* (1957), Arden's first play to be produced at the Court, concerns Krank (real name Sigismanfred Krankiewicz), a Polish refugee from the Second World War turned slum landlord and pimp, who leads a double life as an architect. This uneasy deceit is threatened by a fellow Polish émigré, Paul, who wishes to enlist Krank's extremely reluctant help in a bomb plot against the leaders of the Soviet Union, who are visiting the UK. A Tory MP, who becomes a client of the architectural firm, for which Krank works, is now keeping one of Krank's former prostitutes and is involved in the Soviet visit. Meanwhile, Krank's employer, Barbara becomes attracted to him, and threatens unknowingly to discover his secret. To extricate himself, Krank attempts to buy Paul off with money stolen as part of a local Lottery scam, which goes disastrously wrong. *The Workhouse Donkey* is no less complex. It centres on the power struggle between Charlie Butterthwaite, a self-styled 'Napoleon' of provincial politics (who plays a minor part in *The Waters of Babylon* as Krank's 'fixer'), and the newly-arrived Chief of Police, Colonel Feng. To precipitate Feng's rapid departure from the town, and ensure the embarrassment of his Tory arch-rival, Sweetman, Charlie attempts to engineer a scandal involving the local nightclub-cum-brothel, which is secretly owned by Sweetman and kept open with the connivance of the police. Meanwhile (and there is always a meanwhile in Arden's plays), Charlie is threatened when his 'fixer', Wellington Blomax, calls in his gambling debts (Blomax himself is being cajoled by his daughter Wellseley, who has been proposed to by Sweetman's son). The situation descends into riotous disorder when Charlie decides to pay his debts by stealing from the Council...with results that we shall examine later.

Much of the humour of Arden's plays (and they are often very funny, as well as being comic in the formal sense) arises from the freewheeling intricacy of these highly eventful narratives. However, this complexity of plot also serves a thematic purpose. One of the central concerns of *Waters of Babylon*, for example, is the impossibility of remaining socially, politically and morally uninvolved. Krank attempts to organise his affairs so as to move through life without fear of commitment or contamination. 'I am a man of no one condition' he confides to the audience near the beginning of the play 'having no more no country, no place, time, action, no social soul. I am easy and able to choose whatever alien figure I shall cut, where and wherever I am' (1967: 29). Yet, as the plot demonstrates, such detachment is not possible, since all Krank's action have consequences, which he can neither foresee nor control. Each new strategy rebounds on him, until his death at the hands of Paul, though absurd and accidental, seems like a logical conclusion to a life lived trying to escape history; Krank, who has posed as a former inmate of Belsen concentration camp, is revealed at his death to have been a guard.

The complexities of Arden's plots are contained, like Jonson's, within rigid structures and a series of formal devices, to which the attention of the audience is drawn; the skeleton of the narrative is worn on the outside of the body, as it were, and not concealed beneath the skin. *Waters of Babylon*, *The Workhouse Donkey* and *The Happy Haven* all open with a character addressing the audience directly, a device that establishes both the dramatic situation and the performance register. In the case of *The Workhouse Donkey*, the audience is positioned in a precise way, socially and culturally: the published text makes it clear that different opening monologues are to be used depending on whether the play is performed South or North of the River Trent. And all three plays end with obvious rhetorical devices, designed not simply to conclude but also to *present a conclusion* to the play. *Waters of Babylon* ends with the singing of a round; *The Workhouse Donkey* concludes with a formal chorus addressing the audience in the manner, though not the political purpose, of a Greek drama; and *The Happy Haven*, which is set in an old people's home, is resolved with a formal, if ironic, admonition to the audience to plan better for their old age.

Arden's exuberant theatricality is a celebration of the values of performance, and this links him, once again, to Jonson. Richard Cave has written of Jonson on the contemporary stage that 'the most successful of recent productions have been ones which clearly began in rehearsal by investigating theatricality as the vehicle which would best convey an audience into an imaginative engagement with Jonson's themes' (Cave, 1991: 5). The same approach would clearly work for Arden's plays, too. Like Jonson's, Arden's plays both draw attention to their theatricality through a range of intriguing and imaginative devices and construct the idea of performance itself as complex metaphor embedded in the density of particular texts. The world of many of Arden's plays – and nearly all of Jonson's – is a theatricalised one, in which the vocabulary of performance (self-presentation, dissembling, the playing of roles in specific situations) is both a mechanism of character and narrative construction and, self-referentially, an embodiment of a moral and political statement. Dissembling and the playing of roles are central. There is a moment in *Waters of Babylon*, for example, where Krank disappears behind a screen and re-emerges transformed from slum landlord into respectable architect. As Albert Hunt has pointed out (1974: 38), this is a quick-change routine, a device straight from the music-hall, and appeals to the audience on that level. It is also a potent comment on the malleability of a man like Krank, a survivor of one of the most appalling crimes of human history, constantly required to re-invent himself to survive.

To take another kind of example, for the elderly inmates of the nursing home in *The Happy Haven*, old age is a kind of performance that they are required to give to each other and to the nursing staff who have power over them. In addition, Arden wrote the play to be acted in half masks, of the kind used in the Commedia dell'Arte, and one result of this is that the performative element of each character's role is foregrounded in the mask. One of the functions of the mask is to allow the actor to display, rather than simply inhabit, character. Arden also asks that the elderly residents be played by young people, whose youth should be evident in the way they move, especially when not required to 'perform' their old age for others, thus creating a striking contradiction between actor and role that acquires a social resonance.

The masks also serve another function, which is to experiment with a modern equivalent to a Jonsonian comedy of Humours. For Jonson, the physiology of Humours provides an additional structural device, keeping the characters within the bounds of shared expectations of what is, and is not, possible behaviour. There can be no exact equivalent to this in modern science and philosophy, but Arden's sense of social type (which also parallels Jonson's) fulfils some of the same theatrical function. This is not without its problems, however. As William Gaskell, the director of *The Happy Haven* at both Bristol and the Royal Court, observed: 'If you read any Ben Jonson play, most of the first half is taken up by long, rich, verbal statements of character by Morose, Epicure Mammon, and the rest. In the Commedia dell'Arte the mask by its very nature makes the same statement at once, and goes on making it in a fast-moving situation'(Gaskell, 1960: 19). This tends to underestimate the importance of the dialectic that the play in performance establishes between the fixity of the mask and the playfulness and flexibility of language, which modifies and develops an audience's response to the mask / character.

Indeed, language, simultaneously theatrically exuberant and closely observed, is crucial to the construction and development of social types in Arden's plays, as it is in Jonson's. As Arden noted in a comparison between Shakespeare's and Jonson's representation of an Irishman in *Henry V* and *Bartholomew Fair* '[there] must have been plenty of Irishmen in London at that time: but where Shakespeare seems to have obtained a generalised impression of nationalist hysteria and boozy blasphemy, Jonson actually *listened* to every turn and phrase and noted it down' (1977b: 30). As this comment indicates, Jonson creates character through language – often a wild, extravagant language, which is not designed to 'reveal' character, as if through a window, but rather to embody it often through verbal excess and direct statement. Arden himself created an Irishman in *Waters of Babylon*, Cassidy, who, like Jonson's, is based on close observation married to wild metaphorical inventiveness. Cassidy is clearly a 'stage Irishman', whose fluent verbal felicity catches both the musicality and metaphorical richness of an Irish working-class demotic, whilst referring the audience to social reality and theatrical tradition. Discussing the latest arrival of young Irish women off the boat train (potential fodder for Krank's brothel), Cassidy says 'there they stepped down from it, six beautiful doxies.... all roaring gorse, wild whitethorn, a chiming tempest of girls, turned that dirty Euston station into a true windswept altitude, a

crystal mountain-top for love.' (Arden, 1967: 42). The problem for a
modern audience is that this rich, poetic language is spoken by a
contemporary character ('historical' characters do not pose the same
problems), and this is perhaps a major source of the resistance that Arden's
plays sometimes face on the professional stage. We are returned once more
to the questions of what kind of audience Arden's plays are designed to
address, and how; and here Jonson was, once again, a guide.

Jonson, Arden and the popular tradition

Arden's affinity for Jonson was kindled by seeing a production of
Bartholomew Fair at the Edinburgh Festival in 1950 at the Assembly Hall
in a production directed by George Devine (later to become the first
Artistic Director of the English Stage Company at the Royal Court Theatre,
and an early champion of Arden's work). Writing of the critical reception
of the play, Arden noted:

> [The critics] use words like 'pedantic', 'heavy', 'over-conscientious'. This
> surprised me. There had, it is true, been a lot of long speeches, some of them
> almost incomprehensible: but the overall action of the play was so clear, the
> setting of the fair and its habitués so precise, that it didn't seem to matter. I
> cannot remember the evening in much detail – the main impression I retain is
> one of having been at a fair (rather than having seen a play about some fictional
> people at a fair), and a fair full of very curious happenings and juxtapositions of
> persons, which emerged, as it were, from out of the crowd and then sank back
> into it... There was, in fact, the whole of London, shuffling and prowling about
> on the big Assembly Hall open stage – and each of them, one way or another, as
> cracked as an old carrot.
>
> (Arden, 1977b: 32)

These comments are revealing in many ways. What is at stake here is not
what is often meant when a member of the audience feels that a theatrical
representation has stopped being 'like theatre' and has become 'like life'.
Questions of surface plausibility, of verisimilitude, are not the issue, since
the play was clearly not a piece of unmediated Naturalism. It was rather the
inexplicability of seemingly chance events, of the grotesque, the chaotic
and the unexplained, *the taste of here and now* that attracted Arden, and
which was to prove decisive. Though set in the sixteenth century, this
production brought Arden into contact with a means of dramatising the
contemporary world in a theatrical form that did not simply collapse back
into Naturalism.

'The contemporary' as a critical and descriptive category was a crucial part of the public self-definition of New Wave British drama in the 1950s and an important element in its success. There is not the space here to explore this in depth,[3] but it is important to note that 'contemporary' often functioned as a synonym for 'socially engaged'; to write directly about post-war Britain carried a quasi-political charge, and its absence from the artistic culture of the early 1950s was, from the viewpoint of a new generation of writers, a serious lack. Arden is most often thought of as a writer of history plays, and clearly much of his dramatic output (as well as his novels and stories) is set in the past, often for good 'Brechtian' reasons (to get a proper purchase on the present). However, his early plays, which are the ones most influenced by the Jonsonian 'pattern book', engaged with contemporary Britain in a direct way. *Waters of Babylon* is set at the time it was written and first performed, and is party a satire on the Premium Bond scheme, which had recently been introduced; *Live Like Pigs* (1958) was inspired by a contemporary newspaper article, and concerns the clash of cultures on a post-war housing estate; *The Happy Haven* is set in an old people's home in the late 1950s, and superimposes a post-war concern with the potential of science and technology onto a traditional plot device, the search for 'an elixir of youth'; and *The Workhouse Donkey* is set against the backdrop of the Machiavellian politics of local government and was inspired by Arden's birthplace, Barnsley.

For many of Arden's fellow playwrights, dramatising contemporary Britain meant writing within the Naturalist tradition (Raymond Williams has noted how the contemporary became a defining characteristic of Realism and Naturalism in the theatre[4]). For Arden, it meant something very different, and his work, whether written individually or with D'Arcy, explores pre- and, later, post-Naturalist forms, in particular forms associated with the popular theatre tradition. In this, Arden is most clearly a 'Jonsonian', for, like Jonson, he saw no necessary distinction between 'serious' theatre and popular entertainment. Jonson's plays move easily between broad comedy and serious debate – indeed, it is often *through* the broad comedy that serious issues are explored, and Arden found Jonson's pluralistic approach to form exhilarating and decisive. For Arden, then, the contemporary world could only truly resonate in the popular imagination if it was expressed though the forms, poetic and comic, of the popular tradition.

Arden articulated his conception of this tradition most clearly in an essay written in 1960, 'Telling a True Tale'.[5] 'What I am deeply concerned with' he argued 'is the problem of translating the concrete life of today into terms of poetry that shall at the one time both illustrate that life and set it within the historical and legendary tradition of our culture.' (1970: 125). Arden conceived the popular tradition as a single, unbroken (though not necessarily straight) line, originating in the Dionysiac comedies of Aristophanes and finding expression in the mediaeval jongleurs, the Commedia dell'Arte and, in the British context, the mummer's plays, before arriving at the Renaissance theatre of Shakespeare and Jonson, where it merged with a renewed literary tradition. After this point, the tradition was less visible in the theatre, though it could be identified in the street ballad and, later, the music-hall. Its position in the twentieth century, however, was by no means secure, and in the post-war world the threat of popular culture in its mass-produced and electronic forms threatened to extinguish it entirely. The literary theatre, meanwhile, had become dominated by Naturalism and its variants. 'Telling a True Tale' reads as an impassioned defence of a tradition that still had the potential to represent contemporary life in a way that social realism could not. 'Social realism' he argued 'tends in the theatre to be dangerously ephemeral and therefore disappointing after the fall of the curtain. But if it is expressed within the framework of the traditional poetic truths it can have a weight and impact derived from something more than contemporary documentary facility.' (1970: 126).

One might argue that the notion of a singular popular tradition is misleading, and perhaps a-historical, but it had its roots in a libertarian politics, influential in the 1960s, that saw popular culture of this kind as a source of instinctive and radical opposition to the ruling class, in whatever historical form it took. This conception of the subversive power of the popular has resonated in recent years with the theoretical work of the Soviet theoretician Mikhail Bakhtin on the 'Carnivalesque', which has been a key influence on the re-evaluation of popular performance (though unknown to Arden and his contemporaries in the 1950s and 1960s). There is not the space here to do justice to the rigour and scope of Bakhtin's work, but it should be noted that he argued that popular artistic cultural forms and communal celebrations had the potential to subvert the social and political status quo by a strategy of inversion, parody and satire. As another champion of popular theatre, John McGrath, put it, the Carnivalesque embodied 'The concept of an unofficial, Rabelaisian merry-making which is licensed to mock, parody and create obscene versions of the church and state.' (1990: 153).

A belief in the essentially subversive nature of popular theatre forms animates Arden's plays, much as it does those of Jonson (the relationship between Jonson's work and the Carnivalesque is commented on elsewhere in this book). The best example of both is *The Workhouse Donkey*, which celebrates the Jonsonian values of a fluid, self-referential popular theatre at the level of theatrical convention and political debate. The play is intended for an open stage with the minimum of setting to ensure rapid movement between its many locations. Characters address the audience throughout, and there is a narrator-cum-fixer, Wellington Blomax, who leads the audience through the action. Bakhtinian subversion is represented in a binary opposition between anarchy and order in the play, embodied in the characters of Charlie Butterthwaite (three-times Mayor of the unnamed Northern town in which the play is set, and the workhouse donkey of the title), and the newly arrived Chief Constable of police, Colonel Feng. Charlie is a larger-than-life socialist, driven by his appetites for food and beer, and a destabilising presence from the outset of the play. Feng, by contrast, is correct and ordered to the point of rigidity. The plot brings the two extremes into conflict, with the result that both must be expelled from the community: Charlie is carted off to prison for stealing money from the Town Council, and Feng resigns, compromised by his naïve, failed attempts to protect his integrity.

In the final scene of the play, Charlie, now removed from all positions of power within the ruling Labour group that runs the town, leads a drunken mob to disrupt the opening of a new art gallery (which, in a comic play on the opposition between high and low cultures, was converted from a brothel). The scene is an explicit evocation of the Feast of Fools. Sitting cross-legged on the banqueting table, surrounding by the chaos of a rich buffet lunch and with glass in hand, Charlie 'pulls down a paper chain and hangs it round his neck' and 'picks up a ring of flowers that has been garnishing the buffet and puts it on his head' (1977a: 231). The speech that follows is both a riotous disquisition on the power of Charlie's anarchic presence and a parody of Christ's lament over Jerusalem: 'In my rejection I have spoken to these people. I will rejoice despite them. I will divide Dewsbury and mete out the valley of Bradford; Pudsey is mine, Huddersfield is mine... Black Barnsley is my washpot, over Wakefield will I cast out my shoe, over Halifax will I triumph.' (1977a: 231).

The exuberant theatricality of this scene is evident, but Arden is also asking serious questions about the nature of power and how it might be exercised. Charlie's anarchic sensuality is a danger to the status quo (and much else besides), but it also represents a kind of rough, popular justice (like that meted out by Brecht's Azdak in *The Caucasian Chalk Circle*), whilst the rigid adherence to principle and order, as represented by Feng, provokes disorder and injustice. The play ends with the restoration of a centrist consensus, in which the representatives of the main political groupings (Labour and the Tories) re-establish a mutually beneficial and quietly corrupt order. This political compromise acts as a metonym of the national consensus that prevailed through the 1950s and 1960s in affluent Britain. It is certainly an order of sorts, one which tolerates hypocrisy and corruption as long as its own interests are not threatened.

Arden's intentions for *The Workhouse Donkey* also show a different level of thinking about the potential of the popular theatre to re-define the contemporary stage. In an 'Author's Preface' to *The Workhouse Donkey*, Arden argued that the theatre must 'grant pride of place to the old essential attributes of Dionysus: noise / disorder / drunkenness / lasciviousness / nudity / generosity/ corruption / fertility / and ease' (1977a: 113). These are values that the Comic Theatre was formed to celebrate, but in order to do so in the contemporary context the theatrical event itself needs to be re-invented.

> I would have been happy had it been possible for *The Workhouse Donkey* to have lasted, say, six or seven or thirteen hours (excluding intervals), and for the audience to come and go throughout the performance, assisted perhaps by a printed synopsis of the play from which they could deduce those scenes or episodes which would interest them particularly and those they could afford to miss. A theatre presenting such an entertainment would, of course, need to offer rival attractions as well, and would take on some of the characteristics of a fairground or amusement park; with restaurants, bars, side-shows, bandstands and so forth, all grouped around a central playhouse. The design of the playhouse itself would need careful consideration, as clearly members of an audience continually moving to and from their seats in a conventional building will cause intolerable distraction.
>
> (1977a: 113)

Behind this cheerful notion of a relaxed and casual theatre event is an image of the Elizabethan play-house, placed at the centre of a thriving and lively city, and overlain with the cultural forms of an industrial working class. It is also close to the anarchic immediacy that Arden had responded to so favourably in *Bartholomew Fair*. That Arden was never in a position to achieve this context for his work represents a lost opportunity for the English stage; indeed, the challenge Arden issued to his contemporaries, under the influence of Jonson, was never picked up. The final parallel to be drawn between the two writers here is to note that both have often been marginalised and misunderstood on the post-war professional stage – an irony that would not be lost on Arden. This book is an indication that the tide may be turning for Jonson – let us hope it soon turns for Arden as well.

Notes

1   Michael Cohen, 'Exemplary Drama: Arden's Shifting Perspective on Sixteenth and Seventeenth Century Predecessors', in Jonathan Wilk (ed.) (1995), *John Arden and Margaretta Arden: a Casebook*, Garland, London.

2   John Arden (1977), 'Ben Jonson and the Plumb-Line', in *To Present the Pretence: Essays on the Theatre and its Public*, Methuen, London, p. 26. This essay is substantially the same as an essay published in *Gambit* No 22 in 1972 (a Jonson 400th anniversary issue) under the title 'An Embarrassment to the Tidy Mind'. The later essay is more generally available and contains a postscript concerning Jonson's involvement in the Gunpowder Plot. For these reasons, I have referenced the 1977 version.

3   See Stephen Lacey (1995), *British Realist Theatre: the New Wave in its Context, 1956–65*, Routledge, London for a fuller account of the way that conceptions of the contemporary functioned in the theatre of this time.

4   Raymond Williams (1987), 'A Defence of Realism', in *What I Came to Say*, Verso, London.

5   John Arden (1970), 'Telling a True Tale', in C. Marowitz, T. Milne and O. Hale (eds), *The Encore Reader*, London: Eyre Methuen.

Chapter 10

'A deal of monstrous and forced action': Joe Orton and Ben Jonson

John Bull

The first, and perhaps the greatest, popular comedy-writer was Aristophanes, and his work still retains a boldness and originality which few since his day have managed to attain. ... The outpouring of Elizabethan and Jacobean theatre must be the greatest source of truly popular and great drama. In particular we shall look to Ben Jonson's comedies and Shakespeare's tragedies. ... Never afraid to tackle important contemporary issues head on; always ready to question taboos or satirise the habits of men and women; Aristophanes ... chose the really big issues of the day as his subject matter; no topic was too big to tackle – politics, war, religion, the arts, judicial systems. ... Nothing was sacred. Everything and everybody was fair game.

(MacLennan: 139)

The above comes from the programme for *General Gathering* (1983). It was written by John McGrath on behalf of his 7:84 Theatre Company, an assemblage of socialist theatre practitioners committed to producing radical performances for audiences that would not normally be found in conventional theatres. Interestingly, having started with Aristophanes, he has no problems including Ben Jonson in his catalogue or, indeed, also including a list of more modern playwrights, Brecht, Dario Fo, O'Casey, Odets and Gorki. The point that McGrath is making is crucial to his notion of the creation of a theatre that is both entertaining (popular) and engaged in debate about matters of public issue (serious). It is not difficult to see how Jonson's work might be subsumed into such a catalogue although, obviously, the way in which he understood the dualism of popular and serious is very different to the more avowedly twentieth-century *agit-prop* aspirations of 7:84. The very distance between the work of the two writers might, however, suggest that there are other positions, and other writers, that might lay claim to inclusion in such a list. To seek to add Joe Orton's drama is at first sight, somewhat contentious, and it is done with an awareness that in so arguing I am presenting a case for a rather more serious significance being given to Orton's work than has frequently been the case.

Tracing influences in the work of Joe Orton is both easy and extremely problematic. His plays borrow freely from a variety of theatrical and literary sources, but his stylistic preference was for the creation of a complicated collage of discourses, a collage in which the literary is mixed with street argot, technical and professional languages, and a whole battery of different registers of speech. Consider, for instance, this extract from *Loot* (1966): the nurse, Fay is confronting the young man, Hal, who with his friend Dennis has recently robbed a bank, the proceeds of which will shortly be hidden by the pair in the coffin of Hal's mother, replacing her body.

> **FAY** The priest at St. Kilda's has asked me to speak to you. He's very worried. He says you spend your time thieving from slot machines and deflowering the daughters of better men than yourself. Is this a fact?
>
> **HAL** Yes.
>
> **FAY** And even the sex you were born into isn't safe from your marauding. Father Mac is popular for the remission of sins, as you know. But clearing up after you is a full-time job. He simply cannot be in the confessional twenty-four hours a day. That's reasonable, isn't it? You do see his point?
>
> **HAL** Yes. I'm going abroad.
>
> **FAY** That will please the Fathers. Who are you going with?
>
> **HAL** A mate of mine, Dennis. A very luxurious type of lad. At present employed by an undertaker. And doing well in the profession.
>
> **FAY** Have you known him long?
>
> **HAL** We shared the same cradle.
>
> **FAY** Was that economy or malpractice?
>
> **HAL** We were too young then to practice, and economics still defeats us.
>
> (*Complete Plays*: 199–200)

This is a language that could only exist in a theatre. It moves through a succession of styles, before finally arriving at a pithy epigram in the spirit of his most obvious theatrical antecedent; something recognised by Ronald Bryden's famous description of Orton as 'the Oscar Wilde of Welfare State gentility' in his review of the play (*Observer*, 2 October 1966). However, in the same review Bryden also compared *Loot* to the work of George Bernard Shaw and, rather less obviously, Ben Jonson.

Now, it is not difficult to see why echoes of Wilde and even Shaw might be found in Orton's insistently witty banter, but Jonson seems a less obvious source. It is not that there is not wit in Jonson – there is that aplenty – it is rather that the kind of debt Orton owed, and readily acknowledged owing, to Wilde in particular is one that derives from a 'comedy of manners' tradition deriving from late post-Restoration Comedy, with another Irish playwright, Congreve, playing a key role. Indeed, after the commercial failure of the first production of *Loot* (1965), Orton made the explicit connection to his agent, Peggy Ramsay: 'I've always admired Congreve who, after the absolute failure of *Way of the World* just stopped writing.' ('Introduction', *Diaries*: 13).

But Bryden was not the only reviewer to make such a connection. The previous year the notorious theatre critic of the *New York Times*, Howard Taubman, had used it to damn the American production of *Entertaining Mr Sloane*:

> Joe Orton is outraged by corruption and hypocrisy he finds all around him. He is prepared to cry out mercilessly that protestations of honor and virtue are an obscene sham. ... A perfectly valid job for the playwright in any era. ... William Shakespeare, Ben Jonson and friends ... relentlessly held up the mirror to nature. ... But how does Mr Orton go about it? ... He uses characters so lost in honor and decency, so sunk in dirt and degradation, that his point is vitiated almost before he has begun.
>
> (*New York Times*, 13 October 1965)

It is a curious contrast: whereas Bryden finds something positively Jonsonian about *Loot*, Taubman constructs a model of Jonson as a moral satirist with which to belabour *Sloane*. Now, given the variety of Jonson's dramatic output, it is foolish to over-generalise, but it is reasonable to assume that if Orton was familiar with any of his work, it would be with those plays that have most stood the test of time and have been most frequently revived in the modern period: and this means *Volpone*, *The Alchemist* and *Bartholomew Fair*. Of these, we can only be certain that Orton knew the first, for he invokes it to argue against John Russell Taylor's charge in relation to *Sloane* that 'living theatre needs the good commercial dramatist as much as the original artist'. ('Introduction' *New English Dramatists*: 8). Orton wrote angrily to his agent, Peggy Ramsay (17 October 1964): 'Are they different, then? *Hamlet* was written by a commercial dramatist. So was *Volpone*' (*Prick Up Your Ears*: 206).

The Jonson conjured up by Orton in this letter is, obviously, not the writer of court masques: it is the Jonson who, in the single most important century of English drama, was the only playwright to see a complete collection of his plays in print. His invocation points to a central point about Orton. As a playwright he had two great ambitions, the first of which – to shock his audiences – was always liable to be thwarted to a considerable extent by the overweening pressure of the second, to be commercially successful, with all the fame and fortune attendant on its achievement.

It was a tension that reached its height as he was working on what was to be his last play, *What the Butler Saw*. By this time, the revival of *Loot* had at last started to give him the prominence that he craved, its success guaranteed after it had been voted best play of 1966 by both the *Evening Standard* and *Plays and Players*. He was working simultaneously on the screenplay for a new Beatles' film, and everything augured well.

By 23 July 1967 Orton's agent, Peggy Ramsay, had read the first completed draft of *What the Butler Saw* and rang to congratulate him. Her enthusiasm – 'the very best thing you've done so far' – was tempered by her worries about what the Lord Chamberlain would make of the incest and the deployment of Sir Winston Churchill's penis in the denouement of the play. Later that day, he was phoned by the impresario, Oscar Lewenstein, who had been presented with a copy by Ramsay. He too expressed his delight, adding that if the Lord Chamberlain 'insists on too many cuts we'll have to think about putting it on at the Royal Court'. Orton, however, did not wish his play to be perceived as part of a self-conscious avant-garde: 'I think a short tour and straight into the West End' (*Diaries*: 250). He reiterated the point at a meeting with Lewenstein shortly after: 'I don't think it's a Court play'. The producer's response was to suggest the possibility of a private club performance if the Lord Chamberlain refused to pass it; and, if he did, he mused on the possibility of getting Binkie Beaumont to put it on at the Haymarket. Orton's reaction is interesting:

> 'That'd be wonderful,' I said, 'it'd be a sort of joke even putting *What the Butler Saw* on at the Haymarket – Theatre of Perfection.' We discussed the set. 'It should be beautiful. Nothing extraordinary. A lovely set. When the curtain goes up one should feel that we're right back in the old theatre of reassurance – roses, French windows, middle class characters.'
>
> (*Diaries*: 255–6)

As I will argue later, it is this sense of disruption of a bourgeois model, especially in *What the Butler Saw*, that most obviously places Orton as, in part, a follower of Jonson.

When Taubman argues for a Jonson who 'held the up mirror to nature' as a moral satirist, he is undoubtedly following in the spirit of Jonson's own critical defences of his work – that if he 'sported with vice' it was in order to expose it. In *Every Man out of His Humour*, for instance, he has Asper, the resident satirist, argue on his behalf:

I'll strip the ragged follies of the time
[...] and with a whip of steel,
Print wounding lashes in their iron ribs.
(Every Man out of His Humour: Induction 15–18)

The Prologue to *The Alchemist* is almost entirely taken up with the theme, Jonson apologising for his presentation of the vices of the age, but promising 'wholesome remedies' and 'fair correctives' to please his audience (*The Alchemist*: Prologue 15, 18); and many more such examples could be cited. The quotation in my title comes from the Prologue to Ben Jonson's *Volpone*, and it is a deliberate misappropriation, since it appears to describe a strategy, whereas it actually outlines what it is that Jonson claims he has not set out to do in the play. In the Prologue Jonson denies that he is attempting:

To stop gaps in his loose writing,
  With such a deal of monstrous and forced action,
As might make Bedlam a faction;
  Nor made he his play for jests stol'n from each table,
But makes jests to fit his fable –
(Volpone Prologue 24–28)

This is consistent with his claim earlier in the Prologue that he has sought 'to mix profit [that is, moral instruction] with your pleasure' (Prologue 8). His argument is that the depiction of loose and morally reprehensible behaviour, 'with such a deal of monstrous and forced action', is there not to be savoured by the audience but to be learnt from.

However, not only is this the standard defence of the satirist but also, it does not really square with a more modern reading of Jonson's great comedies. In *Volpone*, the great schemer is finally revealed by over-reaching himself and tried and punished in court, but there is little real sense of a moral world reimposing its values. Volpone's victims, with the exception of Celia, are presented as greedy citizens well deserving of being tricked out of their possessions, and conjure no sympathy from an audience; and when Volpone is finally brought to justice it is in a court that is most notable for its bickering and wheeler-dealing. It scarcely needs the fox to step forward at the end to ask for the audience's applause. In a world such as Jonson depicts, there is no one else to applaud. In *The Alchemist*, the arrival of the master, Lovewit, also brings the trickery of Face and Subtle to a halt; but once more it may well be only a temporary halt as Lovewit is well pleased with the rich young widow provided for him by his servants, and there is no suggestion of punishment being meted out to them,

Face ending the play with a promise to the audience 'to feast you often, and invite new guests' (5.5.165).

In a world divided almost entirely between con-artists and their victims – and the impotent virtues of Celia and Bonario in *Volpone* do little to disturb this dichotomy – it is not hard to see where the audience's engagement, perhaps even its empathy, will lie. For, in as much as we can describe these plays and *Bartholomew Fair* as satires, then, it is evident that not only is the satire aimed at the victims rather than the 'villains' – who are seen to be doing no more than taking advantage of characters who are driven by greed, and whose hypocrisy in pretending that this is not so is unmasked by the tricksters – but there is no formal closure or moral resolution to the action.

Orton's plays all re-enact this refusal of moral closure. The plots may be brought to a conclusion in structural terms, but there is never any sense of what might conventionally be thought of as malefactors – in the way that Volpone can be so defined – being brought to justice. In *Entertaining Mr Sloane* (1964), the central character, who has committed a murder before the action opens and will commit another during it, ends being effectively blackmailed by a brother and sister into acting as a sexual slave (and thus theoretically, if somewhat perversely, being punished), but actually content in the bisexual domestic ménage that he has constructed for himself. At the end of *Loot*, the weak father, McLeavy, is rewarded for his honest and dull citizenship by being the only character to be punished by the due processes of the law he so reveres. As he is dragged away screaming, the criminal trio of Hal (his son), Dennis and the nurse Fay are reassured by Inspector Truscott that there will be no unpleasant repercussions:

McLEAVY	I'm innocent! I'm innocent! (*At the door, pause, a last wail.*) Oh, what a terrible thing to happen to a man who's been kissed by the Pope.
DENNIS	What will you charge him with, Inspector?
TRUSCOTT	Oh, anything will do.
FAY	Can an accidental death be arranged?
TRUSCOTT	Anything can be arranged in prison.
HAL	Except pregnancy.
TRUSCOTT	Well, of course, the chaperon system defeats us there.

(Complete Plays: 274)

And it is left to Fay to suggest that it would be 'nice' to 'bury your father with your mother'. In this connection, Orton's quotation from George Bernard Shaw's *Misalliance* (1910) as a preface to *Loot* takes on a very particular resonance:

SUMMERHAYS	Anarchism is a game at which the Police can beat you. What have you to say to that?
GUNNER	What have I to say to it! Well I call it scandalous: that's what I have to say to it.
SUMMERHAYS	Precisely: that's all anybody has to say to it, except the British Public, which pretends not to believe it.

(Orton, *Complete Plays*: 193); (G.B. Shaw, *The Complete Plays*: 638)

Claudia Manera makes the connection forcefully:

> In both Jonson and Orton the ingredients of the innocuous domestic farce are present, but the use which is made of them challenges the circular structure of comedy and promotes an ongoing situation of chaos, a carnival that does not finish at the end of the revels. Closing the curtain at the end of the play only momentarily interrupts the chaos.
>
> (Manera: 186)

That she is able to make this connection in the context of her application of Bakhtin's ideas on carnival to the work of Dario Fo (one of the playwrights singled out by McGrath in the opening quotation as being both radical and popular) makes it the more pertinent. However, whilst this may be true in terms of the dramatic structure of the plays, it is not really so in terms of theatrical intent. In Jonson we can detect an ambiguity, in Orton a conscious aim.

This does much to define the sense in which Orton might be thought of as a 'Jonsonian'. What Taubman offers by way of criticism, the lack of moral dimension to Orton's work, is not to be thought of as a weakness but as the very point of the plays. In work after work, the playwright presents a series of tableaux in which representatives of a 'straight' society – where straight is to be thought of in terms of bourgeois conformity as well as those of sexual practice – are confronted by bohemian nonconformists who simply refuse to accept the expectations of normal society. In the early plays Orton is clearly confronting the ghosts of his own past in Leicester, and his unhappy straight jacketed family life. In *The Good and Faithful Servant* (1967), for instance, Buchanan, the unquestioning employee who has retired from his firm about fifty years of humble employment, with an electric clock and an electric toaster, both of which immediately cease to function, discovers that he has a grandson, Ray. Horrified that Ray has never worked, he and his wife Edith seek to educate him.

| BUCHANAN | Not work! What do you do then? |
| RAY | I enjoy myself. |

BUCHANAN	That's a terrible thing to do. I'm bowled over by this. I can tell you. It's my turn to be shocked now. You ought to have a steady job.
EDITH	Two perhaps.

(Complete Plays: 167)

Still haunted by his past at this point, Orton has Ray accept work, marriage and respectable domesticity, but the other side of Ray – 'I enjoy myself' – would increasingly preoccupy Orton in his work. In *What the Butler Saw*, Orton has Geraldine say, 'I lived in a normal family. I had no love for my father.' (*Complete Plays*: 382). The point can be stressed further. The young male characters (Sloane in *Entertaining Mr Sloane*, and Hal in *Loot*, for example) in Orton's early plays are all in some fairly clear ways versions of Orton himself, both in their non-conformist attitudes to sexual activity and in their celebration of criminality. For Orton is not simply interested in creating rogue characters who would dominate the action in the tradition of Jonson, he was very aware of the conscious creation of himself as an outsider figure, both rejecting and being rejected by 'straight' society. This is most obviously related to his openly promiscuous homosexuality at a time when such attitudes were not only dangerous in terms of personal reputation but also still regarded as criminal, and punishable by the law. But Orton was also a confirmed hoaxer and player of tricks. He created a series of personas to use in letters to the press. He succeeded, for example, in getting *Plays and Players* to publish a letter from Donald H. Hartley praising his 1967 production of *Loot* in the same edition as one from Edna Welthorpe condemning it. Both letters were actually written by Orton (*Diaries*: 286–87). His tricks were to land him in serious trouble. In 1962, he and his long-term partner, Kenneth Halliwell, were found guilty on five counts of theft and of defacing library books. They served six months in prison. Orton believed that the severity of their sentences was 'because we're queers' (Croft-Brooke: 82). Although he spent most of his time in a series of open prisons, he made the most of his criminality once released. On first meeting Peggy Ramsay, he told her that he had done 'six months in Wormwood Scrubs for a series of minor thefts and that it had been remarkably good for him' (Ramsay to Harold Hobson 1 May 1964; quoted in *Diaries*: 15). Indeed, he thought that prison had made him as a writer: it certainly toughened his attitudes towards the forces of the establishment, defining the parameters of his world in an increasingly 'them' and 'us' way.

However, this opposition to 'straight' society is, even in the early plays, never simply quasi-biographical. Much of the energy of Orton's works derives from its insistent assault on a procession of such British institutions as the Holiday Camp, the monarchy, parliament, the mysterious workings of the public bureaucracy of police, the water-board, and so on, just as Jonson enjoys himself exposing the limitations of the representatives of the world of justice in *Volpone*. Furthermore, it is easy to draw parallels between Orton's *The Erpingham Camp* (1966) and *Bartholomew Fair*. In Jonson's play, the respectable citizenry are attracted to the chaotic fun of the fair, there to be divested of their sense of bourgeois separation from the revelries, their possessions and their clothes. Significantly, the major representative of law and order Justice Overdo, present in disguise, has Adam as his first name. Stripped of his vestments of authority he becomes a kind of Everyman figure, the representative figure of mankind. In *The Erpingham Camp* Orton offered a freewheeling attack on the British Holiday Camp, complete with its regimented fun and exaggeratedly grotesque competitions.

ERPINGHAM	Our disability bonus was won by Mr Laurie Russell of Market Harborough. Both Laurie's legs were certified 'absolutely useless' by our Resident Medical Officer. Yet he performed the Twist and the Bossa Nova to the tune specified on the entrance form.
TED	He fell over, though. Twice.
LOU	They help them a lot, don't they? That blind woman would've never found the diving-board if the audience hadn't shouted out.

(Complete Plays: 283)

The point is reinforced when it is realised that the owner, Erpingham, who is using the PA system, is an obsessively puritan Christian – 'We've no time for hedonists here. My camp is a pure camp.' (*Complete Plays*: 279) – so that the possibility of real as opposed to carefully organised revelry will always be ruled out. Generally, Puritanism is as much a target for Orton as it had been, in very different circumstances for Jonson. Volpone is an outright voluptuary, and Bartholomew Fair is precisely the location for impurity and hedonism: in Ursula's booth, Knockem assures us, 'you may ha' your punk and your pig in state, sir, both piping hot' (*Bartholomew Fair*: 57). In pursuit of Dame Purecraft, the puritan Zeal-Of-The-Land Busy is only too easily drawn into the fair, and in *The Alchemist* the hypocrisy of Ananias and Tribulation make them easy targets for the tricksters' promises of gold. In Orton's *Funeral Games* (1968) Caulfield is employed by Pringle, who calls Christmas 'the Festival of the renewal of Spirit' (*Complete Plays*: 324), to check on his wife's alleged adultery. In the course of his investigations Caulfield breaks into the house of

McCorquodale, who is he assures him 'a defrocked priest' (*Complete Plays*: 331), and the phrase reverberates with images of cross-dressing as well as the more conventional 'sins' that might have brought about his downfall. Organised religion is always a prime target for Orton, offering images both of repression and hypocrisy. 'One might cite the heavily parodied dialect of the Catholic Church which pervades *Loot*, largely in the persons of various imaginary organisations like the Fraternity of the Little Sisters and the Knights of the Order of Saint Gregory.' (Bull and Gray: 93).

Such attacks on the self-ordained arbiters of morality and prohibiters of enjoyment are never merely tangential in Jonson and Orton, even though the reasons for their targeting may differ somewhat. They allow for a great deal of the humour of the plays to derive from the gap between the cloak of respectability and moral uprightness and the human reality revealed once the process of 'unfrocking' takes place. The specific theatrical mode within which such revelations are made is less that of the witty comedy of manners than that of farce. Today, when audiences have even more trouble understanding the minutiae of the witty banter of *The Alchemist* and *Bartholomew Fair* than Jonson's contemporaries did, and when much of what can be understood comes largely as a result of the physicalisation of the verbal thrust and parries, the importance of the farcical elements in Jonson is inevitably foregrounded. However, this is only a matter of stress: farce was always central to Jonson's strategy. In one of his more extended pieces of theatrical analysis, Orton is quite explicit on how he seeks to develop the form. Rejecting the boundaries of modern farce as too 'narrow', he continues:

> As I understand it, farce originally was very close to tragedy, and differed only in the *treatment* of its themes – themes like rape, bastardy, prostitution. But you can't have farce about rape any longer. French farce goes as far as adultery, but by Ben Travers time it was only *suspected* adultery, which turned out to have been innocuous after all. ... A lot of farces today are still based on the preconceptions of half a century ago. But we must now accept the fact that, for instance, people *do* have sexual relations outside marriage: a 30s farce is still acceptable because it is distanced by its period, but a modern farce which merely nurses the old outworn assumptions is cushioning people against reality. And this, of course, is just what the commercial theatre usually does. In theory there is no subject which could *not* be treated farcically – just as the Greeks were prepared to treat any subject farcically.
>
> (*Plays and Players*, June 1966)

Orton's mention of the Greeks is significant. What he sought, in particular in his final play *What the Butler Saw* (1969), was a reanimation of the farcical tradition in ways that look beyond the dreariness of the Whitehall farces, *No Sex Please, We're British* and *Boeing-Boeing* to what he saw as a rougher, more open, tradition. Jonson, too, had looked back beyond his own age for dramatic models. The exact nature of Jonson's indebtedness to the Greek dramatists continues to be a subject of contention, but it is generally agreed that in his middle period comedies it is Aristophanes who most frequently provides a model (Evans: 188, 191, 195, 199). Anne Barton argues that *Volpone, Epicæne – The Silent Woman* and *The Alchemist* are the plays which owe most to Aristophanes, and elaborates on the connection:

> In most of the extant plays of Aristophanes, a character or small group of characters conceives an improbable and extravagant idea. ... The individuals who concoct these apparently lunatic schemes are usually self-seeking and rather suspect. Although the society against which they react, and which their scheme intends to subvert, is corrupt and foolish, Aristophanes refuses to make ... [them] ... into exemplary figures. They are comic rogues, whose own idea of what constitutes a comfortable and desirable life happens to conflict with the self-destructive impulses of the community in which they live. This is one reason why critical work on Aristophanes, as on the Jacobean Jonson, has been so bedevilled with disagreement as to the moral valency of the plays.
>
> (Barton, 1984: 114–15)

This dichotomy in Jonson – moral satirist or amoral 'realist' – points to where Orton is both most Jonsonian and most in opposition. He shared with Jonson a desire to celebrate the chaos of the contemporary world, but with Orton there is absolutely no sense whatever of the possibility of a moral conclusion. His plays, though, do fit perfectly into the model outlined by Barton above, even though it is not possible to hazard a guess as to the extent of his knowledge of the Greek dramatist's work. What it does indicate about Orton's work is that there is a tension between the language of wit, the chief inspiration for which was the comedies of Oscar Wilde,[1] the writer with whose work he had a 'deep-seated and prolonged obsession' (Bull, 2003: 47), and the more robust farcical elements. Orton was able to make a distinction of considerable importance: 'I admire Wilde's work but not his life, it is an appalling life' (*Evening Standard*, 12 January 1967). Prison destroyed Wilde, and Orton could not forgive him that, for it represented a giving-in to the establishment and an admission of personal weakness. For Orton, his prison sentence was a public confirmation of his outsider status and a necessary test of his ability to survive; and he was always proud of his personal strength. In this sense, prison was the final piece of Orton's process of education: 'I tried writing before I went into the nick ... but it was no good. And it suddenly worked. Being in the nick brought detachment to my writing' (*Leicester Mercury*, 4 June 1964: quoted in Lahr, 1980: 152). Two years later, he expanded on the theme, and it is interesting to notice just who he invokes to counter Wilde's passivity:

> I didn't suffer or anything the way Oscar Wilde suffered from being in prison – but then Wilde was flabby and self-indulgent. There is this complete myth about writers being sensitive plants. They're not. It's a silly nineteenth-century idea, but I'm sure Aristophanes was not sensitive. I mean there's absolutely no reason why a writer shouldn't be as tough as a bricklayer.
>
> (*Evening Standard*, 3 October 1966)

Orton's construction of Aristophanes as 'not sensitive' comes from at least some knowledge of his work. What is more intriguing is his epithet 'tough as a bricklayer'. It is an easy simile to make, but it begs the question, did Orton know that Ben Jonson had once been a bricklayer, and, furthermore had also been imprisoned and survived, so that his 'tough' qualities – in Orton's sense of the term – could thus be attributed to both his theatrical and his manual work? It is almost certainly a curious coincidence, and no more, but it does lay stress on another important connection between the two writers' work. Orton once told the impresario Oscar Lewenstein, 'I'm from the gutter. And don't you ever forget it' (*Diaries*: 54). He wasn't. He was actually from a Leicester housing estate. But his rogue characters live near to the street, as do their counterparts in *The Alchemist* and *Bartholomew Fair*.

It is in his final play, *What the Butler Saw* (1969) that Orton really starts to develop the relationship between the satire on bureaucracy and the kind of chaotic energy associated with Jonson and, through him, Aristophanes. On his first entrance the psychiatric Inspector, Rance, asks, 'Why are there so many doors. Was the house designed by a lunatic?' (*Complete Plays*: 367). It is a question that not only lays stress on the function of the psychiatric clinic in the play, but takes us back to the play's prefatory epigram (from Middleton's *The Revenger's Tragedy*): 'Surely we're all mad people, and they / Whom we think, are not'. Farce, as Orton was beginning to reshape it, allowed for a complete abandonment of plot and character in favour of a world in which the repressions and sublimations of life are allowed fully-articulated play. The world depicted is a true Freudian nightmare of unleashed sexuality, free from the burdens of respectability or convention. It is civilisation without its clothes. Indeed, it is Dr Prentice's attempt to cover up the only comparatively straight heterosexual act in the play – his persuasion of a putative secretary, Geraldine (later made to assume the names Nicholas and Nicola as she is alternately clothed as boy and girl), to undress, supposedly for a medical examination – that sets things in motion. The wife he would deceive has just returned from a meeting of a club 'primarily for lesbians' (*Complete Plays*: 369), at which she has had sex with a hotel porter, Nicholas Beckett, who is about to demand money from her for photographs taken during the liaison; having spent a large part of the previous evening molesting an entire hotel corridor of schoolgirls.

The arrival of the Inspector is the signal for an orgy of cross-dressing (with Nicola and Nicholas easily changing gender roles), a sort of sexual *Bartholomew Fair* in which clothing is first removed and then redistributed in a confusion of sexual roles; the whole business being presided over by a lunatic bureaucrat, Rance, who offers a series of psychoanalytical explanations of the characters' behaviour, the unlikelihood of which is only outreached by the truths of the case. The representative of the forces of law, Sergeant Match, arrives to try, unsuccessfully, to sort out the confusion, and is immediately caught up in it. His declaration, 'Marriage excuses no one the freaks' roll-call,' (*Complete Plays*: 409) points to the way in which Orton seeks to celebrate chaotically the confusions of sexuality – no longer held in the simple binary opposition of heterosexual and homosexual practice.

Already, in *The Erpingham Camp* the chief redcoat had persuaded one of the visitors, Kenny, to undress and put on a Tarzan costume, which he continues to wear as he leads the riot in protest against the treatment of the campers. It is a riot that is described by the two 'Christian' authority figures, Erpingham and the Padre, in terms that are comically dyonisiac:

ERPINGHAM   They were running about half-naked spewing up their pork 'n beans. I counted eight pairs of women's briefs on the stairs. There'll be some unexpected visits to the Pre-natal clinic after tonight. (*He mops his brow.*) It would take the pen of our National poet to describe the scene that met my eyes upon entering the Grand Ballroom. My Chief Redcoat was being savagely beaten about the face by a man dressed as a leopard.

PADRE   It was like an allegorical painting by one of the lesser Masters. I was forcibly reminded of a 'Christ, Mocked' which was, until recently, hanging in the cellar of the Walker Gallery, Liverpool.

ERPINGHAM   When I remonstrated with them I was subjected to abuse. I was hit upon the head by a bottle. They were completely out of control.

MASON   (*with wonder.*) Hit an official of the Camp? That's never been done before.

(*Complete Plays*: 304–5)

The allegorical analogy of 'Christ Mocked' is given further weight by its recall of a painting not available for viewing by the public ('in the cellar'), and the significance of the protest is underlined by the immediate entrance of the Chief Redcoat, Riley: *'his uniform is torn; his face bleeding; he is dispirited and ashamed'* (*Complete Plays*: 305). The puritan paradise of carefully regulated fun and competition has been disrupted by a riotous and hedonistic public seen as socially inferior by Erpingham.

In *What the Butler Saw*, Sergeant Match is forcibly re-dressed, at Halliwell's suggestion in 'something suggestive of leopard-skin – this should make it funny when Nick wears it and get the right "image" for the Euripidean ending when Match wears it' (*Diaries*: 237). This reference to Dionysus takes us to Aristophanes' *The Frogs*, where amongst other disguises, including a swap with his slave, Pentheus dresses as the God; and more specifically to Euripides' *The Bacchae*. Having completed the first draft, Orton was pleased with the 'Euripidean ending ... as "all is forgiven" – just as in the later Shakespeare plays' (*Diaries*: 242). It is significant that it should be Match (the name perhaps suggestive of something with the potential to be ignited) who is forced into the role of Dionysus for, as a policeman, he should conventionally represent a world of rules and regulations: in Orton's world, however, such niceties are redundant.

Once more there is no moral closure to the play. The discovery that Geraldine and Nicky are not only sister and brother but (in a parody of the conclusion of *The Importance of Being Earnest*), they are the long lost progeny of Dr and Mrs Prentice, conceived in a linen cupboard in the Station Hotel, is hardly the most shocking revelation in a play that conjures with rape, incest and trans-sexuality. No one is brought to book, and all is concluded with an appropriately Bacchanalian tableaux:

> **PRENTICE**   Well, sergeant, we have been instrumental in uncovering a number of remarkable peccadilloes today. I'm sure you'll co-operate in keeping them out of the papers?
> **MATCH**   I will, sir.
> **RANCE**   I'm glad you don't despise tradition. Let us put our clothes on and face the world.
> *(They pick up their clothes and weary, bleeding, drugged and drunk, climb the rope ladder into the blazing light. Curtain)*
>   (*Complete Plays*: 448)

Because Orton died before the play was first produced, and he was anyway working within the boundaries of what was permissible on stage before the abolition of Theatre censorship in 1968, *What the Butler Saw* did not go as far towards the Dionysiac as Orton would have liked. "'It's the only way to smash the wretched civilisation,'" I said, making a mental note to hot-up *What the Butler Saw* when I came to rewrite. ... "Yes. Sex is the only way to infuriate them. Much more fucking and they'll be screaming hysterics in no time.'" (*Diaries*: 125). Even though the play was eventually produced after the abolition of censorship, the running Dionysiac gag about Sir Winston Churchill's penis had the eventual discovery of the missing object translated into a cigar. It is tempting to wonder about the direction his work might have taken, had he been allowed to continue writing post-1968. For the ultimate extension of the process of his interest in the liberation of libido, in a glorious celebration of chaos and sexual flexibility, might suggest a more truly Bakhtinian notion of carnival than can be invoked for either Jonson or Orton, and the creation of a Dionysian theatre in which no distinction is made between spectators and performers; not the anodyne excesses of the musical *Hair* where, despite the appeal at the end of the performance for the audience to come up on stage, a careful distance is still reserved but, just maybe, a 'happening' where all see and do what the Butler did, no longer content with experiencing it voyeuristically through the lens of the end-of-the-pier machine. Probably not though: Orton was also hooked on the notion of public acceptance. A final fantasy production, however, and one conceived of, in part, in the light of Mosca's celebration of Volpone's hedonistic excess in the first scene of Jonson's play, and the first part of the second scene, where the fox is entertained by a dwarf, a eunuch and an hermaphrodite: Joe Orton working on an extremely free adaptation of *Bartholomew Fair*. Staged in promenade, the audience become as embroiled in the action as do the characters in Jonson's play, and the whole thing concludes in the true realms of sexual carnival.

Such a production, whilst offering possible pleasures – if somewhat dangerous pleasures – in its own right, would, however, not be really in the spirit of Jonson. To posit it is to point to the very important distinctions between the work of the two playwrights. They are divided by more than just time. Orton's work may well have claims that allow him to be considered a 'Jonsonian', but he was already going beyond the bounds of Jonson's deployment of 'monstrous and forced action', and would presumably have gone still further. For all the comical excess of *Bartholomew Fair*, Jonson's targets are still clear. He does not use the seventeenth-century equivalent of a scatter-gun, as does Orton. Jonson's authority figures are scorned and ridiculed for specific reasons: Orton's simply because they are authority figures, whose essential function is to police outbreaks of hedonism and to enforce conformity. Perhaps what ultimately makes Orton most a 'Jonsonian' is that, had they been writing contemporaneously, Orton could very easily have found himself a character, subject to satirical abuse, in Jonson's work, a Jonsonian rogue rather than, to use a totally inappropriate phrase, a camp follower.

Note

[1] The connections between Wilde and Orton are further explored in John Bull's essay 'Joe Orton and Oscar Wilde'. The essay appears in Francesca Coppa (ed.) (2003), *Joe Orton: a Casebook*, New York and London, Routledge. p. 47.

Chapter 11

His very own Ben:
Peter Barnes and Ben Jonson

Brian Woolland

Jonson is subversive. Shakespeare, on the other hand, retired to the Jacobean equivalent of Eastbourne to end his days, thankful no doubt to be finally finished with the sordid business of earning a living. No wonder Shakespeare is beloved of the English Establishment.... Jonson has to be played with balls. It's not just a matter of vitality but of groin heat. A playwright who can kill an actor, quarrel violently with his designer, insult a king, beat up a fellow dramatist, refuse a knighthood and out-drink Shakespeare can't be bad. I wish I'd been that good.

Peter Barnes [1]

The self-professed Jonsonian

Peter Barnes is a passionate admirer of Jonson. Of all the contemporary practitioners whose work is discussed in this section of the book, he would be proudest to be thought of as a 'Jonsonian'. He has edited and / or adapted *The Alchemist, The Devil is an Ass, Bartholomew Fair* for the theatre; adapted and directed *Eastward Ho!, The Magnetic Lady* and *The Devil is an Ass* for radio; and directed *Bartholomew Fair* in the theatre. His enthusiastic championing of Jonson's work is invigorating, provocative and challenging, but his prizing of the Jonsonian cloak more highly than the Shakespearean mantle reveals a wealth of complex personal, social and political attitudes to contemporary culture, and a healthy distaste for the theatrical and political Establishment, in general, and the institutional appropriation of Shakespeare, in particular.

Although several of Barnes' major stage plays have been described as 'neo-Jacobean',[2] his plays are quite unlike Shakespeare's. The title of his 1973 radio broadcast, *My Ben Jonson*, is very revealing. His version (or vision) of Ben Jonson is of a man in his own image: there is something curiously autobiographical about his accounts of Jonson and Jonson's theatre, in that one senses this is how he would like to be thought of himself. Although he wishes he had 'been that good', there is a sense in which he uses great Ben's relative unpopularity at the end of his life to vindicate the unfashionability of his own work for theatre. For all his enthusiasm in embracing the 'Jonsonian' tag, however, Peter Barnes is no mere imitator but, rather, a modernist with an acute awareness of a wide range of theatrical traditions. Given the vigorous inscription of his own passions and ideologies onto Jonson's theatre, the task of this essay is to note the ways that Barnes uses Jonson as a catalyst in mixing all manner of diverse ingredients in a theatrical crucible to create a *'new amalgama'*.[3]

There is a heady eclecticism about Barnes' work: he is as steeped in theatre, film and popular culture as Ben was in the classics, and he proudly acknowledges considerable debts not only to Jonson and his contemporaries (particularly to Marston and Middleton) but also to Feydeau, Brecht and Wedekind and those pioneers of twentieth-century cinema: Eisenstein and Pudovkin. This range of influences gives Barnes' work an elusive and continually shifting tone; a peculiarly Jonsonian characteristic. Plays like *The Bewitched*, *Red Noses*, *Laughter!* and *Dreaming* slip from grand spectacle to claustrophobic intensity, from collective celebration to Beckettian isolation, from horrific Artaudian brutality to high comedy. With the comedy itself ranging from sophisticated verbal repartee to crude slapstick, from scorching cruelty to surprising tenderness, these shifts in style and tone are deeply unsettling and challenging. Beyond insisting that his work is anti-naturalistic,[4] Barnes resists categorisation – and this, rather than his affinity with Jonson, may be why he has become one of the least fashionable of Britain's major playwrights.

Intertextuality and metatheatricality

The danger of claiming a Jonsonian inheritance for Barnes from a set of shared characteristics is that it risks tautology and invites the unworthy speculation that the claim to the Jonsonian cloak is a means of self-aggrandisement. It is, nevertheless, worth remarking on the most visible Jonsonian characteristics of his work: the facility with a variety of comic styles; the masterly control of complex narrative; the elements of the grotesque and carnivalesque; the use of metatheatricality to engage audiences and then to shift the ground beneath them; and the use of cruel, dark comedy as a form of political satire (using the word 'political' in its broad sense). His plays also contain overtly self-conscious references to

Jonson's theatre. In *Leonardo's Last Supper*,[5] these references are explicit and relatively simple. The three undertakers are clearly modelled on *The Alchemist*'s venture tripartite. Lasca, whose name echoes Mosca in *Volpone*, and Maria are essentially tricksters in the mould of Jonson's great tricksters and, as in Jonson, trickery is a means of examining the social and political frameworks within which it operates. In the eyes of Lasca and Maria the medieval Guild of Apothecaries, which attempts to regulate and control their activities, is a corrupt and pernicious means of keeping them at the bottom of the social pile. They are tricksters because that is the only way they can survive. Allusions to *The Alchemist* permeate the play. In *A Hand Witch of the Second Stage*,[6] echoes of *The Alchemist* are distorted, wittily inverting the structures and gender balance of Jonson's play: Marie Blin has been accused of witchcraft. The play opens with her 'spread-eagled on a rack', Father Delmas trying to extract a confession from her, Claude Delmas giving evidence against her whilst Henri Mondor, the executioner, impatiently waits to get on with the torture. But Marie Blin adopts the kind of improvisatory wit, speed of thought and sleight of mind of which Dol Common would have been proud. She tricks her persecutors into believing not only that she is a witch, but that she really does have Satanic powers and that the only way for them to escape her vengeance is to free her. Thus, in an elegant reversal of the psychological structure of *The Alchemist*, Marie Blin uses her persecutors' terrors and anxieties to give them exactly what think they most want: her guilt. And she then uses that against them in the same way that the 'venture tripartite' uses the gulls' own desires to trick them. Such echoes and reworkings permeate Barnes' theatre; but what underpins it, and what is more interesting in this exploration of the Jonsonian, is a celebration of theatre as a site of metaphor and metamorphosis. Jonson and Barnes are each fascinated with the processes and the workings of theatre, with theatre as a metaphor for the mechanisms of illusion and delusion. When Barnes employs intertextuality he does so not as dry conceit, but to remind us that we are in a theatre assisting and collaborating in the making of meaning. Canny playwright that he is, and a realist in his assessment of the general theatre-going public's knowledge of Jonson, the direct allusions to Jonson's theatre within the plays themselves are relatively infrequent. Thus there arises the almost Zen-like paradox that his references to specific Jonson plays are less 'Jonsonian' than his witty misquotations of Shakespeare. *Dreaming* (1999)[7] provides a fine example. The play is set during the Wars of the Roses and follows the fortunes and misfortunes of Mallory and his band of war-weary mercenaries who are trying to escape the horrors of civil war and the implications of their own involvement in it. Throughout the play they are tracked by Richard of Gloucester, a grotesque, pantomimic version of Shakespeare's Richard III.[8] When we first meet Richard, he announces his presence: 'Now is the summer of my deep content... That has a good ring to it. People put words into my mouth. The wrong words usually.' Richard wants Mallory to join him at court: 'I need your cold sword and colder heart at court to help me keep what we steal. I've a high destiny and I'll pull you up in my wake.' (1.1) The wry, jokey Shakespearean misquotation undercuts the dark violence of the opening wordless prologue (a short expressionist evocation of the Battle of Tewkesbury, at the end of which giant crows strut the battlefield, and the solid looking stage floor is revealed as transparent glass beneath which lie piles of twisted corpses and decaying skeletons) thus signalling the tonal and stylistic instability of the play. This playful metatheatrical intertextuality is closely associated with one of the central concerns of the play. Mallory's determination to find 'home' is a dream of rediscovering his own identity, and throughout the play he is trapped in Richard's perception of him as a cold-hearted killer, just as this Richard is trapped in audiences' perceptions of Shakespeare's King Richard. The purposeful irony of this is that Mallory himself does something very similar to his own band of refugee followers and, in particular, to Percy Beaufort's widow, Susan, whom he insists is his own wife Sarah, forcing her to (re-) marry him.

> **KELL** Mallory insists on a wedding. He's convinced Susan she's here for their marriage and cast us as her family.
>
> (2.5)

Kell is to be Susan / Sarah's father; Bess her mother; Skelton her brother; Davy her son from her first marriage. Each of them is aware of the role playing that is required of them. Mallory asks them to play the roles of family in order to 'normalise' the wedding, to make it seem more domestic, to reinforce his sense of coming home. The metaphor of being 'caught in a story that isn't our story, minor characters pushed to the edge' (2.5) is one which most of us can identify. But it is particularly apposite for refugees in wartime. For the majority of those fleeing Kosovo or Serbia in the early summer of 1999 (when *Dreaming* was produced in London) it was a very precise metaphor. War, as *Dreaming* reminds us, heightens the differences between assertive leaders and an acquiescent majority, between those who impose particular versions of history onto others and those who accept these narratives without questioning whether their own interests are really served by the claims that are made on their behalf.

Comedy, humour and audience

Jokes and humour can be used to reinforce hegemonic structures of authority or to subvert them. Comedians on the political right frequently use their act to assert an affiliation with those who deplore difference as evidence of weakness and inferiority. The telling of jokes thus becomes a means both of locating oneself (and all those who share the joke) within a particular social grouping and of excluding the targets of the joke. The same mechanism of identification and complicity is at work in subversive humour. Laughing, sharing a joke, implicates us in a web of social and political attitudes, we become complicit with the joke-teller (often in spite of ourselves). Barnes uses humour and laughter to position and then to destabilise and interrogate an audience's response to the narrative. *Dreaming* contains an excellent example: the stage is set very simply for the wedding of Mallory and Sarah / Susan: '*a life-sized crucifix... behind an altar*', suggests a church. During the scene, as Kell intones the marriage service,

> *The figure of Christ* [...] *stirs and comes down off the cross.*[...] *Kell silently mouths the words of the marriage service whilst Christ stretches and talks directly to Susan....*
>
> (2.5)

Christ then tells Susan and the theatre audience a series of jokes (see Figure 2). The routine ends as he returns to the cross and asks Susan if she thinks his last joke is better than those that have gone before. 'I do!' she says, to which Kell, the godless priest, announces,

> By the power invested in me, I now pronounce you man and wife!
> *Susan bursts out laughing at Christ's joke and the lights snap out quickly.*
>
> (2.5)

The scene is constructed as a 'turn', presenting the marriage service as a ritual in which a woman, well aware of the joke, agrees to participate in a male narrative because it is amusing; or, put another way, Christ tricks her into agreeing to the marriage. As so often in Barnes, the key is to realise that these are not alternative readings, but that they co-exist. The next scene (in which Susan and Mallory are in bed together) offers further inflection of these possibilities, indicating that Susan is acutely aware of being tricked – by both Mallory and Richard of Gloucester. But the juxtaposition of the two scenes suggests that whilst Susan may understand Mallory's deviousness ('When did you know I wasn't Sarah?') and Gloucester's ruthlessness ('He has so many instruments of death in his hands....' (2.6)) she shows no awareness of the connection that Barnes encourages his audience to make between the Judaeo-Christian institutionalisation of patriarchy and the way that this Christ's humour functions ideologically in consolidating patriarchal power. Christ's speech to Susan is constructed as a stand-up comic routine to which Susan and the audience are party, but which is not attended to by the other characters on stage. Christ is presented as a self-deprecating Jewish stand-up comedian: he complains that his father (God) never listens and hasn't created enough money to go round and concludes with a joke about Jewish mothers as self-sacrificing martyrs. Christ's 'act' ranges from the apparently crude ('Golgotha was bad enough but at least it was short. I didn't expect to be left hanging around for centuries' [2.5]), through a philosophical conundrum about the existence of God, to the Jewish mother joke. The constant shift of tone, even within the routine itself, makes it both challenging and uneasily provocative. As an audience, we are being asked to monitor and reflect on our own responses. If, as is likely, we laugh at some parts of the routine and grimace elsewhere that only serves to focus on the ways that the play examines and differentiates between the various levels of complicity in different forms of meta-narrative.

Barnes' use of humour is rich and heterogeneous. As in Jonson, it constantly destabilises audience responses to the narrative. Although the wedding scene in *Dreaming* has no direct parallels in Jonson's theatre, it does create a distorting echo of the strange marriage at the centre of *Epicœne* in which Morose's eagerness to accept Epicœne as his (female) bride is motivated by his desire to inscribe particular qualities on her; in which Epicœne's silence and 'divine softness' gives Morose the space in which to develop his absurd fantasies about his bride-to-be.

Authority and acquiescence

One of the differences between the two marriages is the role of the 'woman'. Whereas Epicœne is apparently a willing party, put up to it by Dauphine, deftly playing the part of the softly spoken easily manipulated woman, Susan is reluctant, tricked into agreement by the metonymic Christ figure and forced to trust in Mallory by the desperation of her situation. But what initially seems to distinguish Barnes from Jonson, closer analysis reveals as a shared fascination. At the heart of almost every major play by Barnes lies an almost obsessive exploration of authority.

PLATE 2: *Dreaming.* Christ comes down from the cross to talk to Sarah. Luke Williams as Christ; Kate Isitt as Susan / Sarah

Photograph © Sheila Burnett. Reproduced by kind permission of Peter Barnes and Sheila Burnett. This image is taken from a colour photograph.

This has often been perceived as a playfully anarchic anti-authoritarianism. But Barnes is much less interested in the assertion of authority than in the tendency to accept it, comply with it and submit to it. Where authority figures appear in Jonson their legitimacy is almost always undermined – either by their failures of judgement (Overdo and Wasp in *Bartholomew Fair*), their dishonesty and self-deception (Zeal-of-the-Land Busy), their incompetence (Sir Paul Eitherside in *The Devil is an Ass*) or their opportunism (Lovewit in *The Alchemist*). As I argue elsewhere in this volume, *Sejanus his Fall* is crucially concerned with responses to authority and tyranny. Tiberius and Sejanus may be presented as monsters, but Jonson's scorn is reserved for those who swim in whichever direction the tides of power are flowing.

Barnes' examination of the social psychology of acquiescence can be seen to have its roots in Jonson's theatre. *A Hand Witch of the Second Stage* concludes with Marie Blin addressing the audience directly:

> The fear that accused me, tried me, condemned me without hope of reprieve was the fear that freed me. So I say: to defeat Authority, use Authority's weapons. Do not deny their fear, increase it, their fear, not your fear.
>
> (1990: 19)

The distinction of Barnes' work lies not in his scabrous attacks on those who wield authority or those who have been granted it by the mediations of history, but rather in his examination of possible responses to it and his ability to explore these responses using juxtapositions of humour and popular theatre forms (music-hall, stand-up comedy, song, dance, allusions to cinema, gothic horror – each of them, it could be argued, a form of resistance to more 'legitimate', high-culture theatre forms) in carefully structured montages. *Dreaming* marks a development in Barnes' work, offering an exploration of authority and acquiescence which is more complex and more ambivalent than in his earlier plays. Jonson also has a strong interest in the relationships between the mechanisms of authority and role play, counterfeit and complicity. What drives *The Alchemist* is every bit as much the gulls' desire to collude in the extravagant devices for relieving them of money as it is the venture tripartite's ingenuity and speed of reaction. The target of the satire in almost all the comedies is not the rogues but those who are taken in by them. Thus, in *The Devil is an Ass*, the inexhaustibly energetic inventiveness of Meercraft and Engine delights us whilst we watch in critical amazement as Fitzdottrel succumbs to their ploys. And again the parallels between Barnes and Jonson become clear, for the metatheatrical devices of *The Devil is an Ass* function in very similar ways to those adopted by Barnes in the example discussed above.

We are encouraged to take pleasure in the tricksters' chicanery, rather than to sit in judgement, and are thereby at least partly implicated in the game. Thus we are shown the theatrical and social mechanisms that they use to fool their prey, but we, too, number amongst their victims and our responses to the on-stage action are problematised in such a way as to make our laughter uneasy and disturbing.

Montage, plot and narrative

Jonson and Barnes each use various strategies to destabilise audience response, to encourage audiences to interrogate their own relationship to what they are watching. In the plays of both playwrights these shifts of tone and style are frequently achieved through a form of montage. Jonson's extraordinarily skill in interweaving and controlling the pace of apparently diverse narratives has often been remarked upon; but the theatre of each playwright demands both narrative clarity and, simultaneously, an emphasis on non-linear rhythmically juxtaposed 'attractions'[9] whose meaning derives as much from their relationships to each other as it does from their place in the overall narrative. This structural use of parallels, juxtapositions, contrasts and resonances to create meaning is perhaps most easily exemplified in Barnes' play *Laughter!*[10] Comprising two distinct parts: the first, *Tsar*, is set in Moscow 1573, the second, *Auschwitz*, in a minor bureaucrat's office in Berlin 1942, with an Epilogue the scene shifts to Auschwitz itself where 'two hollow-eyed comics' appear in a spotlight and are announced as 'the climax of this Extermination Camp Christmas Concert, the farewell appearance of the Boffo Boys of Birkenau.' The play measures Ivan the Terrible's personalised reign of terror against the depersonalised bureaucracy that underpinned the Nazi extermination machine. As in so much of Barnes' work, the play focuses on authority and assent. Acquiescence to authority (on whatever basis that authority is claimed) enables people to deny responsibility for their own actions and for the socio-political structures of the world they inhabit. Although there is no narrative link between them, the two parts and the epilogue all inform each other, with the comedy becoming ever darker and the resonances between the three increasingly alarming. The camp comedians' routine is so profoundly shocking because it presents us with the disturbingly familiar routine of victims turning 'jokes' against themselves, but in a context which poses painfully difficult questions about the function of humour. Is it a token of resistance, the only kind of resistance available to them? Or a form of resignation or even of collaboration with the most obscenely inhumane regime (a regime which the play represents as 'ordinary' and banal, a regime which the bureaucrats insist is part of 'A benevolent brotherhood of man')? By denying their plight do they trivialise their own oppression? By trivialising their predicament do they deny their oppressors triumph? It is the aggressive juxtaposition of the three scenes, the montage, which raises these questions. Whether it works in the theatre as Barnes intends it to, however, is a different matter. Whether it alienates audiences to such an extent that they refuse to see the play as anything other than an assault is open to question. Barnes considered the play an experiment, a deliberate Artaudian attempt to push the boundaries of what is possible in theatre, to explore the relationship between the laughter which heals divisions and alleviates suffering and the laughter which compounds injustice and misery. What Barnes has done, however, is to take a Jonsonian strategy and push it to extremes.

Jonson's use of such juxtapositions is less evident because it is usually tied to plot, but the effect is similar in that so much meaning is created by the montage, by the space *between* scenes. The interweavings of plots and sub-plots is simultaneously linear and lateral. What makes *Bartholomew Fair* and *Every Man in His Humour* so pleasurable in the theatre and so difficult to read off the page is precisely this lateral relationship between scenes and characters. For the purposes of this argument, however, I shall look at *The Alchemist* precisely because it appears on the surface to be the most linear of Jonson's plays.

> Much company they draw, and much abuse,
> In casting figures, telling fortunes, news,
> Selling of flies, flat bawdry, with *the stone*;
> Till it, and they, and all in *fume* are gone.
>
> (The Argument. 9–12)

The final four lines of Jonson's 'Argument' summarise the bulk of the play. The linear mechanics of the plot work so well, with the interventions of the gulls becoming ever more demanding, the pace ever faster, that it is easy to overlook its lateral relationships. Each of the visitors to Lovewit's house (turned brothel / alchemist's den) seeks his own magical transformation, and each becomes a butt of the satire; but the juxtapositions of personal greed, business enterprise, fashionable behaviour, naïveté, lust, narcissism, aggression, credulity, hypocrisy, religious zeal and simple-mindedness create a shimmering montage in which each of these characteristics is individually highlighted but also equated to others. We are invited to draw comparisons between Dapper and Mammon, each of whom parades their sensual fantasies and desires for social eminence or dominance (Ostovich

1997a: 35–8); Mammon's grand excesses and self-serving philanthropy no less absurd than the pathetic dreams of Dapper. Mammon's dream of fabulous wealth is also equated with the Puritans' aspiration to be 'temporal lords' (3.2.52). Helen Ostovich has demonstrated (1997a: 33–5) the parallels between early seventeenth-century Puritanism and alchemy. Tribulation and Ananias are no less opportunistic than Subtle and Face, more than ready to 'deal with widows, and with orphans' goods' (2.5.47) in the hope of 'raising' them through the alchemical process. When reading the play from the page it is tempting to consider the end of an individual scene as a sort of closure. In performance, meaning is generated through rhythmic relationships between scenes. Act 2, Scene 6 ends with Subtle and Face arguing about Dame Pliant.

> FACE   A wife, a wife for one on us, my dear Subtle!
>   We'll e'en draw lots, and he that fails shall have
>   The more in goods, the other has in tail.
> SUBTLE Rather the less. For she may be so light,
>   She may want grains.
> FACE   Ay, or be such a burden,
>   A man would scarce endure her for the whole.

                                              (2.6.85–90)

The following scene (3.1) begins with Tribulation explaining to Ananias that:

> Such chastisements are common to the saints,
> And such rebukes we of the separation
> Must bear with willing shoulders, as the trials
> Sent forth to tempt our frailties.

                                              (3.1.1–4)

Just as the broad structure of the play equates Mammon and Dapper in their dependence on Dol to realise their dreams, so the micro-structure of the scene-change creates a situation whereby the Puritans' speech is assailed by echoes of the previous bawdy exchange; thus Tribulation inadvertently extends the sexual punning (on tails, burdens and wholes), unwittingly relating his self-righteous, martyr-like talk of purification through persecution (chastisements, rebukes, burdens, trials, temptation and frailties) to masochism and sexual humiliation. Off the page this montage effect might seem tendentious; in the theatre Subtle and Face have prepared an audience to read the innuendo.

    Influenced by twentieth-century cinema, Peter Barnes pushes the use of montage to extremes: circus and music-hall, song and dance routines are interposed with scenes of harsh violence and cynical exploitation, anarchy and arbitrariness. But the roots of the technique are Jonsonian.

Open texts

The trajectory of Barnes' writing bears interesting similarities to Jonson's in that his most recent plays (I hesitate to call them 'late plays', in the hope that he has more to offer and they might yet be seen as belonging to his 'middle period') share some of the characteristics of Jonson's late plays. The scabrous, acerbic satire that characterises much of Barnes' earlier work has been replaced by something warmer. The warmth is perhaps the kind that people might find when huddled round a fire in the depths of winter, but the humour is slightly gentler and occasionally whimsical. Barnes seems to have returned to the questions he posed at the beginning of *Laughter!*: 'In the face of Attila the Hun, Ivan the Terrible, a Passchendaele or Auschwitz, what good is laughter?' and come up with a different answer. Laughter may still be 'the ally of tyrants' (Barnes, 1989: 343) but in *Dreaming* it is also, at least occasionally, a defence against the bleak horrors of the world; and whereas in the earlier plays this use of humour was shown to be self-deceptive and self-defeating, in *Dreaming* it is far more ambivalent. Barnes once commented about Jonson that he was 'a master of invective, one of the marks of a good playwright';[11] and whilst there is undoubtedly an element of self-justification in the assertion, there is a parallel mellowing in the later work of both playwrights. Although this may be true of many writers, in the case of Jonson and Barnes the later plays also mark a shift towards a particular kind of experimentation that results in texts which are more openly ambivalent.

In August 1995, the National Theatre Studio staged an experimental play by Barnes, *Luna Park Eclipses*, in a production that he directed himself. Writing about the play, he stated that his intention was

> not to depict plot or character but show directly the contrast between what viewers apprehend and what they provide for themselves as in an abstract painting or collage. The audience is faced with the same dilemma the author faced when writing the play – it must make choices. ... The play's audience is made up of ... individuals who are not coerced by the authority of an omnipotent author and therefore can enter new fields of self-expression.
>
> (1996: 203)

On the surface this seems to be a radically new development in Barnes' work, but the desire to entangle the roles of author and audience in the meaning-making process can be seen as a development of continuing interests in the dynamic and ever changing relationship between the two, and, as such, an extension of the Jonsonian tradition. It is perhaps not surprising that *The Magnetic Lady* has become one of Barnes' favourite plays. He has described it as 'very funny and quite remarkably modern: an extraordinary blend of fairy tale and bawdy comedy, realism and fantasy, romance and social satire'.[12]

Critics' reactions to *The Magnetic Lady* have been remarkably varied. Discounting Dryden's (in)famous dismissal of it (and the other late plays) as a product of Jonson's dotage, C.G. Thayer refers to it as 'The most Chaucerian of all Jonson's plays' and 'the neatest of all Jonson's plots'. Simon Trussler thinks of Jonson at this stage in his career as a critical analyst of romantic comedy rather than as a late convert to its values. Anne Barton writes: 'In *The Magnetic Lady*, Jonson admitted to being a divided and contradictory being, a man whose nature led him to disorder and eccentricity.' (1984: 299). Richard Cave argues that the play is a logical development of Jonson's enquiry into the 'proper relation between audience and play' and that in *The Magnetic Lady* Compass is 'the exemplary spectator... (seeing) through the anarchic follies and deceptions being played around him and comes at the truth of people's psychological and social conditions as a basis on which to fashion potential social harmony.' (1991: 156) For Barnes the attraction of the play lies in the very diversity of responses that it arouses. Whereas in many of Jonson's earlier plays, such diversity is created by dynamic shifts in tone, for Barnes *The Magnetic Lady* is simultaneously 'realism and fantasy, romance and social satire.' It is this openness, the refusal to conform to generic expectations that he finds so appealing about it. In these terms, maybe even *Luna Park Eclipses* can be seen as a wry Jonsonian rejoinder to questions posed by *The Magnetic Lady*'s openness, echoing the terms of The Boy's mischievous reprimand to Damplay: '... conjecture is a kind of figure-flinging, or throwing the dice, for a meaning was never in the poet's purpose perhaps'. (Chorus 4. 25–7).[13] In Robert Speaight's account of William Poel's work on 'The Elizabethan Revival' he writes of the 'Elizabethan' audience as 'athletes, not eunuchs, of the imagination, and when they went to the theatre they demanded the opportunity for exercise.' (1954: 88)[14] The epigram might well apply to the opportunities that Peter Barnes creates for his audiences.

Notes

1 The quotation comes from an unpublished lecture given by Peter Barnes at the conference *Ben Jonson and the Theatre* held at the University of Reading, 1996. See Cave, Schafer, and Woolland (1999).

2 Ronald Bryden used the phrase in his introduction to *The Bewitched* in *Barnes: Plays One*, p. 187, Methuen (1989).

3 *The Alchemist*. 2.3.80.

4 In his introduction to *Collected Plays*, Barnes describes his own theatre writing as 'repeated bayonet attacks on naturalism.' (Barnes, 1981: ix).

5 First produced at The Open Space Theatre, London. November 1969. Directed by Charles Marowitz. Published in *Barnes: Plays One*, p. 126.

6 The first part of a trilogy of short plays. First produced as a television play, broadcast by BBC TV, August 1989. Published as *The Spirit of Man* (1990) Methuen, London.

7 *Dreaming* opened at the Manchester Royal Exchange in March 1999. A revival of the play (this time directed by Barnes himself) was mounted at the Queens Theatre, Shaftesbury Avenue in June and July 1999. The play is published by Methuen. Page references in notes below are from this edition.

8 There is possibly a further Jonsonian reference here: When the fire in Jonson's lodgings destroyed all his books and manuscripts in 1623, one of the manuscripts that burned was *Richard Crookback*.

9 The Russian director, Vsevolod Meyerhold sought to reveal the ruling idea of a play by creating a series of 'attractions', 'constructed according to musical principles, not with the conventional aim of advancing the narrative'. Braun (1969) p. 318.

10 *Laughter!* was premiered at the Royal Court Theatre, London on 25 January 1978 under the direction of Charles Marowitz. Published in *Barnes: Plays One*. (1989) p. 342.

11 From the unpublished lecture given at the University of Reading, 1996.

12 In an unpublished letter to Brian Woolland, July 1996.

13 *The Magnetic Lady*, ed. Peter Happé (2000). The Revels Plays. Manchester University Press, Manchester.

14 Robert Speaight's book *William Poel and the Elizabethan Revival* was published by Heinemann in 1954 as the Annual Publication of The Society for Theatre Research for 1951–52.

Chapter 12

The Language of Carnival: Strategies of Overthrowing from Ben Jonson to Caryl Churchill

Claudia Manera

Why Churchill and Jonson?

In the following pages I am not going to attempt a thorough comparison between the two playwrights, nor will I claim a direct link of inspiration passing through the centuries. If, on the one hand, the diversity of the work produced by both authors provides in itself a good enough reason to compare them, on the other hand it makes the analogy potentially imperfect and vague.

What I propose to do, therefore, is to develop a discussion, more than a comparison, based on the central idea of *carnivalesque overthrowing*. In particular, I would like to consider the notion of *carnivalesque language* in its wider sense, as a language of multiplicity, a multi-layered idiom, which breaks boundaries and which is, I would argue, pertinent to both Jonson and Churchill. The discussion of carnival and language will inevitably start from Bakhtin's aesthetics of the carnivalesque, as well as from his work on language, and it will move on to later interpretations of his theories.

In his well known work on Rabelais, *Rabelais and His World*, Bakhtin provides probably the most extensive discussion on the 'carnivalesque spirit', a festive spirit of countercultural overthrowing, which Bakhtin links to the 'medieval culture of the marketplace':

Celebrations of a carnival type represented a considerable part of the life of medieval men [...] large medieval cities devoted an average of three months a year to these festivities. The influence of the carnival spirit was irresistible: it made a man renounce his official state as monk, cleric, scholar, and perceive the world in its laughing aspect.[1]

In Bakhtin's view, the carnivalesque is a force which pervades the medieval popular culture of the street fair, and which finds a later literary expression in works such as Rabelais' *Gargantua and Pantagruel*. It is identified with the irreverent laughter, and expresses a desire for dismantling hierarchies and hegemonies.

The 'culture of the marketplace' finds expression through the celebration of what Bakhtin defines as the *lower bodily stratum*. In particular, the language of the 'grotesque body' becomes the quintessential expression of the carnivalesque spirit. The image of the grotesque body becomes in Bakhtin's theorisation the emblem of transgression and transformation. The grotesque body is opposed to the classical body, it is the visual rejection of decorum, it is the open body. In order to illustrate this idea, Bakhtin describes the Kerch terracotta collection:

> In the famous Kerch terracotta collection we find figurines of senile pregnant hags. Moreover, the old hags are laughing. This is a typical and very strongly expressed grotesque. It is ambivalent. It is pregnant death, a death that gives birth. There is nothing completed, nothing calm and stable in the bodies of these old hags. They combine a senile, decaying and deformed flesh with the flesh of new life [...] it is the epitome of incompleteness. And such is precisely the grotesque concept of the body. [...] the grotesque body is not separated from the rest of the world. It [...] transgresses its own limits.
>
> (Bakhtin, 1984: 25–26)

The carnivalesque celebrations realise themselves through the perpetual circle of life and death, which, in turn, takes place via the bodily functions of the grotesque body itself. According to Bakhtin, therefore, the Medieval culture of the marketplace undermines, by using the language of the 'body', the canons of classical decorum, and, by extension, it hints at the possibility of shaking the foundations of authority.

It is by referring to such categories as 'the grotesque' and such images as the marketplace, that I propose to develop a discourse which relates the work of Caryl Churchill to that of Ben Jonson. The crossing of boundaries and overthrowing of expectations will concern the visual as well as the verbal. The category of the grotesque will be stretched to the analysis of a language which rejects closure and definition, to a language which rejects and sometimes appropriates and overturns the language of classic composure.

Pigs and markets: *Bartholomew Fair*, *Serious Money* and *A Mouthful of Birds*

Discussing Jonson and carnival would not be possible without mentioning *Bartholomew Fair*. With its insistence on the body and the confusion of social distinctions and class boundaries, this play seems quintessentially carnivalesque. I will use *Bartholomew Fair* to open up a discussion of two quite different plays by Caryl Churchill, *A Mouthful of Birds*[2] and *Serious Money*.[3]

I previously mentioned how, in Bakhtin's terms, the 'grotesque body' becomes the image of rebellion, of unruliness, of the undetermined. What is normally defined as base, vulgar, even filthy, can be seen as an instrument for subversion. With this in mind I am going to choose the iconography of the pig, as it appears in both *Bartholomew Fair* and *A Mouthful of Birds*, as a graphic representation, and at the same time a metaphorical one, for the disruptive potential of the grotesque body.

In *The Politics and Poetics of Transgression*, Stallybrass and White devote a section to an 'attempt to sketch out a social semiotics of the pig in relation to low discourses, the body and the fair'.[4] The main concern of this 'social semiotics' seems to be the identification of a fundamental ambivalence in the symbolism associated with the pig, whereby instances drawn from high and low culture, art and religious iconography appear to indicate an alternation between celebration and vilification of anything associated with this animal. In particular, it finds three 'symbolic processes' at work in the carnivalesque use of the pig: demonisation, inversion and hybridisation. The first of the three is probably the most familiar of all, insofar as it refers to the derogatory features usually attributed to the pig (at least in Western culture): filthiness, excessive eating, fatness. 'Inversion' is the process of overturning which takes place in a carnivalesque representation, where the master becomes the slave and the animal replaces the human: it was not rare for pigs to be elected 'king' of the carnival in popular festivities of Medieval origin. Finally, 'hybridisation' is not always distinguishable from 'inversion'. It is, to some extent, a more complex way of trespassing boundaries between high and low, official and unofficial or, in this particular case, human and animal.

In the same study Stallybrass and White choose to develop the illustration of the marketplace, and of the 'social semiotics' of the pig by referring to Ben Jonson's *Bartholomew Fair*. I certainly agree with Herry Levin in his definition of *Bartholomew Fair* as Jonson's 'broadest and most atmospheric evocation of low life in its sights and sounds and smells'.[5] We are in the Bakhtinian realm of the 'lower bodily stratum' and the pig imagery is of paramount importance. The common denominator is vulgarity and greed. Everything becomes obscene and grotesque when it is transported inside the confines of the fairground, where the figure of Ursula, strongly associated with the image of the pig, dominates. The pig is crucial to convey the sense of attraction and repulsion which emanates from the fair. In the play everybody longs for pig's meat. The puritan Busy is more attracted than the others and employs his rhetoric to justify the attraction.

It is almost as if, by eating pig, the characters assumed some of its proverbial filthiness. In the case of Ursula the borderline between human and animal is certainly very thin. Knockem describes her as 'mother o' the pigs' (2.5.70); and Winwife says that 'her language grows greasier than the pigs' (2.5.125). The pig is, however, like the fair, simultaneously attractive and disgusting.

These symbolic processes, combining reactions of attraction and repulsion, seem also to be at work in the pig episode in *A Mouthful of Birds*. The play is constructed in episodes, and explores the possibilities of 'blurring boundaries', of overcoming static structures imposed by society, as well as challenging in various ways a monolithic discourse on form. The episode to which I am referring sees a businessman (Paul) gradually falling in love with a pig after having visited the pig farm where the animal is about to be slaughtered. Paul eventually tries to save the pig but he arrives at the farm too late to do so. The episodes comprise alternating words and dance.

The 'demonisation' of the pig, its identification with the unpleasant, is ensured by Paul's friend (in a dialogue preceding the dance episodes), who tends to redirect the conversation within the parameters of normally accepted views:

> **FRIEND**   If you drive past a pig farm you notice the smell. [...]
> They lie about in the mud. Filthy pig. [...]
> Of course they are fat. Fat pig. Pig ignorant.[6]

Inversion and hybridisation are mostly interwoven, since the very fact of falling in love with the pig is at the same time a reversal of categories and a grotesque violation of boundaries between the animal and the human. An obvious overturning of parameters occurs in Paul's remarks during the conversation to which I have just referred:

> **PAUL**   But really they are very clean animals. [...]
> Pigs. Are very intelligent. Like a dog. More than a dog. [...]

> It could sleep on the end of your bed. [...]
> They are not fat. [...]
> They have a huge bite. [...] And at the same time they are so
> gentle. You can stroke their ears.[7]

The inversion does not only happen at the level of spoken language. The characterisation of the pig takes place through a sensuous dance performed by an agile dancer (Stephen Goff in the original production). Paul's vision corresponds, therefore, to the actual vision we are offered.

Once again, the hybridisation affects a number of aspects. At the immediately available visual perception, the dance offers a striking juxtaposition between a virtually naked human / animal body and a man wearing a formal business suit. During the final part of the dance, when the pig has been killed and then been brought back to life by Paul's love, the jacket is 'ripped off,' the businessman has lost his bourgeois integrity, control is lost. The fact that the pig materialises by using dance offers another occasion for hybridisation, this time the hybrid is the form of communication. At a later stage I will discuss in more details the notion of multi-layered language and the extension of the notion of carnivalesque overthrowing to the use of language. It is true, though, that the ambivalent imagery connected to the pig is accompanied by a polymorphic use of language in both *Bartholomew Fair* and *A Mouthful of Birds*. In the former, the language of the marketplace, with its bodily images, confusion of human and animal, vulgar expressions and metaphors, dirty dealings brings about the ultimate undermining of authority, in the person of Justice Overdo. In the latter, the experiments in 'different languages' encourage the breaking of narrative boundaries.

Having discussed the pig as an exemplification of what Bakhtin defines 'lower bodily stratum', I would like to extend the analysis to other aspects of the culture of the marketplace, linking *Bartholomew Fair* with Churchill's *Serious Money*, defined by Francis King as 'a play remarkably Jonsonian in tone, [where] every character is motivated by the single humour of greed'.[8] Here the reference is obviously to the Jonsonian theory of Humours; what is more, Churchill immediately refers to the play as a 'city comedy', a frequent denomination associated to Jonson's comedies.

The direct link with 'city comedy' is established at the start of Churchill's play by introducing a scene taken from a comedy of the Restoration period, *The Volunteers or the Stokjobbers* by Thomas Shadwell. Although Shadwell's play belongs to a theatrical practice which is very different from Jonson's Jacobean drama, Shadwell proclaimed his admiration for Jonson, and for his comedy of Humours. What is more, both Jonson's and Shadwell's comedies are mostly about London, about 'The

City'. Churchill chooses a playwright who can function, I would argue, as a transition between the original tradition of city comedy and the late twentieth-century setting. In both cases (the Jonsonian comedy and Churchill's play), as well as in the scene from Shadwell which is presented at the opening of *Serious Money*[9] the market economy and the greedy logic of acquisition and ownership come under close examination.

The notion of 'trading', whether on the financial market, or in human relationships, is undoubtedly at the centre of much of Restoration drama, and of Jonson's comedies. For instance marriage, or 'the market of matrimony', as Shadwell calls it in *The Volunteers* (Shadwell, 1927: 165), is usually an instrument of economic transactions in both traditions. I previously discussed the implications of the 'language of the marketplace' in Bakhtinian terms, for both Churchill and Jonson: I will now briefly concentrate on the marketplace as the site of 'trading' in *Serious Money* and *Bartholomew Fair*. In *The Politics and Poetics of Transgression*, Stallybrass and White discuss at length various aspects of the 'fair', in particular, when dealing with the character of the marketplace, they insist on the importance of both 'spectacle' and 'trade'. In the coexistence of the two, they see a source of strong threat for the established order:

Although the bourgeois classes were frequently frightened by the threat of political subversion and moral licence, they were perhaps more scandalised by the deep conceptual confusion entailed by the fair's inmixing of work and pleasure (Stallybrass and White, 1986: 30).

I would argue that both Jonson's *Bartholomew Fair* and Churchill's *Serious Money*, two 'city comedies', contain the spirit of the fair and its 'inmixing of work and pleasure', with similar and different results.

I have already talked about the ambivalent reactions caused by the emblematic image of the pig, a recurrent feature in *Bartholomew Fair*, in particular among the stalls of the market and around Ursula's stall. The Jonsonian market contains both spectacle and trade, a sense of commodification is what governs transactions both in goods and in human relationships. This mixture of spectacle and trade is certainly not an isolated episode in Jonson. An eloquent example is to be found in *Volpone*, where the illicit trade becomes in itself a staged demonstration of Volpone's and Mosca's theatrical skill: to the extent that Volpone himself cannot resist jumping on an improvised stage, to carry out his sinister and lascivious courting of Celia. In *Bartholomew Fair*, the spectacle of illicit trade happens all around Ursula's stall, which functions as a centre of energy, a disruptive energy which generates thefts, tricks, misunderstandings, dethroning of authority, improvised marriages. In the words of Quarlous, marriage is really a 'market of matrimony':

Why should I not marry this six thousand pound, now I think on't? And a good trade too, that she has beside, ha?

$$(5.2.76-7)$$

The language of the play, the language which communicates the high amount of energy involved in the transactions of the fair, is an eloquent example of 'heteroglossia', to use another Bakhtinian concept, which I will further discuss at another point in the chapter. It is a mixture of lower class jargon, regional variations, pompous rhetoric, stereotyped phrases and useless Latin quotations. The fair has its own language and, in many ways, its own rules. The characters of higher social status who enter the fairground become disoriented and lose sight of the parameters which govern the outside world. In its own way, the fair is in itself a spectacle, a theatrical world, where the game will be pushed to the limit during the final puppet show. About this final show within the show Richard Cave observes:

> Is proffered as an entertainment for most of the characters we have seen elsewhere and in some measure it heightens our appreciation of the themes of the play overall. [...] the performers are all puppets. This is wholly in keeping with the demotic setting of the play at a popular fair; so too is the style of the play on offer – a bawdy, farcical debunking of a fashionable work of high culture (Marlowe's *Hero and Leander*) which is transposed to a Thames-side tavern where it becomes an excuse for much sturdy knockabout.[10]

Once again, the use of low comedy, of vulgar language, is functional to the debasement of authority, in this case, at least partially the authority of literary tradition. In addition to this, having a puppet show on stage threatens to blur yet another boundary, the one between spectator and spectacle. The choices in staging reflect, to some extent, the confusion of identity portrayed by the fair, which, in this case, itself becomes a kind of theatre artefact. As is frequently the case in Jonson, the authority of the spectator is undermined, in the same way as any possible notion of authority in the play. But how does the mixture of trade and spectacle, of attraction and repulsion, work in Churchill's *Serious Money*? What is the effect of the vulgar language of 'trade' in a theatrical portrayal of a contemporary financial market?

The depiction of the stock exchange to some extent reproduces the confusion and energy of the fairground. Highly technological equipment substitutes for the fair booths, but the simultaneity of actions recreate the fervent activity of the market. Even more than in Jonson's somewhat allegorical fair, the high level of energy which emanates from Churchill's financial market results in converging and contrasting feelings of repulsion and attraction.

The following are some extracts from reviews of the play:

> *Serious Money* is a socialist play about capitalist pleasure, conjuring up the exhilaration of the chase after millions.
>
> (Jim Hiley, *Listener*, 2.4.1987)

> A suavely complex financial horror cartoon, in which the pursuit of money lends life a savage, aphrodisiac energy, and where characters thrive or die according to their fitness for this gangster pace. [...] the juggling of naturalism and cartoon turn the City's fiscal squalor into a high-spirited bacchanal.
>
> (Andrew Rissick, *Independent*, 30.3.1987)

The dominant idea emerging is of a play which succeeds because it is highly entertaining thanks to its exuberance. Images of unrestrained sensual-sexual energy are also evoked, such as 'high spirited bacchanal'.

In *Serious Money* the universal greed and corruption which dominates the world of financial capitalism is shown with much more directness than the widespread amorality of *Bartholomew Fair*. The 'longing for the pig' is replaced, in Churchill's play, by uncompromising declarations such as:

> Greed is all right. Greed is healthy. You can be greedy and still feel good about yourself.
>
> (p. 45)

Jonson's Puritan Busy seems almost pathetic when compared with the world of Churchill's *Serious Money*, where hypocrisy is programmatically on the agenda:

> **BIDDULPH** We will make profit. But at the right time and in the right place,
> With a smile on our very acceptable face.
> You do so much good, you give so much
> Enjoyment.
> **DUCKETT** Youth unemployment.
> **BIDDULPH** Yes, youth unemployment,
> Swimming pools, pensioners, toy libraries, art –
> **DUCKETT** What's this about art?
> **BIDDULPH** You don't give a fart,
> I know it, they know it, you just mustn't show it.
>
> (pp. 80–81)

The use of verse enhances the grotesque depiction of the unscrupulous world of finance. The verses contribute to the satirical tone of the piece and function as 'alienating' devices. The mechanism at play is the one of paradox, whereby the rhymes create a paradoxical juxtaposition between the form used and the content described. But the use of verses also has the effect of increasing the comic potential of the piece, thanks to the clever wordplay, and simultaneously exposing the sinister reality. The mechanism at play is not very distant from the Brechtian idea of 'laugh[ing] when they weep',[11] a mechanism which undoubtedly wants to entertain and instruct.

Although this play genuinely aims at denouncing the corruptive forces embedded in Western capitalism, and although its satirical potential is striking and the objectives are clear, the well documented audience reactions to the play raise some interesting and problematic issues. As I noted before, the play was praised by the reviewers for its exuberance and 'sexual' energy. If, on the one hand, the portrayal of the world of financial trade shows an unavoidable contamination with corruption and unscrupulousness which does not save anybody, on the other hand the disgust is somewhat dimmed by a glamour which runs the risk of being self celebratory. To some extent the play exemplifies Dolcie Starr's (one of the characters) ideas about public relations:

STARR   Let Duckett be good. And a bore.
                Then you can be bad. And glamorous.
                You'll have top billing by tonight
                Everyone loves a villain if he's handled right.
                Bad has connotations of amorous.
CORMAN   Bad and glamorous?

                                                  (p. 91)

The fact that the play was particularly successful among those who were targeted in its satirical and direct attacks raises some questions of interpretation. The play was originally performed in 1987 at the Royal Court Theatre, a theatre with a tradition of intellectual and innovative experimentation. It then moved to the West End, to the Wyndham's Theatre. Here the success among reactionary audiences seems to have been generated, at least in part, by a misinterpretation of the original intentions.

In Jonson's *Bartholomew Fair* the use of base and vulgar language is a clear extension of the depiction of the 'grotesque body', especially in the case of the pig woman Ursula. As is the case in Bakhtin's idea of 'grotesque body', the effect is one of trespassing the limits of acceptable decorum, of classical restraint, and of bringing about the general confusion of the market, of the carnivalesque fairground. In *Serious Money*, the use of obscene and vulgar language is closely associated with the manipulation of money at high levels. There are times when the play verges on the 'pornographic', in that it positions an audience as voyeuristic spectators taking pleasure in watching the display of an unattainable object of desire. The world of financial trade is undoubtedly repulsive, as it appears in the play, but at the same time its energy and wealth can be highly desirable.

If *Serious Money* remains a controversial play in terms of audience response, this should not obscure its subversive potential. The play remains highly political, certainly carnivalesque, and, precisely because of the problematic audience response, even more Jonsonian. Its 'Jonsonian' characteristics become all the more evident when one thinks of *Volpone*, at a performance of which we, as an audience, are likely to share the delight that Volpone and Mosca experience in transforming their greed into skilled performance. It is probably fair to describe Churchill's and Jonson's carnivals as unpredictable and sometimes dangerously sinister and, probably because of this, even more challenging.

Carnivalesque language: *Volpone*, *The Alchemist* and *The Skriker*

In the chapter 'Word, Dialogue and the Novel' which forms part of *Desire in Language*, Julia Kristeva elaborates on Bakhtin's use of the idea of carnivalesque, with particular reference to the use of language in the novel as literary form.

> Carnivalesque discourse breaks through the laws of a language censored by grammar and semantics and, at the same time, is a social and political protest. There is no equivalence, but rather, identity between challenging official linguistic codes and challenging official law.[12]

Here Kristeva creates a connection between Bakhtin's work on the carnivalesque, and his work on the novel and the fundamental concepts of 'heteroglossia' and dialogism. The bridge provided by Kristeva seems to me particularly useful in analysing much of the potential for 'carnivalesque overthrowing' present in Jonson and Churchill. Because of the limited scope of this study, I will limit the references to Churchill's *The Skriker*, although many other plays could be analysed in the same light, particularly *A Mouthful of Birds*. I will also refer to some examples from Jonson's *Volpone* and *The Alchemist*.

While describing the language of the novel, Bakhtin finds it 'dialogic'.[13] In other words, it is a language which manifests itself through a multiplicity of voices, and which challenges predetermined patterns. He opposes the potential for transformation typical of this language, to the monolithic structure of more ancient forms, such as epic narrative. In her discussion of 'carnivalesque language', Kristeva appropriates the concept of 'dialogism' and maintains that it 'challenges God, authority and social law, by bringing to surface the underlying unconscious [of] the structure of [...] literary productivity', in other words 'sexuality and death' (Kristeva, 1984, 78–79).

Although both Bakhtin and Kristeva apply these theories to the realm of the novel, they seem to me applicable to the theatre, a form which offers even more opportunity for interaction of different codes of communication.[14] Certainly much of Churchill's work seems to be challenging in various different ways an idea of monolithic and definitive discourse. The intertwining of forms and the constant shaping and reshaping, as it manifests itself in *The Skriker* is not far from the transgressive potential of Kristeva's carnivalesque language. The following are some extracts from the reviews of the play, after its first production at the National Theatre in 1994:

> Caryl Churchill's fairy tale for the 1990s is poised [...] between the domestic and the grotesque, between reality and magic. [...] In this performance, movement and language don't just complement each other, they are luminously inseparable.
>
> (J. Mackrell, *Independent*, 29.1.1994)

> Churchill offers a Joycean deconstruction of language, a surreal stream of consciousness that addles the brain with the sheer volume of its inventiveness.
>
> (Neil Simon, *What's On*, 2.2.1994)

These latter observations draw attention to a use of language which seems to be anything but definite and predetermined. In the same way as the central character, the Skriker, 'constitutes a complex, contradictory meshing of transformative powers',[15] the play not only shifts between 'the domestic and the grotesque', but also transforms itself by moving from words to dance, to singing, simultaneously exploring and critiquing established dramatic forms. I would argue that the 'grotesque' pervades the play at many different levels. The protagonist itself, the Skriker, is a hybrid, particularly in the initial and final appearance as an ancient, deformed, mysteriously grotesque creature. The audience is immediately faced with the image of a non-definable being, possibly coming from the underworld. The contorted figure which comes to occupy the empty stage of the original production at the National Theatre[16] has an apparent kinship with the medieval grotesques displayed on street scaffolds. In the same way as the grotesque body at the centre of many medieval street spectacles is – as

Bakhtin defines it – a body in constant transformation, the Skriker is a 'shapeshifter' about to undergo a series of chameleonic impersonations.

Before being allowed to witness the actual body breaking the boundaries of identity, the audience is confronted with waves of words, phrases, and free associations which emanate from the 'creature' on stage. Finding herself in constant transition, the hybrid fairy produces a language which does not have a referent, or at least not only one. Elaine Aston defines the Skriker's speech a 'mouthful of words',[17] a definition which not only creates a clever pun by referring to another 'dialogic' play by Churchill, but clearly points at a language constantly shifting between distorted nursery rhymes and advertisements:

> SKRIKER   Heard her boast beast a roast beef eater, daughter could spin span
>   spick and spun the lowest form of wheat straw into fold, raw,
>   into roar, golden lion and lyonesse under the sea, dungeonesse
>   under the castle for bad mad sad adders and takers away.
>
>   (p. 243)
>
>   Eating a plum in the enchanted orchard, cherry orchid, chanted
>   orchestra was my undoing my doing my dying my undying love
>   for you.
>
>   (p. 245)

The Skriker's speeches could almost be said to illustrate Derrida's idea of 'différence'.[18] Words, or rather, signifiers, follow one another in a chain of assonances where the process of moving further along the chain appears to become more important than a permanent decodification of the message. The language itself shifts its shape, and, like the grotesque body it emanates from, extends beyond its limits whereby each word becomes the source for others.

Both this idea of constant transformation, and the specific use of a language which expresses such shifts and turns, prompts me to bring Jonson back to the foreground of the discussion. Two of his best known plays, *The Alchemist* and *Volpone* are examples of unstoppable transformative energy. In both plays, the process of grotesque overturning of reality takes place, to a large degree, at the level of language. It is through his rhetorical skills that Mosca persuades Corbaccio to disinherit his son:

> MOSCA   Now would I counsel you, make home with speed;
>   There, frame a will, whereto you shall inscribe
>   My master your heir.

CORBACCIO	And disinherit
	My son?
	[...]
MOSCA	[...] When I [...]
	Last produce your will, where without thought
	Or least regard, unto your proper issue,
	A son so brave and highly merit in
	The stream of your diverted love hath thrown you
	Upon my master, and made him your heir:
	He cannot be so stupid, or stone dead,
	But out of conscience and mere gratitude -
CORBACCIO	He must pronounce me his?
MOSCA	'Tis true.
CORBACCIO	This plot did I think on before.

(1.4.93–110)

Within a few lines the state of things is turned upside down and, thanks to the ability to play on the longing for the 'forbidden fruit', the most unnatural act – disinheriting one's son – becomes the most obvious step to take. This is certainly carnivalesque, with its bringing forward of chaos and its celebration of misrule. The disguise is here the disguise of language, which becomes a mask to be laid on an ultimately inconsistent reality. Jonson's is a dark carnival, a carnival that goes beyond the joyous festivity, a carnival where misrule is perpetual and inherent in any form of human interaction or communication. The power of a distorting rhetoric strikes throughout the play and persuades Corvino to become a recognised cuckold, in the same way as it convinces the court first of the guilt and then of the innocence of Celia and Bonario.

Language is also used in *The Alchemist* as a powerful tool to express one's and to manipulate others' desires. An audience which had attended *The Skriker* would recognise in *The Alchemist* the Babel of sounds, in which the alchemy of social roles and heterogeneous linguistic registers combine to form an 'explosive' theatrical product. What follows is an example of the almost nonsensical language used by Epicure Mammon to express his aspirations in *The Alchemist*:

I will have all my beds blown up; not stuffed:
Down is too hard. And then, mine oval room,
Filled with such pictures as Tiberius took
From Elephantis, and dull Aretine
But coldly imitated: Then, my glasses,
Cut in more subtle angles, to disperse,

And multiply the figures, as I walk
Naked between my succubae

                                                                    (2.2.41–48)

We'll [...] go with all, my girl, and live
In a free state, where we will eat our mullets,
Soused in high-country wines, sup pheasants' eggs,
And have our cockles boiled in silver shells,
Our shrimps to swim again, as when they lived,
In a rare butter, made of dolphins' milk [...]

                                                                    (4.1.155–60)

In both *The Alchemist* and *Volpone,* the chaos expressed by the manipulative use of language is maintained till the end, although with much darker tones in *Volpone,* where the Fox's final appeal to the audience is anything but a resolution. The passivity with which the two innocent victims succumb to the power of rhetoric does not leave any room for hope. Besides, the audience is faced with an embarrassing wish to identify with the tricksters, and finds itself a victim of the same drive towards a perpetual renewal of the role which constitutes the trap for the protagonists of the play.

It is a 'dark carnival', a carnival which does not have resolution, in Jonson and in the grotesque fairy tale about the Skriker. One of the languages which is employed and subverted in Churchill's play is the codified language of the fairy tale. One of the ways in which this language is subverted is by the openness of the ending. What some critics have found inconclusive and puzzling, is surely a programmatic decision. The never ending transformations, the loose chain of signifiers are part of a discourse which challenges a possibility of resolution.

I started this section by referring to Kristeva's notion of carnivalesque language, and I will conclude with her attempt to explain the dark sides of carnival:

> The word 'carnivalesque' lends itself to an ambiguity one must avoid. In contemporary society, it generally connotes parody [...] The laughter of the carnival is not simply parodic; it is no more comic than tragic; it is both at once, one might say that it is serious.
>
> (1984: 80)

The carnival of Jonson's theatre and of Churchill's *The Skriker* is as serious as it is disturbing.

Classical theatre and violence

My reasons for including Caryl Churchill among the 'Jonsonians' have been so far grounded in the *aesthetics* of carnival, with reference to the grotesque as a vehicle for overturning content and form. I would like to conclude by drawing attention to another possible common ground between the two playwrights: an interest in the classics. In the space available here I will limit myself to an indication of possible paths of enquiry, and will not delve deeply into Jonson's relationship with the classics, of which there are many studies available.

Plays such as *Poetaster*, *Sejanus*, *Catiline* are overtly set in ancient Rome, while references to the classics appear in one way or another in many of Jonson's works. His use of the classics is certainly 'dialogic', insofar as it further problematises the author's involvement with his contemporary world, and adds to the multi-layered language of his plays. Even where he claims close adherence to the original sources, such as in *Sejanus*, he does it in a polemical fashion, to argue a case relevant to his contemporary world and to his position as artist. What is more, *Sejanus* ends with yet another unresolved dark carnival, the violent solution having left the political uncertainty and the threat to freedom of speech as it was before. Sejanus, somewhat like Volpone, is brought down by his inability to interrupt his skilful performance before it becomes too dangerous, and the audience, as in *Volpone*, is left with serious doubts about the morality of the process which has brought the 'trickster' to justice.

A Mouthful of Birds finds its starting point in Euripides' *The Bacchae*. I would argue that the use made of this classical play and myth, in itself very problematic, contributes to what I previously described as 'carnivalesque language', a language that defies predetermination and stasis. Churchill states that *The Bacchae* offered a number of interesting starting points for a 'workshop' exploration of the potential for violence in women and of the state of 'possession', of going beyond oneself.[19] The contemporary play, therefore, does propose an adaptation of the Greek play, but rather derives from it some ideas and possibly methods to tackle specific issues. Churchill's and Lan's play is closely interwoven with Euripides' but in such a way that reinforces its own polyphonic and 'carnivalesque' nature.

In both plays Dionysus is the driving force, the carrier of the energy which brings about the collapse of a superimposed structure. In the case of Euripides, the choice of Dionysus is rather self-explanatory, insofar as the Dionysiac festivals are generally recognised to be at the origin of western theatre, besides being occasions for a 'carnivalesque' freedom from restraint, for a celebration of fertility and violence at the same time. The

City Dionysia festivals were apparently characterised by 'reversal and blurring of political and sexual hierarchies [...], unusual masks and costumes or no clothing at all, dramatic role-playing, wild dancing'.[20] Most of these characteristics apply to *A Mouthful of Birds*, where the programmatic exploration of violence passes through an ongoing experimentation with dance and words, and layers of role-playing and gender blurring.

A similar experimentation with form and violence is carried on into another performance and collaborative piece, where the world of the classics surfaces again in the form of the myth of Medea: *Lives of the Great Poisoners*.[21] This piece which once again combines dance, singing and drama, and which has at its core the theme of poisoning, opens with a movement piece where Medea kills and restores to life and youth Aeson, father of Jason. She then concludes the opening scene with these words:

> Hurting you I heal you
> Killing you I cure you
> Secrets of death and new life
> Poisons that heal
> Fill your blood fill your breath
> By my skill
> I kill you and give you new life
>
> (*Lives of the Great Poisoners*, Prologue)[22]

This circle of life and death, intermingled with research into violence and passion seems to be very much in line with the exploration carried out in *A Mouthful of Birds*. These are Lena's remarks at the end of the play, after she has been possessed by a spirit which has persuaded her to kill her baby in order to acquire personal integrity and independence:

> It's nice to make someone alive and it's nice to make someone dead. Either way. That power is what I like best in the world. The struggle is every day not to use it.
>
> (*A Mouthful of Birds*, p. 51)

The killing and dismembering of one's offspring is a recurrent theme in classical mythology, which is where popular festive forms such as carnival probably have their origin. The act of tearing flesh apart and eating it seems to recall in a rather explicit fashion the process of knowledge and self expression through 'swallowing' which Bakhtin sees as fundamental to the carnivalesque. Within the realm of the 'marketplace culture', the functions of the body are those which determine the flow and renewal of life. The violence of the mother (or the father) who kills and dismembers the offspring carries further the process of interacting with the world through the body, through the 'grotesque body' in perpetual transformation.

The theme of killing in the family is central to *Thyestes*, Seneca's tragedy of revenge, translated by Churchill and produced in 1994. In the introduction to the play, Churchill explains the choices she made during the process of translation, while at the same time tracing the influence of the Senecan tragedy in much well known Elizabethan theatre, in particular Shakespeare:

> 'Now could I drink hot blood,' says Hamlet, 'and do such bitter business as the day would quake to look on.' He wants to be a hero in a Seneca play. I didn't know that until I read *Thyestes*.[23]

In Churchill's translation, *Thyestes* comes across as a particularly blunt tale of unstoppable human cruelty. As she notes in the introduction, 'Seneca could have brought a god on at the end of his play, but he's made a world where gods either don't exist or have left' (1998: 301). As well as testifying to the playwright's interest in the classics, this exploration of myths of primordial violence is in line with much of Churchill's recent work, where the economy of language and of images is sometimes juxtaposed to a disquieting study of alienation. The carnival has certainly become serious in *Far Away*, *This is a Chair* and, despite the farcical aspects of *Heart's Desire*, also in *Blue Heart*.

I am going to conclude on this rather sombre note, which although seemingly distant from Bakhtin's festive laughter, looks back to my original argument. The notion of 'carnivalesque language', as a language of transformation, of polyphony, of experimentation and of challenge has served as a useful starting point to discuss Caryl Churchill's work as 'Jonsonian'. Although much has been left out (not least the recurring 'Bakhtinian' banquets, such as in *Top Girls*, *The Poetaster* and *Bartholomew Fair*), I have pointed to some of the ways in which the vast and diverse work produced by both Churchill and Jonson can be looked at from parallel paths; and shown how these paths cross each other in the name of culture and counter-culture, plurality of sources and intertextuality, enriched by a carnivalesque laughter which remains defiant even when it turns bitter.

Notes

1   M. Bakhtin, (trans. H. Iswolksy) (1984), *Rabelais and His World*, Indiana University Press.
2   *A Mouthful of Birds* was first performed by Joint Stock Theatre Company at Birmingham Repertory Theatre, 2 September 1986. Directed by Ian Spink and Les Waters.
3   *Serious Money* was first performed at The Royal Court Theatre, London, 21 March 1987. Directed by Max Stafford-Clark.
4   P. Stallybrass and A. White (1986), *The Politics and Poetics of Transgression*, Methuen, London, p. 44.
5   Herry Levin (1987), *Playboys and Killjoys*, O.U.P., Oxford, p. 373.
6   *A Mouthful of Birds*, in Caryl Churchill (1998), *Plays Three*, Nick Hern Books, London. p. 30.
7   Ibid.
8   *Sunday Telegraph*, 5 April 1987.
9   T. Shadwell, (ed. M. Summers) (1927), *The Volunteers and the Stockjobbers*; V. 5, The Fortune Press, London.

> **2ND JOBBER** There is likewise a Patent moved for, or bringing some Chinese Rope-Dancers over, the most exquisite in the world; considerable men have shares in it.
>
> **1ST JOBBER** But verily I question whether this be lawful or not?
>
> **HACKWELL** Look thee, brother, if it be a good end and that we ourselves have no share in the vanity or wicked diversion thereof by beholding of it but only use it whereby we may turn the penny, always considered that it is like to take and the said Shares will sell well; and then we shall not care whether the aforesaid dancers come over or no.

10 Richard Allen Cave (1991), *Ben Jonson*, Macmillan, London, p. 95.
11 Bertolt Brecht (ed. and trans. John Willet) (1992), *Brecht on Theatre*, Methuen, London, p. 71.
12 Julia Kristeva (trans. T. Gora et al) (1984), *Desire in Language*, Blackwells, Oxford. p. 65.
13 The two essays which discuss the concepts of heteroglossia and dialogism are included in the collection: Mikhail Bakhtin (trans. C. Emerson and M. Holquist) (1981), *The Dialogic Imagination*, University of Texas Press, Austin.
14 What I claim here seems to be in apparent contradiction with what Bakhtin himself states in *Problems of Dostoevsky's Poetics*, where he includes drama among the monolithic forms of discourse. I would argue, in agreement with Kristeva, that Bakhtin interpretation of drama largely derives from limiting its definition to the Aristotelian unities. Aristotle's prescriptive dogmas are not even entirely applicable to Greek tragedy, let alone to multi-shaped contemporary pieces, such as Churchill's.
15 Elaine Aston, (1997), *Caryl Churchill*, Northcote House, Plymouth. p. 99.
16 *The Skriker* was first performed at The Cottesloe, Royal National Theatre, London, 20 January 1994. Directed by Les Waters. The role of the Skriker was performed by Kathryn Hunter.
17 Aston, op. cit. p. 96.
18 The English word *deferral* only partially translates Derrida's use of *différence* as neologism. This word includes both the idea of difference and of deferral, where the latter indicates a movement forward.

[19] See especially the interview with Caryl Churchill 'The Common Imagination and the Individual Voice', in *NTQ* vol. IV.13 (1988). 7–10. The issue of possession is also explored in *The Skriker*.

[20] M. Flaumenhaft, (1994), *The Civic Spectacle*, Rowmen and Littlefield, London, p. 64

[21] *Lives of the Great Poisoners* was first performed at the Arnolfini, Bristol, 13 February 1991. Directed by James Macdonald, the piece was the result of a collaboration with the composer Orlando Gough and the choreographer Ian Spink, who had already worked with Churchill on *A Mouthful of Birds*.

[22] Churchill (1998), p. 191.

[23] From the author's introduction to *Thyestes*, in Caryl Churchill, (1998), *Plays Three*, Nick Hern, London, p. 295.

Chapter 13

'Real but not Realistic':
Alan Ayckbourn and Ben Jonson

Richard Allen Cave

It was Peter Hall on reading *A Small Family Business* (staged 1987) who first drew parallels between Jonsonian comedy and Ayckbourn's work. Ayckbourn himself refers to this when introducing the four plays contained in Faber's edition, *Plays One*; he informs us that he went away and 'read some Ben Jonson but I must confess I didn't understand much of it. Still, I was very flattered'.[1] The inference on first looking at this remark is that Ayckbourn did not himself see any analogies because he found the Jonsonian text difficult to comprehend (a common enough problem if one merely *reads* a text of Jonson's). Indeed comedies and farces, even Ayckbourn's, yield little at a reading unless one has a tutored imagination. But the fact remains that Ayckbourn chose to recall Peter Hall's observation and to do so in the context of a selection of his later plays written between 1984 and 1987, which he designates his 'social' period (p. vii). This argues that at some level his mind perceived resonances significant enough later to prompt the process of recall. Given that both dramatists favour writing comedies with a high component of farce and enjoy depicting the range of human folly, some shared techniques and themes would seem inevitable.[2]

But Hall, as a politically and socially aware director of the National Theatre, would seem to mean more by his remark than a spotting of such superficial resemblances. Hall had long admired Ayckbourn's style. As early as 28 August 1973, he was recording in his diary this response to viewing the London production of *Absurd Person Singular*:

It is a hard, beautifully constructed play. ...I love farce. It is so merciless. I have never directed one as cruel as this and would dearly love to.

(1983: 55)

'Cruel' is not a word that any twentieth-century theatre practitioner will use lightly, and assuredly not Hall, who as Director of the RSC had with Peter Brook in 1964 presided over a Season of Cruelty at the Aldwych Theatre, which actively engaged with Artaud's manifesto about the ideal nature of theatre. It may seem surprising nonetheless to find Hall using the term for a playwright generally at that date considered 'popular' in the sense of 'commercially viable' (1983: 55). On reflection, it seems more surprising that Ayckbourn has sustained his popularity, given the evident (and increasingly marked) cruelty in his plays, which pitch audiences into strange emotional territory, a no-man's-land in feeling poised between hilarity and shock. Why exactly do we laugh in *Things We Do For Love* (staged, 1997–98) when the pains of love are literally experienced by Barbara and Hamish (one black eye, one split scalp in need of stitches, several bruised ribs) so that their final reconciliation is a matter of careful, tentative and tender physical negotiations (the stage directions read: '*As they clasp each other tighter they are reminded of former injuries*')?[3] A play which finds a place for sustained knockabout, rendering the characters physically vulnerable whenever they are caught in the grip of feeling is not in the traditions of romantic comedy. There is no place here for sentiment or sentimentality, only a harsh sense of the characters' utter absurdity. The pain may be mitigated somewhat for the audience by their appreciation of the actors' expertise in negotiating the intricate choreography of the knockabout, but it takes a toll on the performers and not just in terms of stamina.

Peter Hall again is a fit informer here, writing in his *Diaries* (3 March 1977) of the cast's response to playing in Ayckbourn's *Bedroom Farce* at the National Theatre:

> ...there's nothing sadder than playing uproarious comedy. There can be no emotional release. The satisfaction is manipulative rather than sharing a feeling.
>
> (p. 285)

Two years later (26 April, 1979) he was still boosting the morale of the cast even though the play, after a long run in the West End, was now succeeding on Broadway beyond expectation without losing its particular 'edge' ('plenty of laughs, but thankfully the seriousness was intact'). The paranoia, as he saw it, of the actors caused him to meditate more deeply on both the demands and consequences of playing in this style:

> ...to play Ayckbourn properly you have to dig deep, be serious and then get laughed at. It wounds the personality.
>
> (pp. 432–3)

There is, in other words, no place in this genre of comedy for archness, for complicity between performer and spectator at the expense of the role, for geniality. This is the sense in which Ayckbourn is to be defined as *cruel*. It would be hard to think of better prescriptions than Hall's for playing most of the roles in Jonson's comedies too (all those sad victims of their own folly). The prescriptions are the more welcome in being phrased by a practitioner, since they tackle head-on and dismantle from the actor's perspective the oft-reiterated criticism levelled at both dramatists: that they deal in stereotypes (or Humours as they tend to be termed in Jonson's case) and that playing stereotypes is *easy*. What Hall's words highlight is the complexity of the demands made on a performer playing in any manifestation of the theatre of cruelty.

How appropriate is it to label Jonson with Ayckbourn as cruel?[4] In the finest work of both playwrights there is the same lack of a *dramatised* fixed moral centre. For all Jonson's concern with drama as a medium of education as well as delight, from *Sejanus* onwards any moral reading of the action of his plays is left entirely to the private responses of the individual spectator. One has to find one's moral ground with little or no endorsement of one's viewpoint by the dramatist. The same is true of Ayckbourn's later plays too. We may relish Volpone and Mosca's gulling of money-hungry obsessives like Corbaccio, Corvino and Voltore, but do we continue to relish their endeavours when they plan adulterous rape or shamelessly taunt their gulls by tartly reminding them of the behaviour that exposed their stupidity? The brilliance of invention that keeps Surly, Face and Doll in control of an increasingly frantic range of plots and disguises is thrilling to experience, but how should one react to Lovewit's cool take-over of their profits or to Face's vicious rebuffing of his accomplices, especially of Doll, when he thinks the game is up and sees a need to save his own skin?[5] What too of Dauphine's systematic unmanning in *Epicœne* of Daw, La Foole and his uncle, Morose, within a play that is preoccupied with the nature of gender and gender differentiation? Or of Quarlous's clever manipulations which result in his placing most of the middle-class characters of *Bartholomew Fair* in situations where they are wide open to the possibility of his blackmailing them? Having got them all under his subtle control, he generously invites them to dinner at another man's expense. The fact that Jonson does not offer a secure moral standpoint challenges spectators in the very act of laughing by holding a mirror up to contemporary society that reflects its profound and determined cynicism. If Jonsonian comedy is both uproarious and *dark*, then here is the source of that ambivalence. The extremes of that ambivalence are what render his plays *cruel*.

How this differs from conventional farce may be appreciated by comparing *The Alchemist* or *A Small Family Business* with *Tons Of Money* by Will Evans and Valentine, the first of the famous Aldwych farces dating from 1922 which starred Ralph Lynn. Interestingly Ayckbourn chose to revive this play with some adaptations by himself at the Lyttleton Theatre in 1986, the period when at Peter Hall's invitation he was directing a company of selected actors at the National Theatre, while on a year's sabbatical from his own theatre in Scarborough. (The same group were in time to perform *A Small Family Business*.) All three plays are about lust for wealth and about using money to generate more money. Both Jonson's and Ayckbourn's plays are set in a sharply realised society. Jonson's Jacobean characters are discontented and, desperate to be upwardly mobile, seek any means to come by social advancement. Alchemy is about the transmuting of base metals into gold; the visitors to Subtle, Doll and Face's establishment give them money in the hope of aid in transforming their humdrum lives into some more satisfying form of existence. They long for gold, but perhaps more importantly for a golden age in their experience.[6] Inevitably as the trio are working a scam, their clients are all frustrated. The poetry of the play seethes with references to the details of daily existence in Jacobean London during the plague-ridden months of a summer. This realism is offset by extended fantasies in which the characters envisage for themselves what each imagines would be an ideal lifestyle. In the stark contrast between actuality and dream lies both humour and a rigorous social critique. Ayckbourn's play is set in Thatcherite Britain amongst a family that for years has been defrauding their own firm by selling goods on at a profit to an Italian company who trade under a trendier and therefore more expensive label. The whole workforce is involved in the scam and are the richer for it. During the play we watch Jack, a relatively decent man, compromise repeatedly with his values in a vain attempt to impose those values on the firm he has recently been appointed to direct. Relentlessly the Ten Commandments are transgressed from stealing through to murder, while the Italian connection reveals itself as a cover for illicit drugs dealing that has links with the Mafia. Here Thatcher's *laissez-faire* policies run riot, while her advocacy of Victorian decent family values undergoes a complete trouncing. Ayckbourn harnesses the breathless inexorability that is characteristic of farce to the steep moral decline of Jack's family as the humour becomes ever blacker. When his wife and two daughters struggle like maddened Maenads with a private detective for possession of a case containing thousands of pound notes and inadvertently kill him when they topple him backwards into their bath, spectators are left unsure whether to laugh or cry out in shock. Similarly the women's shrieks of laughter when Jack discovers them express an immediate release into hysteria, but this quickly dissolves into tears. Here all the characters share a seemingly ordinary middle-class existence, but have privately acquired the cash necessary to live out their various dreams of a wealthier lifestyle. They have gone a stage further than Jonson's gulls; they have actually succeeded in creating a scam that fuels their upwardly mobile desires and now their efforts are directed at protecting their gains. How a spectator responds to their endeavours will depend on the degree to which he or she can comfortably relate to *laissez-faire* politics. Only the increasingly frantic physicality of the farce offers any criticism of what is going on.[7]

Tons of Money centres on a willed bequest and one living and one missing heir: two brothers, Aubrey and George Maitland respectively. Aubrey is over the ears in debt so his wife concocts a scheme whereby he should feign death, assume his brother's identity and claim the whole inheritance while avoiding paying his creditors. Inevitably things go wrong with the attempt to create an accidental death; George himself turns up, but so does someone fraudulently impersonating him in hope of getting the money. With each fresh challenge to her powers of invention, Louise (Aubrey's wife) devises a yet more preposterous role for him to play or another disappearing act for him to attempt. When the plan goes awry, the consequences (usually timed for an end-of-act curtain) allow for a spectacular or hilarious appearance by the star actor in the role of Aubrey: at one time he is catapulted through the ceiling (*'his face blackened with gunpowder, his clothes...hanging on him in shreds'*);[8] later, when he should feign drowning, his getaway clothes are removed by a tidy-minded servant, so he is forced to enter *'practically naked, soaking wet and covered in duckweed. He has managed to find a couple of boat cushions which he clasps to him to preserve his modesty'* (p. 38). This is highly diverting but hardly *dark*. *Tons of Money* never negotiates credible experiences of pain; though Aubrey is blown sky-high and nearly drowns, it is not his suffering that is dramatised but his seemingly endless capacity for survival. Though Louise invents the scams which inevitably go wrong, she always knows in consequence of Aubrey's comic 'resurrections' that she is only playing the role of weeping widow. We are in a never-never-land where events are propelled by a comic logic rather than by social circumstance. Geniality is the prevailing tone. Though the action is situated amongst the propertied classes, that social sphere is never defined: it exists as a *given* factor, which remains unexamined. The farce exists to exploit the comic techniques of the cast in terms of eccentric characterisation, caricature impersonations, impeccable timing of fast and furious activity; but it invites no form of moral enquiry, despite its preoccupation with people's lust for money. By comparison with the plays by Jonson and Ayckbourn, *Tons of Money* seems curiously innocent, because lacking in serious engagement with anything but the actual medium of farce in performance. If the play seems 'thin', it is because the farce has no serious moral or social imperative to direct its mechanisms. It lacks both the urgency and the cynicism of Jonson's or Ayckbourn's work.

A particular satirical tone is not the only quality the work of Jonson and Ayckbourn share. There is also the critical attitude to prevailing culture, especially an awareness that a once challenging form of theatre has a tendency to lose its special 'bite' once it has become overly popular. Both dramatists can be seen to deploy strategies (which current critical theorists would define as forms of intertextuality) to achieve precise satirical ends. In *Bartholomew Fair*, for example, we find Jonson in the character of Adam Overdo investigating the trope of the figure of authority who disguises himself the better to understand the wicked ways of the world he is required to rule or legislate. Invariably the disguise takes the figure down the social scale. One recalls Shakespeare's Henry V indulging in his 'little touch of Harry in the night' when he visits the common soldiers in his camp the night before Agincourt in an attempt to discover how they view him and the responsibilities of his command over them. Or again there is Duke Vicentio in *Measure for Measure* in his habit as a friar struggling to subvert the hypocritical and criminal intentions of his deputy, Angelo. And there is Marston's Duke Hercules in *The Fawn* who dons the garb of a servant the better to observe and in part tutor his own son's abilities as a diplomat (especially with regard to organising his own dynastic marriage with Dulcimel, daughter of the Duke of Urbin).[9] All are discomfited, usually physically but often psychologically, in their assumed role, learning more than they bargained for and finding in themselves an unexpected vulnerability. By the time Jonson picked up the trope it was long-since dated, but that may partly be Jonson's point. His disguised 'ruler' is a bourgeois Justice of the Peace, struggling to come to terms with the 'enormities' (as he sees them) of the great London fair. Adam, as his name implies, is a commoner, one who tends to over-do and over-react; it is symptomatic of the pomposity that underlies his anxious pretensions to 'make discoveries' and so be a fair dispenser of justice that he should chose a hackneyed theatrical device as the means to his end and, moreover, a device normally reserved for enactment by kings and dukes. The choice of role as Mad Arthur, a beggar in Smithfield, is fit enough to allow him access to all levels of the carnival crowd at the fair, but that epithet 'mad' is equally a comment on Adam's utter absurdity, particularly since he defends himself with preposterous reference to classical precedent ('On, Junius Brutus'). Name, choice of role and inflated verbal register all mark out Adam Overdo as a fool. He wishes to contain, confine and limit the carnival spirit but, as he discovers unexpectedly, it is relatively easy to elude the restriction of the stocks (that emblematic demonstration of justice in action) and, when he chooses finally to 'uncover' and reveal his true self, no one respects him as a representative of the majesty of the law. Far from being the one in control of events and with the right to dispense the final ordering expected in the conclusion of a play, Overdo finds himself somewhat at the mercy of Quarlous (also significantly disguised as a madman) who has deviously gained control of the fates of most of the bourgeois visitors to the fair, not for judicial ends but to consolidate his own future financial security. The intertextuality at work in the representation of Overdo deepens the characterisation, showing how utterly over-parted the man is, whether as madman or as justice: the disguise defines Adam's want of proportion, his lack of the sharp, *original* intelligence, insight, self-awareness or scruple necessary to succeed as a spy. All he discovers at the fair, as Quarlous reminds him, is his own 'frailty'.

Jonson does not signal his intertextual strategies in *Bartholomew Fair* (one can assume he relied on extensive audience-familiarity with the trope he was deploying) but in *The Devil Is An Ass*, the sign-posting is extensive, indicating that Jonson is deliberately inviting spectators to appreciate his cultural critique as complementary to his many metatheatrical strategies in the play, which continually remind audiences that what they are watching is the performing of an intellectual and artistic construct.[10] The central character of this comedy, Fitzdotterel, is besotted with plays about devils; not only does he desire his own personal familiar, he is anxious to get out of the action and take himself off to the theatre to see Jonson's latest play with a devil in its title, the very play audiences are watching. Before the plotting gets afoot, the Prologue invites spectators to show Jonson's work 'the same face you have done / Your dear delight, *The Devil of Edmonton*'. The play begins with a scene in Hell where Pug is begging Satan to send him to Earth to work evil on humankind. Asked to choose a Vice to assist him, he selects Iniquity who arrives deploying the antiquated verbal register of a medieval Morality drama. We next see Fitzdotterel attempting to conjure up Beelzebub in a sequence that echoes the similar episode in Marlowe's *Dr Faustus*. Within some fifteen minutes of playing time we have been introduced to a panoply of references to once-popular devil plays and their particular means of representing Evil. As the play evolves, the strategy draws attention to the ways in which Jonson's play is *different* in its conception and its mode of representation. Jonson refuses on the grounds of social realism to personify evil: that is a dated theatrical convention based on a dated moral conception. Although he has a devil onstage, Pug is continually being outwitted in his efforts to tempt others by their far subtler forms of depravity and fraud. He is a novice beside such worldly experts in vice. This devil is indeed rendered an ass because he cannot keep pace with the complexities of human duplicity in a society like that depicted in the play, which is wholly motivated by material considerations. The magus who outwits the demon, Coreb, in *The Merry Devil of Edmonton*, uses his special powers to bring about a happy solution to a complicated marriage plot in what, despite the title, is basically a romantic comedy. Again the difference from Jonson's play is significant. Frances cannot be redeemed from a disastrous marriage to Fitzdotterel, except by either his dying or her committing adultery, however much an audience may yearn for a romantic outcome. Instead Wittipol can only express the extent of his ardour and respect for Frances by finding the means to protect her future financial security. That is the measure of the power of the vicious in the play to control the lives of those who wish to preserve their integrity. The intertextuality in *The Devil Is An Ass* continually indicates the darkness of Jonson's vision and his refusal to manipulate experience to conform to comfortable dramatic conventions. Intertextuality is Jonson's means of defending of his particular moral artistry.

Ayckbourn frequently establishes his thematic purpose in a play by presenting the generic features of farce in ways that run completely counter to audiences' conventional expectations of the form, which is a mode of intertextual referencing that relies for its effect on cultural conditioning. When, for example, the curtain rises on *Bedroom Farce* (1977) spectators see an arrangement of three adjacent bedrooms which hints at possibilities for complex adulterous liaisons in the manner of Feydeau and his French contemporaries. But the play that ensues concerns the frustrated efforts of the three married couples who occupy those rooms to get a good night's rest since their slumbers are continually being disrupted by a fourth couple and their endless squabbles. Far from being about adultery and permissiveness, the play offers a wry look at the quixotic ways in which couples contrive to live together amicably; it is less concerned with capricious instincts than with the waywardness of affection in regulating marital harmony. Intertextuality here comprises a visual *given*, which continually defines the *difference* of Ayckbourn's psychological rather than physical preoccupations which provide the motor for his farce. Similarly the setting of *A Small Family Business* presents us with the array of doorways which farce conventionally deploys as the action accelerates to manic speeds, but typically Ayckbourn pushes the convention to an extreme, since here we see simultaneously multiple doors on two floors of an entire house (including the all-important hatch between dining room and kitchen and the bedroom wardrobes, this amounts to some twelve practicable doors in all). Normally the doors in farce are used to facilitate rapid entrances and exits, discreet hidings away and sudden revelations of persons who ought to be elsewhere: the focus is on physical agility and the actors' technical panache. But it is Ayckbourn's technical panache we admire in his farce as he brilliantly contrives to shift our perceptions such that a setting which starts as Jack's home serves in time to represent three other houses (Ken's, Desmond's and Cliff's) of identical style and proportions. By the climax of the second act the action has diversified to such a degree that we credibly watch events occurring in three different homes simultaneously within the same playing space. It is not persons that need to be kept hidden, but the family scam which affects all four households and which to succeed desperately requires that all four families preserve their appearance of middle-class respectability. Again, the perceived difference from the conventions of farce in the deployment of the setting emphasises the social satire that propels Ayckbourn's dramaturgy.

In both these instances Ayckbourn is signalling a precise use of intertextuality, since it is in the interest of communicating his satire that he highlights a difference from conventional cultural usage, much as Jonson invites audiences to recall contemporary popular dramas the better to perceive his specific thematic focus. A technique of verbal intertextual 'quoting' is developed extensively by Ayckbourn in *A Chorus of Disapproval* (1984–85), where the rehearsals of an amateur dramatic society allow him to stage whole episodes from Gay's *The Beggar's Opera* within his own action. Gay's play inhabits the underworld of eighteenth-century London with a cast of highwaymen, pickpockets and whores. Much of the amusement for Hanoverian audiences in Gay's comedy derived from an original use of intertextuality: the songs through which the characters in this ballad opera communicate their petty rivalries and animosities were sung to airs drawn variously from folk song and from the more popular arias in Italian *opera seria*, which was then culturally in the ascendant. Gay's satire resides in the disjunction between earthy, low-life lyrics and his choice of a naïve or grandly florid melody to express them. Duplicity and insincerity inform the actions of most of the characters, and their songs continually emphasise their absurd pretensions to sensibility, honour and integrity. Ayckbourn's amateur group call themselves a society and rehearsals and performance in part mimic the integration and interaction that term implies. Privately, however, they are riven with petty jealousies, adulteries and attempts to get the better of each other financially. The double-crossings between them (which relate to the value of a parcel of land that may or may not be ripe for development) are legion and their capacities for moral equivocation profound: 'If I did that [being fair and warning the person who's selling the land], I'd be betraying my own client, wouldn't I? Wouldn't be ethical' (p. 52).

Where Gay's satire exploits disjunctions between context and voiced feeling, Ayckbourn continually deploys sequences from Gay's opera to define the moral complexion of his amateur thespians: their performed eighteenth-century roles continually expose the reality masked by their solid, middle-class, conservative lifestyles. Sharks inhabit both plays, intent only on financial gain; the techniques of manipulation and barter may be more subtle in the 1980s but the difference is only in degree. Here intertextuality again defines difference: not the difference between a received mode of cultural expression and the dramatist's own artistry, but rather now between the characters' inner motivation and their social facades. Where the modern characters would prefer to perceive differences from their eighteenth-century prototypes, none fundamentally is found to exist: a moral myopia permeates both societies to the point where the whole concept of *society* comes under scrutiny. As with *The Devil Is An Ass*, the cultural reference extends inexorably to embrace a rigorous social and political critique.

It could be argued that with his creation of Face, endlessly inventing scams on the spur of the moment, or Meercraft, devising mad inventions for luckless gulls to invest in with no hope of getting them patented, Jonson was anticipating our world where 'hype' and 'spin' run rampant, and that in staging that suspect institution, the Staple of News, he was foreseeing the rise of the tabloid press. In all these sequences we watch individuals being induced to suspend their scepticism. More startling are the final scenes of *The Devil Is An Ass*. Though Meercraft attempts to persuade his gulls and cronies that Fitzdotterel is possessed by a demon of his wife's invoking, it is Meercraft himself who in fact possesses both Fitzdotterel's and his (on-stage) audience's imaginations to such a degree that by power of word he can manipulate them into fancying they perceive whatever he wills them to see. Jonson appears to have been fascinated by this power in language and rhetoric to control or distort people's perceptions, so frequently does he dramatise the situation: one recalls Tiberius playing sadistically with the senators' perspective of Sejanus through the vacillating terms of his letter to them, or Volpone's ability to convince the court of Venice that Voltore on falling into a feigned swoon has emitted a devil in the form of a 'blue toad with bat's wings'.

Ayckbourn addresses a similar issue in *Man of the Moment* (1988–90), which looks at the darker manifestations of contemporary society's obsession with what Baudrillard has defined as the 'simulacra' which inhabit 'hyper-reality'.[11] Ayckbourn investigates the confusing of the boundaries between documentary and docu-drama within contemporary television programmes. 'Documentary' implies as exact ('faithful') a replication or copy of previous events as is manifestly possible, whereas 'docu-drama' with its connotations of (re-en)acting begins to embrace the possibility of fictionalising the events, which immediately brings with it pressures to shape the material to fit received conventions. Jill Rillington is endeavouring to bring together a former criminal Vic Parks and the man, Douglas Beechey, who tackled him, frustrating his attempt at armed robbery of a bank. Vic, now a television star, host of chat shows and the like, patronises both Jill (she gave him his first break) and the 'staggeringly unimpressive' Douglas, who, incapable of taking offence, is impervious to Vic's sarcasm and lofty superiority. Jill has chosen to stage the encounter at Vic's Spanish villa, hoping that the marked disparity now between the men's lifestyles will provoke Douglas's envy so that she can create a 'story' and give him televisual 'interest'. Douglas will not be drawn into complying with her agenda. Nonetheless, his quiet factual accuracy frequently discommodes Vic, exposing his self-vindicating manipulations:

JILL	But the gun was loaded –
VIC	Well, yes, it was loaded. What's the point of carrying an empty gun?
JILL	So you knew you might use it?
VIC	(*sharply*) I've said I had no intention of using it, all right? Is my word not good enough?
	A pause.
DOUGLAS	The safety catch was off, though. ...I remember the police saying so at the time.

(p. 485)

Jill continues to try and coerce Douglas into meeting the expectations that she wants fulfilled by the meeting: 'Now, I don't feel in our case that I've really got at the truth of you. Do you see? I haven't – I don't feel I've allowed you, yet, to say what you really truthfully want to say'(p. 515). For all her blandishments Douglas is too decent to play her game. Just as decency may make bad television, as Jill opines, so it is often argued it is difficult to dramatise a decent individual and endow him or her with any spark of theatrical life; but Ayckbourn does precisely that in this comedy by having Douglas blithely expose the double thinking of everyone around him. It is out of this fundamental decency (in the form of a dated chivalry) that Douglas finally attacks Vic, unwittingly bringing about his death, when he observes Vic verbally abusing his children's nanny on account of her obesity and physically abusing his wife, Trudy, in whom Douglas has recognised someone wrestling with a sense of conscience and of social unease. Vic's death gives Jill her story; and Ayckbourn's play finishes with a re-enactment of the death by a different set of actors impersonating the characters who have till now peopled the play and who participated in the actual event. This docu-drama is beautifully shaped to allow Jill to end her programme (entitled 'Their Paths Crossed') with her commentary neatly poised between possibilities for assessing Vic's life: 'Hero or villain? ... The arguments will continue' (p. 560). Douglas is marginalised right out of the conclusion; the circumstances of the death, Vic's callous attitude to women which provoked Douglas for a second time to attack him, are ignored as Jill, in suitably reverent tones, begins a process of mythologising the former television 'star': 'Next week at this time – and quite coincidentally – the start of *The Very Best of Vic* – a series of twelve special programmes featuring selected highlights from his recent series' (p. 560). Or to put it in Baudrillard's words: 'The event, the meaning, disappears on the horizons of the media.'(Baudrillard, 1990: 85).

The simulacrum that is the docu-drama will be the record stored in media history but Ayckbourn has used the resources of live theatre to expose the dangers and limitations of such *recorded* 'art'. Douglas may be marginalised by the camera as unspectacular, but the playwright has situated this representation of ordinariness wholly in the centre of his conception the better to define the duplicities and self-deceptions which all the media exponents share in being trapped within the demands of the medium. It is an educational, corrective satire which operates by inviting us to look critically at the familiar verbal registers associated with the medium of television. The intertextuality here lies in playing (seriously) with familiar styles of mediaspeak from the unctuously descriptive to the bogusly authoritative, from the deceptively constraining to the invasively rude. Jill and Vic are shameless experts and her ultimate eulogising defence of him is in part a closing of the media ranks about a fellow 'showman' (her final term in reference to him). Vic's arrogant self-defence is the perfect expression of that shamelessness: 'I mean, you talk about villains, you talk about heroes. But what is that? It's very often a value judgement made by society, which has no basis in fact whatsoever' (p. 484). Given what we see in the play of the power of television to shape the value judgements of society, that defence sounds hollow in the extreme. Ayckbourn, like Jonson, judges to a nicety how long to leave the resonances of a specific verbal register sounding for us as audience before familiarity breeds dubiety or contempt. His intertextual references in these plays are the index as with Jonson of a profound moral anger at certain manifestations of contemporary culture or at the trivialising in contemporary practice of the genres of farce and comedy.

In *In Contact With The Gods: Directors Talk Theatre*, Augusto Boal is recorded opining in an interview (where he was being asked to outline the subject of the book that was eventually to be titled, *The Rainbow of Desire*) that 'to be real is to make images of my life and what I feel, not necessarily the image that someone else can endorse'. He continued: 'I don't want people to be realistic, because to be realistic or naturalistic is to reproduce what we already know. I want to discover new things. [...] You should be real but not realistic' (Delgado and Heritage, 1996: 32). Behind Jonson and Ayckbourn's various strategies with intertextuality seemingly lies a similar imperative: a rejection of the familiar in an effort to impel audiences to adopt new modes of perception or, rather, new modes of cultural awareness which will encourage them to resist the pressures of conservative art-forms to condition spectators' responses. 'Impel' is a strong term, perhaps, but it would seem fully to embrace both the anger and the sense of urgent necessity which fuel both playwrights' comic dramaturgy. At his best, Ayckbourn, like Jonson, requires audiences to discriminate meticulously between the 'realistic' and the 'real' for their cultural health.

Notes

[1] Alan Ayckbourn (1995), *Plays One*, Faber and Faber, London, p. ix. The volume contains: *A Chorus of Disapproval*; *A Small Family Business*; *Henceforward*; and *The Man of the Moment*. All future references to these plays incorporated in the text are to this volume. Original dates of performance are given in brackets after the initial reference to a particular play by Ayckbourn.

[2] It would be misleading to imply that there are no significant differences between them. There is Ayckbourn's famous facility, often commencing composition a matter of days before the planned start of the rehearsal schedule, which contrasts markedly with Jonson's painstaking efforts where plays were generally gestated over some months. But a consequence of that facility, mostly noticeable in Ayckbourn's earlier plays, is a tendency to shape plays to fit a specific technical challenge. There is no denying that Ayckbourn's sense of structure can be brilliant as in the interlocking plays that make up *The Norman Conquests* (1974), but sometimes as in *Sisterly Feelings* (1980) the effort at being original technically is conspicuous. Here the action is designed to follow a variety of possible developments depending on the precise flip of a coin in the opening scene but

the sense of potential free-wheeling improvisation is curtailed because whatever development occurs in any performance is limited by the fact that all possibilities lead inexorably to the same final scene. Jonson can devise long stretches of performance which give the impression of being improvised (the scams in *Volpone* and *The Alchemist* are obvious examples). Moreover his plays never give the impression of being contrived to meet some need of the author's nor do they work towards *closed* endings in the way of *Sisterly Feelings* or Ayckbourn's strangely allegorical *Way Upstream* (1982). A further difference between them relates to plot: Ayckbourn generally relies more heavily on narrative event than Jonson, whose major plays from *Every Man in His Humour* tend to be held together by a dominant organising theme.

3 Alan Ayckbourn (1998), *Things We Do For Love*, Faber and Faber, London, p. 119. In the conclusion a third character sustains a broken leg, while a fourth responds to outright rejection by laying waste one of the rooms in which the action is set and shredding her former lover's clothes.

4 Artaud's writings (where he makes repeated reference to English Renaissance drama) and his schemes for a suitable repertoire for his ideal theatre (which include plans for staging plays by Tourneur and Ford) amply justify thinking of Jonson in the context of Artaud's conception of cruelty in the theatre. For further discussion of this issue, see Richard Allen Cave (1994), 'Cruelty in the Theatre and the Theatre of Cruelty: Observations on Artaud and the Modern Director', in G. Ahrends and H-J. Diller (eds), *Chapters from the History of Stage Cruelty*, Gunter Narr Verlag, Tubingen. pp. 153–71.

5 Face consigns both Subtle and Doll to their former social roles: he, as homeless, starving wastrel; she, as prostitute (he offers to write references for her to 'mistress Amo... / Or madam Caesarean' (5.4.141–3). Both fates are a dreadful waste of the intelligence and skills in impersonation of which we have previously observed them capable. Face will shave off his beard and become Jeremy the butler and manservant but, though this is a return also to the status quo, his ingenuity has won him a new relation with Lovewit and he has contrived to maintain his own security and a home. As he rightly observes: unlike Doll and Subtle, he has 'clean / Got off' (5.5.159–60). For references, see Ben Jonson, *The Alchemist*, ed. F.H. Mares (1967), The Revels Plays, Manchester University Press, Manchester.

6 For a detailed examination of this aspect of *The Alchemist* see Richard Allen Cave (1991), *Ben Jonson*, Macmillan, Basingstoke and London, pp. 76–92.

7 It is interesting to compare Ayckbourn's Jonsonian qualities in *A Small Family Business*, particularly as a critique of Thatcherite Britain, with a recent staging of *The Alchemist*, directed by Joss Bennathan at the Riverside Studios, London (2002). Bennathan chose to update the action to the mid-1980s. From the moment Deni Francis arrived on stage as Doll sporting a copy of Madonna's famous pointy-bra, the production occasioned much comic anticipation over how the various gulls would look, what style of period dress they would be wearing to identify their 'type'. Finlay Robertson's Surly really did live up to the name with his scowling looks and dirty black leather gear; Rosalind Adler played Ananias as a fresh-faced convert to the American Evangelical movement; Gavin Molloy as Kastril sported tweeds and a minor public-school accent but clearly longed to be taken for a bit of rough; Adrian Penketh's Lovewit was a nicely observed study of an impeccably dressed cockney spiv (quiet, contained but disconcertingly threatening); while David Florez's Dapper looked the perfect Savile-Row-dressed yuppie. The production had great energy and moved at a phenomenal pace (while allowing for telling comic lines to make their full effect); and there really was evoked on stage that sense of

the city speeding up in the new IT age, which Caryl Churchill also caught so memorably in her Jonsonian *Serious Money*, as if the inhabitants of London were living on an overdose of 'speed'. But energy and clever costuming do not together add up to a rethinking of Jonson's comedy in Thatcherite terms: the modernising seemed eventually to be no more than cosmetic; it did not offer insight into the particular moral and social climate of Thatcher's London. It was fun but that fun sprang from a kind of bemused nostalgia; and so the production lacked grit and rigour. Many of the references to Jonson's London which root the fantastic happenings in a credible social context were cut in the interests of the onward rushing activity of the plot. Fair enough, perhaps; but nothing was substituted to root the production within the living conditions of 1980s England. It was a valuable experiment more ultimately for what it revealed about Jonson's artistry through its omissions than for what it actually achieved.

8 Will Evans and Valentine, *Tons of Money*, Adapted by Alan Ayckbourn (London: Samuel French, n.d.), p. 18. All subsequent references in the text to this farce are to this particular edition.

9 These are three of the finest examples but the trope of the disguised ruler was common, especially in plays of the period before 1600. For a fuller discussion of the trope, see Anne Barton (1994), 'The King Disguised', in *Essays, Mainly Shakespearean*, Cambridge University Press, Cambridge. pp. 207–33.

10 To some extent this conscious sense of the play as construct is achieved in *Bartholomew Fair* through the device of the extended Induction devised for the occasion of the public performance at the Hope Theatre in 1614. This introduces us to a Stage-Keeper who complains that there are none of the side-shows that he associates with the great fair so what spectators will see is hardly realistic; he is dismissed by a Scrivener and the Book-Holder who proceed to read out legal articles defining the precise degree of critical judgement individual members of the audience may assert according to the price of their particular ticket of entrance. These are normally workers in the theatre whom spectators do not see but the mechanics of running a theatre and mounting a performance are being deliberately paraded before spectators to emphasise that dramatists must select their material and that this cannot always meet with the taste and expectations of so socially wide-ranging an audience as that assembled at the Hope.

11 See Jean Baudrillard (1983), *Simulations*, Semiotext(e), New York. Is it absurd to see Jonson as also engaged in (serious) play with simulacra (Baudrillard dates the first cultural manifestation of such games with reality from the Renaissance)? One recalls, for example, the ease with which a dress, make-up and a convenient wig allow Dauphine to pass off a boy as a woman in *Epicœne* and the obsession in that play with creating plausible illusions of masculinity and femininity. Epicœne him / herself is a simulacrum of what conventionally passes in the period for a 'woman' in terms of appearance and behaviour, whether *she* is pretending to be a demurely silent model of dutifulness or a downright scold. Then there is the case of Frances in *The Devil Is An Ass* who has to stand silent like a doll in a revealing dress while her husband displays her to Wittipol to gain his own ends. She is allowed no voice (or identity) of her own but has to be in public only what Fitzdotterel permits: she is a cipher, a simulacrum of *his* values and desires. When she does finally speak, later in the play, it is to give voice to a forceful and highly independent integrity. She resists the role of simulacrum because it renders her a nobody. Typically Jonson works a variation on these two incidents in *The New Inn*, all in relation of the signification of a dress (the one that has been ordered to allow Pru to assume a suitable appearance for her role as Queen of the Revels). The dress fails to

appear in time and Pru dresses in her mistress's gown; later the dress turns up at the inn but worn by the tailor's wife, Pinnacia Stuff, as a private signifier in their sexual games and fantasies. On Pinnacia the dress suggests to the wilder inmates of the inn that she is a whore. Later when worn by Pru the same dress enriches spectators' perception of her as a woman who, despite her origins as a chambermaid, is fit to assume a regal style, given her qualities of insight and judgement. The dress was ordered as a token, a symbol of queenliness; yet it is found to be an empty simulacrum which gains meaning not by what it is in itself but only in relation to the purpose being pursued in wearing it and the particular mind-set of the wearer. The use of the dress in the comedy is a subversive riposte to the sumptuary laws of the time, which attempted to define social and class signification through the precise nature of a given suit of clothing. The laws were an attempt to give absolute social signification about an individual through her or his appearance; Jonson is arguing that such appearances are illusions, simulacra void of meaning. This is perhaps carrying Baudrillard's argument into other areas of enquiry than he chose to pursue, but his thesis opens up new ways of reading these episodes in relation to issues of class and gender.

Chapter 14

Tricksters, Hucksters and Suckers: Jonsonian Cinema

Brian Woolland

Why do we pay so little attention to Ben Jonson,
whom Eisenstein regarded as his teacher? [1]

Jonsonian cinema is something of an oxymoron. Cinema, what cinema? After considerable research, I have only been able to find three film versions of any Jonson play: a French *Volpone* directed by Jacques de Baroncelli in 1941,[2] a 1988 Italian production of *Il Volpone* (also known as *The Big Fox*) and *The Honeypot* (also known as *Mr. Fox of Venice*), a 1967 American adaptation of the same play. This was directed by Joseph L. Mankiewicz; and the writing credits are to Mankiewicz and one Ben Jonson. It is at least reasonably faithful to the co-writer's original stage play: 'Hearing that Cecil Fox doesn't have long to live, some of his former lovers travel to Venice to be near him or maybe to be near his money...'. The film starred Rex Harrison as Cecil Fox and Cliff Robertson as William McFly.[3] There have also been several television versions of *The Alchemist* and *Volpone*.[4] This hardly constitutes a 'Jonsonian Cinema'; but it is at least partly a reflection of the relative invisibility of Jonson in the theatre, and especially the American theatre. If Jonson doesn't play in theatres, directing or performing in a Jonson adaptation is not likely to accrue any of the cultural capital to be gained by working on a film version of a Shakespeare play.

Although it seems that Jonson is virtually invisible in the cinema, it might be that his influence on cinema, both direct and indirect, is perhaps greater than has previously been suspected. The great Russian film director Sergei Eisenstein, who was very influential in developing the theory and practice of cinematic montage, acknowledged his own debt to Jonson. In 1919, Meyerhold gave him project assignments to design productions of *Bartholomew Fair* and *Volpone*. For about a year, in 1921–22, he formally became a pupil of Meyerhold at the GVYTM (State Higher Theatre

Workshop). The work he did on *Bartholomew Fair* stuck with him; and in Jonson he recognised both a precedent and an inspiration for his own work:

> I think that an unsurpassed example of the contrapuntal montage of fragmentary scenes, in which several plot-lines are pursued simultaneously and whose totality adds up to a marvellous generalised image – an image of the dizzy whirl of a fairground – is Ben Jonson's structuring of *Bartholomew Fair*.
>
> (Eisenstein, 1991: 186)

Figure 1: Eisenstein's sketch of a set design for *Bartholomew Fair*

Although Eisenstein's published writings do not elsewhere directly examine a relationship between his own montage theory and the influence of Jonson, the montage-like structure of Bartholomew Fair clearly sowed some fertile seeds. In the two parts of *Ivan the Terrible* (1943–47), the influence of several Early Modern English dramatists is evident. The two parts of the film abound in echoes of Shakespeare's histories and tragedies. Much as he admired Shakespeare, however, he also stated that his own preference was for what he referred to as the 'more primitive' dramatists of the Early Modern period, in particular Marlowe, Webster and Jonson.[5] There is a moment in Part 1 of *Ivan the Terrible* where Ivan is on his death bed, the last rites are performed and he is surrounded by boyars impatiently awaiting his death so that they can resume their divisive plotting. The situation brings Volpone to mind, especially given that we (and the boyars) are not certain whether Ivan is feigning his imminent death. Eisenstein was also intrigued by Jonson's approach to characterisation. Comparing the influence on his work of Shakespeare and Jonson, he wrote: 'The nature of Ivan's environment is really contained more in the canon of Ben Jonson's teaching about Humours....' (Eisenstein, 1987: 105–6)

Meta-Cinema and Meta-Theatre

Ivan the Terrible is a fine example of the way that cinema often uses highly theatrical effects; but can cinema have metatheatrical qualities? It is often self-reflexive, certainly, and meta-filmic: the device of the film within the film is as common as the play within a play. I would argue, however, that a film which interrogates character as presentation, which problematises relationships between identity and selfhood, which inquires into the nature of cultural performance, could be usefully be termed metatheatrical. Such interrogation of performance is a key distinction of Jonsonian theatre.

The film-makers whose work I consider in this essay – Preston Sturges, Spike Lee and David Mamet – are all writer-directors who have enjoyed considerable authorial control over their own output. I am not making any direct comparisons between them, except to argue that each can be thought of as producing work which, in various different ways, can usefully be thought of as Jonsonian. Whilst their work appears to have little in common, they do share an approach to characterisation which eschews and challenges the dominant mode of twentieth-century acting style, the psychologically-based Method system. Many of the characters in the films discussed below are insecure in their own sense of themselves. In relation to the social (and often the sexual) world they inhabit, their identities are unstable. But where this might lead many film-makers to explore their characters in terms of personal psychology, Sturges, Lee and Mamet each place their Jonsonian character types in specific social contexts; and use those characters as weapons in their satirical armoury

Preston Sturges

Preston Sturges (1898–1959) was the first Hollywood scriptwriter to become a director and producer of his own scripts. At his peak, he had a control over his own output that Jonson would have envied. Although, like Jonson, he lost favour, and with it almost all control over his work, he is now regarded as one of Hollywood's most accomplished writer-directors. André Bazin claimed that 'He restored to American film a sense of social satire... equalled only in Chaplin's films.' (1982: 44).

Although it is rarely useful to consider personal biography when examining a writer's or a director's work, in the case of Sturges his personal history is enlightening. His mother, Mary, was a socialite who adored Europe and all things European. She came to an agreement with Preston's step-father that she and Preston would spend six months of each year in Europe and that the boy would spend the other six months in America. Thus, as a child Preston was torn between his mother and step-father; between their respective tastes in art and culture; and between continents. This is perhaps one of the secrets of his success, in that his childhood and adolescence embodied those tensions between the Old and New Worlds that seem to have fed the anxieties at the heart of much American popular culture of the 1940s and 1950s. As his mother, often in the company of Isadora Duncan (a close personal friend) and occasionally Edward Gordon Craig, whisked him around Europe, he was immersed in high culture. When back in America with 'Father' (as he called his step-father) they would go to vaudeville and the Wild West Shows of William Cody (Buffalo Bill).

His work can be seen as a product of the cross-fertilisation created by these cultural tensions – tensions which echo those in Jonson's work between classicism and the demotic. Whilst Sturges proudly asserted his populism, his writing is remarkable for its literary skill. The films of his 'golden period'[6] are elegantly structured and boast a shimmering literary quality, full of word games. For Sturges, populism most certainly did not entail dumbing down.

Sullivan's Travels

One of Sturges's best known films, *Sullivan's Travels* (1942), poignantly dramatises those tensions between high art and popular culture that inform much of his best work. The film begins with a fight on the roof of a freight train boxcar, roaring through the night. As the two figures wrestle with each other, they fall into the swirling waters of a dark river; the words THE END appear and the finale music swells. The lights come on in a Hollywood projection room and we realise that we are watching a private screening of director John Sullivan's latest movie. An argument ensues between Sullivan and the studio bosses: Sullivan (often known as Sully) enthusiastically asks:

You see? You see the symbolism of it? Capital and labour destroy each other. It teaches a moral lesson. It has social significance.[7]

(Sturges, 1985: 540)

But the studio boss is dismissive. He wants a film 'about nice clean people who fall in love, with laughter and music ... and legs.' Sully insists that it's no longer appropriate to make light-hearted films with the world going through such difficult times. 'What do you know about trouble?' asks the studio boss, but the challenge backfires. Instead of dissuading him from making *Oh Brother Where Art Thou*, the socially committed picture that he wants to make, Sully agrees that he has no personal knowledge of hardship and undertakes to go on the road as a tramp and find out 'what it's like to be poor and needy.' Thereafter the film follows Sullivan on his travels, in his high-minded attempts to seek out hardship.

Whilst there are certainly echoes of Justice Overdo here, the device is not peculiar to Jonson, although, as in *Bartholomew Fair*, what Sullivan learns from the disguise is not what he anticipates. The film may be predominantly light in tone, but there is a dark edge to it. While he is sleeping rough in a refuge, his shoes are stolen by an old bum who is then run over by a train in a railroad yard. The bum's body is mangled beyond recognition; but the shoes survive and, with them, Sullivan's identity card which the studio bosses had hidden in the sole. Thus, when the body and shoes are found, Sullivan is presumed to be dead, possibly murdered. In the meantime Sully himself (dressed as a tramp) is found in a boxcar by a railroad guard who catches him and knocks him down. His indignation at being treated as a 'real' tramp gets the better of him, and he retaliates by hitting the guard with a rock, before himself losing consciousness. At his trial Sullivan, still suffering amnesia from concussion, is convicted of trespass and brutal assault. He is sentenced to six years imprisonment. In a labour camp his insistence that he is John Sullivan, the famous film director, is met with derision. When he sees headlines in an old newspaper proclaiming the 'STRANGE DEATH OF HOLLYWOOD DIRECTOR', Sullivan demands to see his lawyer and tries to explain to one of the prison guards that the newspaper article is referring to him. To his horror and amazement, his pleading results in a beating and solitary confinement. Ultimately Sullivan escapes by 'confessing' to the murder of John Sullivan, thereby getting his picture in the papers again, so that the studio can intervene on his behalf and get him a reprieve. But while at the labour camp the prisoners had been allowed to visit a local 'negro church'. At the end of the service they are given 'a little entertainment': a Disney cartoon of Mickey Mouse appears on a makeshift screen. The congregation and prisoners roar with laughter; and although initially Sullivan refuses to get drawn in, he finally succumbs. From this pivotal, transformative moment onwards Sullivan begins to believe in the redemptive power of comedy to transform lives, and in the final sequence of the film he announces that he no longer wishes to make the tragedy, *Oh Brother Where Art Thou?*

> I say it with some embarrassment. I want to make a comedy. ... There's a lot to be said for making people laugh. Did you know that's all some people have? It isn't much, but it's better than nothing in this cockeyed caravan.
>
> (Sturges, 1985: 683)

If this is to be taken as a statement of Sturges's own ideology, then it is disappointingly glib; but by this time in the film Sturges has surely taught us to be vigilant to Sullivan's easy fixes. There is no point in the film when we are encouraged or even briefly allowed to trust his judgement, although several critics and film-makers seem not to have noticed this.[8]

Although some have claimed that the feel-good ending undermines and trivialises the satire of the film, it would be fairer to suggest that it destabilises the film. The character of Sullivan has sometimes been seen as an autobiographical sketch, but Sully's 'conversion' to comedy is not worked through in the way that the darker subject matter of film is. And it is absurdly reductive to think of Sullivan as a Sturges self-portrait. Sullivan is earnest, smug, sober and high-minded, where Sturges is a restless experimenter and a canny manipulator of audiences, an artist who has faith in popular culture, who uses comedy and laughter to introduce satire by the back door. His comedy, although light on the surface, is barbed; and his ability to disguise incisive social criticism as popular comedy, enabled him to make films that dared to ridicule America's complacent image of itself. An extract from the Hays Office[9] report on a late draft of the script indicates the extent of Sturges's achievement in this respect. It had warned:

> In shooting this picture, we strongly urge that you give serious thought to avoiding anything that could in any way reflect in a derogatory manner on Hollywood or the motion picture industry, or that might cause us to be accused of deliberately befouling our own nest. Some of the lines we ask eliminated below as sex suggestive, are also doubly questionable, from the standpoint that they might be considered as reflecting unfavourably, and possibly unfairly on the habits of the motion picture industry. We strongly urge that you give unusual care and attention to this phase of the picture. [10]

The film that Sturges actually shot offers an effective riposte to this preposterous moralising: you patronise your audience at your peril. *Sullivan's Travels* may be lighter than Jonson's social satires but it is a mistake to underestimate its strength as satire. The film may be sentimental about tramps and hoboes, but it shows us the American underclass through Sullivan's eyes; and it is far from soft on Sullivan himself. His motive in playing at being poor is a self-righteous pose of humility. 'I want to hold a mirror up to life,' he claims. 'I want this to be... a true canvas of the suffering of humanity.'(Sturges, 1985: 541). But the image of himself that he creates as he sets out on his travels is patently absurd: he is 'wearing his tramp outfit and carrying a little bundle over his shoulder' (Sturges, 1985: 559) and is followed by a sumptuous land yacht with secretary, reporter, photographer and 'studio strong-arm man'. For all his petulant insistence that they leave him to his own devices, he is shown to be completely incapable of looking after himself. When he eventually does come up against reality, he hits the railroad guard over the head with a rock and is then surprised to find himself imprisoned. 'They don't sentence people like me to places like this for a little disagreement. ... You can't do things like this to people.' (Sturges, 1985: 663). What he means is that they shouldn't do it to him. His interest in poverty and social injustice is a sham, highlighted by the fact that once released he does nothing to help any of those still imprisoned.

Sullivan may be a 'type', but the film shows him attempting to construct a new version of himself: in his own eyes more humble, more sensitive, and more aware of the inequities of the world. Much of the humour in the film comes from the disparity between his own projected image of himself and the way we view him; and the film thus echoes *Bartholomew Fair* both structurally and in the characterisations of Sullivan and Justice Overdo.

It is also worth commenting briefly on the opening of the film in which first the fight on the box-car and then the argument between Sullivan and the studio bosses function as a kind of Prologue and Induction. And just as Jonson's inductions dramatise the contested possibilities of the function of theatre, so these sequences debate the function of cinema; and, as is frequently the case in Jonson's plays, the significance of the two sequences arises not only from the spoken word, but also from the juxtaposition of scenes. Sturges opens with action-packed spectacle in order to permit himself the luxury (in cinematic terms) of the sharp word play which follows and at the same time establishes a dialectic between action and reflection which (although conducted in comic terms) runs throughout all his films.

Sturges the Satirist

Sturges's satire may not be Swiftian, or indeed Jonsonian, in its acerbity –

he often goes for soft targets – but in his method he is certainly a
Jonsonian. In an introduction to the Preston Sturges season at the National
Film Theatre (London), Philip Kemp wrote that in all Sturges's great
movies 'the cross-currents of comic energy swirling through the films
deflect any sustained satirical thrust. In *Hail the Conquering Hero* the
'hero' is greeted at the railroad station by four brass bands all playing
different tunes; it's an apt metaphor for Sturges' tumultuous brand of
comedy.' (Kemp, 2000). But it is precisely these shifts in tone that make
Sturges so effective as a satirist. Sturges's ability to interweave social and
political satire with slapstick, lightning fast verbal repartee and visual gags
enabled him to take on some of the great taboos of American culture:
notions of self-betterment, small town morality, patriotism, national
heroism, political corruption, the institution of the Hays Office and the self-
importance of Hollywood itself.

At a time when the Hays Office subjected every script and film to
intense scrutiny, the subject matter of his comedies is an extraordinary
achievement in itself. In *The Miracle of Morgan's Creek* (1943) the Press
celebrate the achievement of Trudy Kockenlocker[11] (whoever saw that
script in the Hays Office can surely not have read it aloud) in giving birth to
sextuplets as a glorification of American motherhood, conveniently
ignoring that the children are illegitimate, and that Norval Jones, the
'father' they are intent on promoting as a fine example of American
manhood, is a pathetic cuckold. We are not shown how Trudy conceives
her all American brood; but we do know that it occurs while Norval is
sitting alone in a deserted cinema, waiting for her to return from a drunken
round of parties in the company of numerous soldiers on leave. Norval may
be utterly devoted to her (he agrees to go to the cinema to provide cover for
her high jinks), but he is as sexually reticent as she is active. Although it
may transgress the laws of human biology, the logic of the film wryly
insinuates that Trudy's sextuplets have as many as six different fathers.

The satire here, as so often in Sturges, is sharply double edged, tying
hypocrisy, nationalism and journalistic sensationalism together in a
somewhat unedifying bundle. *Hail the Conquering Hero* (1944) adds
'heroism' to the cocktail. Woodrow Truesmith (now there's a Jonsonian
name to conjure with) is lingering dolefully in a bar in San Francisco. He's
been rejected for war service because he suffers from hay-fever; but he
does the patriotic thing and buys a group of marines on leave several
rounds of drinks. He's dreading returning home because it will mean telling
his mother and sweetheart that he's unable to fight for his country. When
the marines hear his tale of woe, they insist that nobody need ever know
that he's not been on active service. They dress him in one of their own

uniforms (complete with medals) so that his Mom will be proud of him. But when their train arrives in Oakridge, the whole town has turned out to greet him. He has suddenly become a war hero, and all his attempts to tell the truth are interpreted as modesty. The more reticent he becomes, the more his humility is celebrated, and against his better judgement he is persuaded to stand for election as mayor. The townspeople adore him – until he can stand the deception no longer and he confesses all at a political rally.

Although Woodrow is always an unwilling participant in the deception, the subject matter of *Hail the Conquering Hero* is a political confidence trick. And, as is the case with confidence trickery in *The Devil is an Ass*, *The Alchemist*, *Volpone* and *Bartholomew Fair*, the target of the satire is not the tricksters but the gulls and, more precisely, what drives the gulls in their need to be tricked. Sturges may not share Brecht's politics, except in the broadest sense, but the satirical thrust of *Hail the Conquering Hero* could easily be summed up in Brecht's epigram 'Unhappy the land that needs heroes'.[12] The film is lighter in tone (and has a far more upbeat ending) than *The Great McGinty*, but both films examine political corruption – not in the sense of a Machiavellian dissection of the mechanisms of manipulation, but in the way that they expose the fickleness of the crowd, the crowd's desire to be taken in, and the way that the crowd is implicated in constructing the performance of those it chooses as its heroes and leaders. Although the reported actions of the populace at the end of Act Five of *Sejanus* are far more horrific than anything that occurs in Sturges's political satires, the impulse to dramatise the mechanisms of acquiescence to authority is stronger in both Sturges and Jonson than is usually recognised.[13]

Confidence Trickery and Negotiated Identities

The interest in the confidence trick runs through much of Sturges's work and, as in Jonson's plays, is manifest both thematically and structurally. In *The Lady Eve* a pair of confidence tricksters, Jean Harrington (Barbara Stanwyck), who later disguises herself as The Lady Eve, and her father, 'Colonel' Harrington (Charles Coburn), are travelling on a luxurious ocean liner 'working' the affluent passengers with the evident complicity of the crew. When the ship stops to pick up an important passenger, who has been up the Amazon studying and capturing snakes, they recognise him as Charles Pike (Henry Fonda), the naïve bachelor heir to a vast family fortune.

They determine to clean him out and initiate a series of clever scams. When Jean finds herself falling in love with Charles – much against her father's better judgement – it's as if Doll in *The Alchemist* falls for Mammon. Although the film is no more an adaptation of *The Alchemist* than *Sullivan's Travels* is of *Bartholomew Fair*, there are some structural parallels: just as the gullible Mammon is accompanied by Surly, so Pike is chaperoned by his streetwise minder, Muggsy (William Demarest), whose dramatic function is similar to Surly's. He remains sceptical throughout, a touchstone against which to measure Charles's credulity, but ultimately powerless as Charles's desire to be taken in by Jean / Eve is far greater than his appetite for the truth. As in *The Alchemist*, the pleasure that we take in the ingenuity of the tricksters places us in a position which makes it impossible to raise any real sympathy for the gulls. These tricksters prey on a deeply snobbish society in which only the supremely naïve Charles Pike is not corrupt – and Pike is the heir to an enormous fortune which he has not himself earned and does not have the wit to keep.

Towards the end of the film 'Eve' starts to play honest. Pike's father cynically tells her: 'I think you're a sucker'. But she is no fool: her new found honesty suits her purposes as much as her earlier deviousness; she invents herself anew to suit her circumstances, in a way that Face and Doll, Meercraft and Engine would have been proud. It is she who shows the initiative, she who gains the spoils, she, as Eve, who will end up in charge of the Pike house; just as Face, as Jeremy, resumes charge of Lovewit's. And if her identity is a performance, it is also a commodity to be exchanged at will. Her identity is fluid because she is confident of her sexuality – unlike Pike whose sexual insecurity makes him easy game. He is only truly at ease with himself when alone: in the penultimate sequence of the film, his response to the bitter disappointment of his apparently failed marriage is to head back to South America to further his study of snakes. His performance of masculinity has been inadequate. The con may feed on his inherent snobbishness, but it is driven by his desire to believe that Jean / Eve is interested in him as a man. There are clear parallels with several relationships in Jonson, most notably those in *The Alchemist* between Doll and Mammon, Doll and Dapper (whose humiliation at the hands of Doll as the Queen of Fairy is at least partially sexual) and Fitzdotterel in *The Devil is an Ass* (whose willing acceptance of Wittipol as the Spanish Lady is as indicative of his own insecurities as it is of Wittipol's skill with disguise). Disguise and mistaken identities may be the stuff of much comedy; but what characterises Sturges recurrent use of the device, and relates it directly to Jonson, is the way in which each relates the comic device to explorations of personal and sexual identities as a social negotiation.

'Unfaithfully Yours' and the performance of sexuality

This fascination with the performance of identity is nowhere more evident than in *Unfaithfully Yours*. The film was something of a new departure for Sturges. Not only was it his first film for 20th Century Fox (he had previously worked for Paramount), but it also marks a move into far darker territory than he had hitherto explored. This mixing of comedy and the very dark content of the film unsettled audiences and critics alike. The plot is relatively simple for Sturges: when Sir Alfred de Carter (Rex Harrison), a English conductor of classical music, returns to America after a tour of Europe, he is wracked with jealousy, fearing his beautiful American wife, Daphne (Linda Darnell) has been having an affair with Tony (his private secretary) while he has been away; his anxiety is at least partly driven by the social differences between them. The film contrasts three extended fantasy sequences that Sir Alfred indulges whilst conducting (in which he is in total control of the orchestra and the emotional authority of the music) and his ever more disastrous real-life attempts to act out those fantasies. These fantasies each represent what Henry Jenkins has referred to as 'a series of ... solutions to the perceived threat of female infidelity' (Jenkins, 1985: 238). In each fantasy sequence Daphne is clearly guilty, a projection of Sir Alfred's anxiety; but in each he plays out a different version of himself: in the first the meticulous, coldly calculating killer, (as he cuts Daphne's throat with a razor, but successfully implicates Tony as the murderer); in the second the noble and magnanimous patriarch, keeping his composure as he proclaims his forgiveness and understanding and writes her a cheque for a hundred thousand dollars; and in the third the recklessly brave melancholic, as he challenges Tony and Daphne to a round of Russian roulette. Even in this final fantasy, where the 'game' results in him shooting himself, what is at stake is not who lives or dies, but who can keep a steady hand. The fantasy here is not vengeance or retribution, but that he remains totally calm as he pulls the trigger and takes his own life, that he can keep control of his emotions while the others are reduced to panic – a distorted echo of the power he has as a conductor, cool and unemotional in himself while evoking passionate feelings in the audience. After the concert Sir Alfred rushes home, ignoring the audience's rapturous applause, and sets about trying to enact the murder fantasy. The result is an extraordinarily clever slapstick sequence which is extended beyond comedy into cruel humiliation as every attempt to put his plan into action results in the trashing of his apartment. When Daphne returns home to find the apartment strewn with broken glass, damaged chairs and smashed ornaments, she is deeply concerned for his welfare; but Sir Alfred insists that he can do what he likes in his own apartment. Surrounded by the destruction he has wrought, like a child sitting in a playpen with only broken toys and a tantrum for company, he announces pompously that 'An Englishman's home is his castle', undermining his own authority even as he attempts to claim it.

When they are finally reconciled he begs her: 'Will you put on your lowest cut, most vulgarly ostentatious dress ... and then accompany me to the vulgarest, most ostentatious, loudest and hardest to get into establishment this city affords... I want to be seen in your exquisite company.' Whereas at the beginning of the film he does not want to leave their apartment so long as she is there, now he wants to parade her because her company will confirm his masculinity. Her public sexual display – providing it is in his company and on his terms – will assuage all doubts about his own sexuality. Superficially, *Unfaithfully Yours* bears little resemblance to anything in the Jonson canon – except in its uneasy shifts of tone – but there are strong resemblances between Sturges's ridicule of Sir Alfred's desperate equation of control and masculinity and Jonson's far more acerbic treatment of Fitzdotterel, Mammon and Morose, each of whom is revealed to be bordering on madness when their obsession with control breaks down. In each case what is both disturbing and potentially comic about their behaviour is that their personal relationships (and would-be relationships) are constructed in almost wholly narcissistic terms; their wives (or would-be wives) are each to be presented for display as commodities to bolster their own sense of sexual selfhood. The resemblance between what Morose says when he first meets Epicœne and Sir Alfred's exhortation to Daphne to dress up is remarkable:

> I do also love to see her whom I shall choose for my heifer to be the first and principal in all fashions; precede all the dames at court by a fortnight; have her counsel of tailors, ... and then come forth, varied like Nature, or oftener than she, and better, by the help of Art, her emulous servant.
>
> (*Epicœne*, 2. 5. 66–74)

The brutality of *Epicœne* is nowhere matched in Sturges's work, notwithstanding the critics' almost universal dismissal of *Unfaithfully Yours* for its unstable mix of slapstick comedy, psychological angst and murderous cruelty. But what Sturges does with this shifting of tone is indeed Jonsonian: he makes the comic routines deeply unsettling; he positions us in such a way as to encourage us to laugh at Sir Alfred's accidental destruction of his own apartment, only to remind us that what he is doing is planning Daphne's murder. We are, of course, laughing at his incompetence and his feelings of sexual inadequacy, but we are also forcefully reminded that the pleasures of slapstick are in the humiliation of others; and that, were it not for his own ineptitude he would achieve what we have seen him do in his fantasy – slit her throat.

Although the structure of the film, with each of the fantasy sequences echoed in the slapstick reality that follows, demands a reflexive response from its audience, *Unfaithfully Yours* is less obviously meta-filmic than *Sullivan's Travels*. It is worth noting, however, that Sturges places a wittily self-reflexive moment at about the mid-point of the film. When Sir Alfred returns to his apartment, having become convinced of Daphne's infidelity, she asks him where he has been. He tells her that he has been to a film, 'which questioned the necessity of marriage for eight reels and then concluded it was essential in the ninth.' His tone is clearly cynical: he is wholly unconvinced by the argument of the final reel. His description of the film he has seen is, however, an accurate account of *Unfaithfully Yours* and his own scepticism encourages us to read the reconciliatory final moments as deeply ironic. As I have argued above in respect of *Sullivan's Travels*, the endings of Sturges's films, which reach for neat resolutions are often far less determined and far more ambiguous than they appear on the surface. Whether the endings of Jonson's plays were as open to interpretation in the early seventeenth century as they are now is itself open to question; but when, at the end of *Volpone*, the old fox is 'punished by the laws' but seeks the indulgence of the audience, and, at the end of *The Alchemist*, Face is reinstated with Lovewit but concludes the play by promising that he will 'invite new guests', a twenty-first-century audience is not likely to read these as offering straightforward narrative closure.

Character and humours

Much of the comedy in both Jonson and Sturges arises out of the difference between characters' self-perception and audiences' perceptions of their anxieties and aspirations. The situations in which they find themselves may change, but the characters do not, although they manifestly try to do so. The names that Sturges gives many of his characters (Woodrow Truesmith, Mr Bildocker, Dr Kluck, Trudy Kockenlocker) offer a kind of descriptive verbal shorthand for behaviour. The names, a source of humour in themselves, are characteristically though not peculiarly Jonsonian. What is more significant is that characters conceived in this way as types, and in the tradition of Jonson's theory of Humours, may seek to affect change but their 'humour' remains the same. Focusing on behaviour traits and character dispositions, rather than on the 'psychological' development of character, enables a dramatist to examine the social (and political) structures that give rise to particular kinds of behaviour. Sturges may not be didactic in a Brechtian sense, but he and Jonson both seek to reveal and ridicule the follies and hypocrisies of the social worlds they dramatise. Both Jonson and Sturges dramatise social mobility and its concomitant anxieties.

Spike Lee's *Do the Right Thing*

In November 2000, whilst at a conference in New York, I discussed the term Jonsonian with Barry Edelstein,[14] the director of a rare, recent American production of *The Alchemist*. He proposed Spike Lee, amongst others, as a present day Jonsonian, and I am grateful to him for that insight. Edelstein proposed Lee as a Jonsonian because of 'his energy, his wit and urban rage'. The phrase 'urban rage' is perhaps an exaggeration of Lee's position, which seems warmer-hearted than Edelstein would allow; but it does conceivably equate with Cordatus's mocking description of Asper in the induction to *Every Man out of His Humour* as 'furor poeticus'.

Spike Lee is a Black American film maker working out of New York and, more specifically, Brooklyn.[15] His work is highly controversial. *Do the Right Thing* (henceforth *DRT*)[16] has been eulogised and denounced by black critics and political activists[17] on various counts; eulogised for its accurate depiction of modern urban life, for daring to provoke public discussion about racial issues, and as one of the American film industry's most serious treatments of contemporary racism; pilloried for presenting stereotypical images of Black Americans, for failing to examine class and racial oppression in any depth, for generalising racist attitudes and for celebrating consumerist culture.

The film is highly specific: it is set in a single street in the predominantly Black Bedford-Stuyvesant neighbourhood of Brooklyn on one of the hottest days of the year. On the corner is a Pizzeria, owned and run by an Italian American, Sal (Danny Aiello), and his two sons, Vito (Richard Edson) and Pino (John Turturro); nearby a general store run by recent Korean immigrants. Early in the film Buggin' Out (Giancarlo Esposito) gets into an argument with Sal in the pizzeria about a collection of photographs that Sal displays on what he calls the 'Wall of Fame.'

SAL   You want brothers up on the Wall of Fame, you open your
                       own business, then you can do what you wanna do. My
                       pizzeria, Italian Americans up on the wall.

BUGGIN' OUT Sal, that might be fine, you own this, but rarely do I see any Italian Americans eating in here. All I've ever seen is Black folks. So since we spend much money here, we do have some say.

Sal has Mookie (Spike Lee), who works for Sal as a delivery boy and general dogsbody, persuade him to leave. Buggin' Out makes a rather desultory attempt to organise a boycott of the pizzeria, which comes to nothing. Gradually, during the course of the day, as it gets hotter and hotter, tensions grow and are finally sparked into violence when Sal loses his temper with Radio Raheem (Bill Nunn), a burly black teenager, smashing his ghetto blaster into pieces with a baseball bat. Young black guys, who have a grudging respect for Raheem but hitherto had little time for him, are outraged by Sal's actions and confrontation rapidly escalates into a riot. The Famous Pizzeria is smashed up, and the brawling spills onto the street. When the police arrive, one of them puts Radio Raheem in a choke hold and suffocates him. Mookie hurls a trash can through the plate glass window of the pizzeria, which is then set on fire. The film ends the morning after the riot, when Sal and Mookie meet outside the burned out shell of the pizzeria. Mookie, who has come to collect his wages, is paid off by Sal. This is followed by an epilogue in which a quotation by Martin Luther King, advocating peaceful resistance as the ultimate solution to racial oppression, is immediately followed by a contradictory quotation from Malcolm X, proposing that the only way to fight violent oppression is through violence. Although Malcolm X has the last word, the epilogue is highly ambiguous, as is the exchange between Mookie and Sal. Even when the final credits have finished rolling it is not at all clear what Lee considers doing the 'right thing' to be.

This account of the film actually describes less then a tenth of it. The violent riot is the culmination of an undercurrent of minor disagreements, but much of the film comprises a montage of relatively good-natured civility, in which racial tensions are played out and, if not resolved, do not appear to be cumulative. That the explosion of violence at the end of the film is so unexpected is surely part of Lee's project.

The racial tension, which appears to be the central concern of the film, is clearly not Jonsonian, although the riot contains echoes of the 'People's beastly rage' at the end of *Sejanus*. Lee, however, is ambivalent about the riot in a way that Jonson most certainly is not. It has been argued that when Mookie hurls the trash can through the window of the pizzeria he is deliberately deflecting the anger of the crowd away from Sal and against the building, thus saving his boss's life. The end of *Sejanus* is bleakly pessimistic; in spite of the riot and the ruined pizzeria (which functions as a community meeting place), the end of *DRT* is highly provocative.

Narrative structure and montage

If the dialectic of the twin quotations functions as an epilogue to *DRT*, the title sequence doubles as a 'prologue'. It comprises an extended dance sequence performed by Rosie Perez in front of studio backdrops resembling the Bed-Stuy street on which the rest of the film takes place. In *DRT*, Rosie Perez plays Tina, Mookie's girlfriend and the mother of his child, Hector. The dance that she performs is vigorously aggressive, as is the role she plays in *DRT*; she dances to 'Fight the Power' performed by rap group Public Enemy. Lee uses this rap in no less than nine scenes within the main body of the film. It is usually heard initially from off-screen, heralding the arrival of Radio Raheem, who plays it continually on his giant boom box, an assertive statement of his own identity.

The aesthetics of rap, as has been argued by Victoria Johnson,[18] are eclectic; it is a form that appropriates freely from other sources, with references to multiple styles and genres. Rosie Perez's dance sequence visually echoes the aural forms of rap. The camera is focused on her throughout. Through the sequence she wears three different outfits, and the dance is cut to action so that her clothes change even in mid-movement: a tight fitting short red dress with wide waist band, black shoes and red earrings; a stylish version of boxing gear – black sports bra, shiny white shorts, sports shoes, large chrome earrings and wide black belt; and a blue spandex leotard and low-cut body stocking – again with earrings. Rap is a black music form, and boxing is closely associated with black achievement; but Rosie Perez and Tina (the role she plays in *DRT*) are Puerto Ricans, not Black Americans. In *DRT* Tina lives with Mookie, she is the mother of his child (Hector); but she is striving to assert her own racial origins, torn between her own mother who wants her to speak Spanish with Hector, and Mookie, who wants their son to grow up Black.

The 'prologue' offers a similar dialectic of style – the rap of Public Enemy sandwiched between the pre-title cool blues (folk-jazz) and the sequence immediately following the dance in which the DJ (Mister Señor Love Daddy) plays soul music. The prologue shows us Perez trying out styles of dress, trying out roles; the dance itself borrows movement from a boxing match as well as from the dance floor (bel hooks (1991) reads these as male dance movements). What all the movements have in common is a feisty determination to inhabit each of the costumes and to make the dance her own. Tensions around cultural identity are foregrounded, not through narrative, but through a complex juxtaposition of cultural signifiers. This is highlighted still further by the decision to shoot this sequence in a studio. The polished floor may allow Perez freedom of movement, but it also functions as a meta-cinematic, and indeed a metatheatrical device, drawing attention to the performative elements of the dance; this is emphasised still further by the use of photographic backdrops – a significant contrast with the main body of the film, most of which is shot on location. Structurally, the connection with the main body of the film is also significant, alerting us both to Lee's fluid use of montage and to the thematic concerns of the film.

After the 'prologue' the film cuts to an alarm clock; the camera slowly pulls back to reveal the DJ of the neighbourhood radio station, Mister Señor Love Daddy, exhorting his listeners to 'Wake up, wake up, wake up, wake up; up you wake, up you wake, up you wake'. As he delivers his friendly patter, the camera pulls back again to reveal that on the shelf in front of him are no less than five different hats (he's wearing a sixth), and then still further to locate the radio station on the street. This really is *local* radio. In the following sequences we are introduced to a range of characters: Da Mayor, an old alcoholic stumbling out of bed, reluctant to heed Love Daddy's alarm call; Smiley, a stuttering, semi-articulate black man (with an almost evangelical desire to sell copies of a photograph he has of Martin Luther King and Malcolm X together); Mookie, counting money and then waking his sister, Jade; Sal, Pino and Vito arriving at the pizzeria and arguing about who is going to sweep the sidewalk; then Mookie walking down the Bed-Stuy street, heading for Sal's Famous Pizzeria, where he works. On his way he meets children and Mother Sister, the wise black matron. It is ten minutes into the movie before Mookie gets to work, and a narrative, of sorts, begins. In spite of the violence in the final reel, the 'events' of the film are not motivated by the need to advance a story. Instead, what we offered is a series of juxtaposed meetings, greetings and exchanges, and what we get is a strong sense of a specific social world. But this account of the structure of the film begs a key question: if *DRT* is not driven by a linear narrative, by the impending racially motivated destruction of the pizzeria, what is its focus? What connects these people is the street in which they live and eat and work; and what gives the film its thematic focus is its close examination of the relationships between style, appearance and identity. As in *Every Man in His Humour*, the key theme is never precisely stated – an audience has to infer it: the close juxtaposition of Mister Señor Love Daddy's collection of hats with Perez's many-costumed dance suggests at the very least a fascination with the way that people in this community play with clothing and social roles.

DRT is interested in identity as a negotiated cultural phenomenon. Its characters attempt to construct their identity largely in terms of cultural style rather than through considered political action; and this apparent refusal of an overt political agenda has itself created considerable controversy. But whilst it may be a source of disappointment to some, it does place his work in a Jonsonian tradition – in which personal identity is a cultural struggle. Lee's characters, like Jonson's, may be types (Da Mayor, the friendly alcoholic; Buggin' Out, the windy, ineffectual self-styled political activist); but Lee uses types as a means of positioning an audience in relation to these characters. We think we know what to expect of them. But the action of the film unsettles us, disturbs us; plays with our complicity – in attitudes and actions that we would otherwise judge and / or deny. Although *DRT* is predominantly illusionist, Lee never allows us to forget that this is a film; a film which interrogates the nature of performance in remarkably theatrical style. His use, for example, of the three older, long-term residents of the street, who talk directly to camera, creates a kind of (wittily unreliable) chorus.

A comedy of humours

If *DRT* is a comedy, it is certainly dark and disturbing. As the embers cool and the dust settles on what remains of Sal's pizzeria, Smiley pins one of his photographs of Martin Luther King and Malcolm X to the 'wall of fame'. It's a hollow triumph. Nobody wins... and none of the characters escapes 'furor poeticus'. Lee presents us with a cast of characters who can be seen as recognisable 'types'; he has been heavily criticised on the grounds that some of these veer towards negative stereotypes. Douglas Kellner[19] has argued that although the film can usefully be seen as Brechtian in its production of an epic polyvocal drama which attempts to pose difficult moral problems and thereby functions as a kind of Lehrstück or 'teaching play', Lee ultimately refuses the political agenda because he makes no attempt to dramatise the processes of marginalisation and oppression which results in non-blacks running the only businesses in a predominantly black area. Whilst agreeing the point, I would argue that the film functions as a Jonsonian comedy of Humours; and that as a provocative social satire its function is to stimulate precisely the arguments about political cause and effect which motivate much of the negative criticism that the film has attracted. It is Brechtian in that it asks the question 'How does this come about?' and plainly the answers do not lie within the confines of this street. The only characters in the film who seem to have any sense of a political context are Smiley, who is tolerated but largely ignored, and Buggin' Out, who may be highly articulate but is no better at organising or leading than Smiley. The low-level, often relatively good-natured racial tensions that run through the film until the final explosion of violence are not orchestrated – either by the director of the characters. And this begs the question whether the violence erupts as a direct result of the absence of strong political leadership.

In a comedy of Humours, characters may seek change, but their attitudes, their mindset, will not. The focus of the drama is not the psychology of the characters, but the social exchanges that feed into and are fed by such behaviour. In the case of *DRT*, the 'humour' of every character is clear. In one way or another every character (with the possible exception of Mother Sister, the all-seeing observer and wry commentator) seeks to negotiate their identity through the commodities they buy, through display. Even the key central event of the film – in which Buggin' Out wants Sal to change the photographs on his wall to reflect the achievements of Black Americans – can be seen in these terms. Kellner's discussion of Lee as a modern day Brechtian is useful on this point: Lee encourages his audience to view the incident through what Brecht would term 'complex seeing', from several points of view. He doesn't try to teach us that Buggin' Out is right, although the character voices persuasive arguments for the boycott of the pizzeria.

The film constantly shifts our perspective, encouraging us to sympathise with Sal and Buggin' Out, even as we grow impatient with them. Perhaps this is a liberal position, a refusal to accept political realities; but if Lee's project is social satire, his decision to allow Sal and Buggin' Out and Radio Raheem each to undermine the strength of their own position is a calculated provocation. The two black radicals in the film are each full of anger; but their anger is either generalised or misdirected. Buggin' Out rants against Sal and tries unsuccessfully to organise a boycott of the pizzeria, and then he gets into an argument with a white guy who accidentally dirties his trainers. The white guy may be lucky to escape a beating – the altercation quickly attracts the attention of other black guys who take Buggin' Out's side, without ever indicating that they particularly like or sympathise with his politics – but the incident reveals Buggin' Out as the modern day equivalent of a Jacobean 'roaring boy'. His easy rage undermines his own intelligent position about the 'Wall of Fame'. The explosion of violence at the end of the film, however, is not triggered by Buggin' Out, but by Radio Raheem insisting that he keep his boom box – still playing 'Fight the Power' – at full volume in the pizzeria.

'Fight the Power' is heard on no less than ten occasions during the film. The lyrics are significant; the rap has a powerful political charge:

> While the black man's sweatin'
> In the rhythm I'm rollin'
> Got to give us what we want
> Got to give us what we need
> Our freedom of speech is the freedom of death
> We got to fight the powers that be
> To revolutionise make a change
> What we need is awareness
> Power to the people, no delay.

As we begin to associate it with Radio Raheem, however, it becomes anthemic; repetition begins to anaesthetise its own power. Radio Raheem is not making music, but buying in to it.[20] He may 'win' his showdown with the Puerto Ricans playing salsa on the stoop (each turning their own music up progressively louder), and his victory may confirm his sense of his own identity, but he is a lonely and isolated figure. The rap emphasises what 'we' got to do, insists on collective action. Raheem, however, uses 'his' music to intimidate: far from uniting or connecting with 'brothers', he separates himself from all the other groupings in the street. This is perhaps most evident at the scene with the fire hydrants are being let off. The young guys spraying everyone may divert the water to avoid wetting Raheem, but as he wanders by, the rap booming out as loud as ever, what we see is his isolation from a community engaged in carnivalesque celebration.

Negative criticisms of the film have focused on the way it tends to represent all racisms as equally pernicious (thus characterising racism as individually, rather than politically motivated), and to ignore the specific white oppression of African Americans as a manifestation of late capitalism. It is argued, furthermore, that the film fails to develop any critique of consumerism and its inextricable relationship with class oppression. It is beyond the scope of this essay to enter that debate in any depth, except to note that the tone of the film, as in a Jonsonian comedy of Humours, is critical of all its characters; there is no heroic figure, no mouthpiece for the author. Whilst none of the characters specifically articulate criticisms of consumerism as such, the film's thematic focus is the negotiation of identity through style and consumption. The continuing debate – as to whether the film offers a celebration or critique – is one which will certainly be familiar to anyone engaged in critical arguments about Jonson's plays.

David Mamet

I wish to conclude this essay by briefly considering some of David Mamet's work as a film director and screenwriter, together with a brief reflection on something he has written about directing for cinema. Although Mamet is better known for his plays than his films, he is an accomplished and successful screenwriter and cinema director[21]. His first film as a director was *House of Games*, for which he also wrote the screenplay. Since then his work as screenwriter / director has also included *Things Change* and *The Spanish Prisoner*. Mamet's work bears little superficial resemblance to Jonson's: although Mamet's plays and films are far funnier than is often allowed, he rarely writes comedies as such (*State and Main* being a recent exception). His plays are usually for small casts, and even the films with larger casts focus on a very small group of central characters. Where Jonson creates a strong sense of the wider social world through populating his plays with a panoply of metonymic characters, Mamet tends to deal with particular character traits that typify specific aspects of contemporary interpersonal exchange. He has stated: 'There is no such thing as character other than habitual action....' (1991: 13). This places Mamet very close to Jonson in his conception of characterisation. Mamet's version of Humours can be seen at its most transparent in *Things Change*, a wittily ironic title. When one of the central characters is mistakenly identified as a Mafia Godfather, he and his minder relish the attention which is lavished upon them. But they rapidly find themselves totally out of their depth. 'Things' may change, but the fundamental attitudes of the characters do not. As in Lee and Sturges, this does not necessarily reveal pessimism about human capacity for change. It is simply a dramatic strategy, a particular means of developing socially driven drama.

The Confidence Trick

House of Games generically belongs to the group of movies that involve elaborate 'stings' or confidence tricks, in which the viewer is also taken in by the 'con'. *The Sting* and *The Usual Suspects* are two of the best known examples, but *House of Games* differs from most other examples in that the interest lies less in the mechanics of the confidence trick, where we, the audience are always trying to see through the trick, than in the psychology of the character(s) who are gulled. In a conventional 'sting' movie the pleasure for an audience lies largely in the roller coaster ride offered by the plot. In *House of Games* and *The Shawl* (a play for the theatre which has been adapted for television) the focus is on character rather than plot.

Although Mamet clearly has an interest in the personal psychology of his victims, his fascination seems to be with the interaction between that psychology and the social world the characters inhabit. As in Jonson,[22] the gulls are presented as having a need to be conned; and that need is metonymic of the broader social world. In *House of Games* Margaret Ford (Lindsay Crouse), a brilliantly successful psychiatrist, and the author of a best-selling psychology book with the title 'Driven: Compulsion and Obsession in Everyday Life' is lured by one of her own patients, Billy Hahn (Steve Goldstein) to a gambling den, where she is caught up in a complex and ingenious con game. Billy has claimed that his life is at risk if he does not repay a large gambling debt. She goes to the 'House of Games' to deal with the threat and the debt. Mike (Jo Mantegna), to whom Billy apparently owes $800, not $25,000, agrees to wipe out the debt if Ford helps him by spotting a 'tell' at a poker game. She is flattered and, before she knows it, is caught up as a victim in what becomes a complex sting. She, who has authored a book about compulsion, who claims the authority to write about obsession in others, who claims to know better than they do what drives people in their 'everyday' lives, is caught out by tricksters who know far better than she does how to use people's drives against themselves. The sting works because they massage her self belief; they convince her that what she wants to believe is true: that she is sharper than they are.

Mamet's dramas are almost invariably set in 'men's worlds'. This is as true of *House of Games* as it is of *Glengarry Glen Ross*. In her own world she is powerful. She is proud of her ability as a woman. When she seeks advice in her personal and professional life, she goes to an older woman, Dr. Maria Littauer (Lilia Skala). But as soon as she sets foot in the House of Games she enters a male world which is far more hostile than it first appears. The 'hook' occurs when she is allowed to think that, as a stranger in this strange land, the very same qualities that make her a successful psychiatrist and author will enable her to succeed here. She is hooked into the con at the moment she is allowed to think that she is smarter than the field. She loses thousands of dollars – all the money she has earned from her best selling book. Her confidence in her own abilities is turned against her; or, to be more precise, she turns that confidence against herself. The further she gets into the world of the con, the more determined she becomes to 'beat' it; a determination which becomes an extremely dangerous compulsion; an obsession that eventually drives her to murder, for ultimately that is the only way she can beat the sting, by killing the man who has allowed her access to this dark side of her own world. And it has become evident that what drives her is an obsession with control. The insights she can offer her patients and the readers of her books give her authority, but she is drawn into the world of the 'House of Games' because she wants to extend that control. The desire to save Billy (who evidently doesn't need saving) is the catalyst that takes her ultimately into madness. In the final scene of the film, she meets with her mentor, Maria. 'There was something on your mind,' says Maria. 'That's right,' she replies. 'And you said, when you've done something unforgiveable, forgive yourself, and that's what I've done.' She has murdered her tormentor and assumed the right to forgive herself for it: a strong suggestion that the psychiatrist has become psychotic. Ford's desire to take unrealistic control of the world around her places her in the strange company of Sejanus, Fitzdotterel and Morose.

Many of Mamet's plays for the theatre examine the mechanisms of entrepreneurial capitalism and its effect on human relationships; and in that respect he shares with Jonson an interest in the commodification of human exchange. But although he and Jonson both use the confidence trick as a dramatic device to reveal self-delusion, Mamet has taken it into new directions. If Meercraft's various 'projects' (in *The Devil is an Ass*) and the mystical wiles of *The Alchemist*'s venture tripartite are metaphors for early seventeenth-century obsessions with material self-improvement, the scams of the tricksters in the *House of Games* are equally revealing of late twentieth-century psychiatry feeding on and feeding into a potentially deluding obsession with the new Philosopher's Stone of self-knowledge.

Mamet's authorial control

Mamet has written extensively about theatre and cinema.[23] His often stated insistence that actors playing in his films and plays should not indulge the American obsession with Method Acting and avoid a psychological approach to character may relate to his assertion about 'habitual action' noted above; but it is also revealing of a thoroughly Jonsonian tendency to want total control of his texts. Consider the following:

> When the film is correctly designed, the subconscious mind and the conscious are in alignment. The audience is ordering the events just as the author did, so we are in touch with his subconscious and his unconscious mind. We have become involved in the story.... The only thing that dramatic form is good for is telling a story.
>
> (Mamet, 1991: 62, 65)

Mamet's insistence on the primacy of narrative line makes him an unlikely candidate as a Jonsonian, as does his argument that drama is essentially driven by what the protagonist wants and whether or not s/he gets what s/he wants. What is so intriguing, however, about Mamet's theoretical position on narrative order and his profound dislike of modernism[24] is that it contrasts with the openness of the texts themselves. His insistence on authorial control of meaning would deny an audience the multiplicity of readings which are evidently available to them. Given the nature of his dialogue, which is often clipped, elliptical and self-reflexively performative, this is a deep – and profoundly Jonsonian – contradiction. *House of Games* dramatises the inability of a woman who thinks she is in authority to retain control – even as she is convinced that she is running the game – in ways which echo Jonson's attempts to exert meticulous control over the publication and reception of his texts when the plays themselves often display a curiously modernist tendency towards fragmentation and irresolution.

Filmography

Christmas in July (1940), Dir. Preston Sturges.
Do the Right Thing (1989), Dir. Spike Lee.
The Great McGinty (1940), Dir. Preston Sturges.
Hail the Conquering Hero (1944), Dir. Preston Sturges.
The Honeypot (1967), Dir. Mankiewicz.
House of Games (1987), Dir. David Mamet.
Ivan the Terrible (1943–7), Dir. Sergei Eisenstein.
The Lady Eve (1941), Dir. Preston Sturges.
The Miracle at Morgan's Creek (1944), Dir. Preston Sturges.
Sullivan's Travels (1942), Dir. Preston Sturges.
Things Change (1988), Dir. David Mamet.
Unfaithfully Yours (1948), Dir. Preston Sturges.

Notes

[1]   N. Kleiman, (1993), p. 39. Naum Kleiman is Director of the Eisenstein Museum in Moscow.

[2]   This starred Harry Baur as Volpone and Louis Jouvet as Mosca. It is regrettably not available in any video collection that I could find.

[3]   The film was based on Frederick Knott's play, *Mr. Fox of Venice*. The play was produced at the Piccadilly Theatre, London, opening on 15 April 1959. It closed in less than a month. The film was no more popular. One critic described it as 'one of the talkiest pictures ever made'. Unfortunately, little of this talk owes anything Jonson. What is interesting about the film, however, is that it becomes far more misogynist than

Jonson's play. Cecil Fox's imminent death is feigned in order to punish his former
lovers.

4 There have been at least 4 television productions of *Volpone*. The best known of these is
the BBC TV early 1950s production starring Sir Donald Wolfit as the old fox. The other
productions are: 1995 Norway; 1972 France; 1978 West Germany. In 1969 *The
Alchemist* was produced (in Dutch) for Belgian television.

5 '...we cannot consider Eisenstein's relation to Shakespeare alone. We also need to
remember the relevance of Marlowe, Ben Jonson and Webster (possibly his favourite
"Elizabethans"). He soon learned to see Shakespeare in relation to these other
playwrights. He was helped in this by his friend, the scholar, critic and translator of
Elizabethan and Jacobean plays, I.A. Aksyonov (who also wrote two studies of
Eisenstein and one of Picasso), and by T.S. Eliot's *Sacred Wood*, which he read with
close attention.' N.M. Lary, in I. Christie and R. Taylor, (eds) (1993), p. 140. See also:
S. Eisenstein, (1987), p. 105.

6 The first film that Sturges directed from his own screenplay – *The Great McGinty* – won
an Academy Award. There followed a remarkable run of seven films, each of them
successful commercially and artistically: *Christmas in July* (1940), *The Lady Eve* (1941),
Sullivan's Travels (1942), *The Palm Beach Story* (1942), *The Miracle of Morgan's Creek*
(1944), and *Hail the Conquering Hero* (1944). Although these are the films that are
usually thought of as representing the high point of Sturges's career, *The Great Moment*
(1946) and *Unfaithfully Yours* (1948) are each fine films, though troubling because of
their shifts between comedy and dark pessimism.

7 The shooting script of *Sullivan's Travels* is published in Brian Henderson (ed.) (1985),
Five Screenplays by Preston Sturges. Also in this collection: *The Great McGinty*,
Christmas in July, *The Lady Eve* and *Hail the Conquering Hero*. All subsequent
references to Sturges's scripts will be to this edition. This extract: p. 540.

8 The Coen Brothers' *Oh Brother Where Art Thou* may not be a remake of *Sullivan's
Travels* but they claim to acknowledge a debt to Sturges beyond borrowing his title. It's
certainly not, however, the film that Sullivan had been intending to make. The brothers
seem to have taken Sullivan's final lines at face value and made a comedy almost totally
devoid of satirical edge. There is, however, an episode of *The Simpsons* with the same
name which is probably closer in spirit to the work of Sturges, and includes a direct
reference to *Sullivan's Travels* with its opening that pretends to be an ending, only to
turn out to be a film within a film.

9 Although a formal Production Code was announced in 1930, it was not until 1934 that
the film industry agreed to distribute any films that had not been given PCA (Production
Code Administration) approval. From 1934 until the early 1950s, just beyond the end of
the studio era, the Hays Code (as the PCA came to be known) defined the ideological
boundaries within which classical Hollywood film could operate.

10 Cited in B. Henderson, (1985), p. 526.

11 The role is played by Betty Hutton.

12 B. Brecht, *Life of Galileo*, Scene 13.

13 This argument is pursued further in my essay on *Sejanus* (Chapter 3 of this volume).

14 Barry Edelstein is the artistic director of the Classic Stage Company, New York. He
describes himself as 'a huge partisan of rare Ben'.

15 Lee has produced a substantial body of work (other films include *She's Gotta Have It*,
Mo' Better Blues, *Jungle Fever*, and *Malcolm X*). His work with Denzel Washington,
Wesley Snipes, Lawrence Fishburne and Samuel L. Jackson brought those actors to

public notice. He has achieved considerable advances for Black Americans working in the American film industry.

[16] *DRT* received an Academy Award nomination for (Lee's) best original screenplay and the best Director and Best Picture Awards from the Los Angeles Film Critics Association.

[17] Amiri Baraka, for example (in *Spike Lee at the Movies*), has asserted that Lee 'is the quintessential buppie, almost the spirit of the young, upwardly mobile, Black, petit bourgeois professional' and that Lee's films embody those values. Cited in M. Reid, (1997).

[18] *Polyphony and Cultural Expression* in M. Reid, (1997).

[19] Kellner's argument comparing Brecht and Lee appears on pages 74–8 of his essay, *Aesthetics, Ethics and Politics in the Films of Spike Lee* (1997).

[20] Lee is particularly interested in the politics of music making – as evidenced in *Mo' Better Blues* and *Crooklyn*. In both these films black musicians assert their own identity through the music they make. Lee's father, William Lee, is a jazz musician and composer. He wrote the score for *DRT*. A more extended discussion of the uses of music in the film can be found in Victoria E. Johnson's *Polyphony and Cultural Expression*, in M. Reid, (1997).

[21] His screenplays include *The Postman Always Rings Twice*, *The Verdict*, *The Untouchables*, *Hoffa* and the cinema adaptation of his own play *Glengarry Glen Ross*.

[22] For example, in *The Alchemist*, *The Devil is an Ass*, *Bartholomew Fair* and *Epicœne*.

[23] His collections of essays include *On Directing Film* (1991) and *Writing in Restaurants* (1988).

[24] 'The audience ... may indulge you for political reasons – which is what most of modern art is about. ... The audience can endorse the triviality of modern art, but they can't like it. I suggest you think about the difference between the way people talk about any performance artist and the way they talk about Cary Grant. And to you lovely enthusiasts who will aver that the purpose of modern art is not to be liked, I respond, "Oh, grow up".' (Mamet, 1991: 60).

Bibliography

Aristophanes (1964), *The Wasps, The Poet and the Women, The Frogs*, Penguin, London.

Arden, John (1967), *Three Plays*, Penguin, London.

Arden, John (1970), 'Telling a True Tale', in C. Marowitz, T. Milne and O. Hale (eds), *The Encore Reader*, Eyre Methuen, London.

Arden, John (1977a), *Plays One*, Methuen, London.

Arden, John (1977b), 'Ben Jonson and the Plumb-Line', in *To Present the Pretence: Essays on the Theatre and its Public*, Methuen, London.

Ashton, John (1883), *Social Life in the Reign of Queen Anne*, Chatto and Windus, London.

Aston, Elaine (1997), *Caryl Churchill*, Northcote House, Plymouth.

Ayckbourn, Alan (1977), *The Norman Conquests: A Trilogy of Plays*, Penguin, Harmondsworth.

Ayckbourn, Alan (1995), *Plays One*, Faber, London.

Ayckbourn, Alan (1998), *Things We Do For Love*, Faber and Faber, London.

Ayckbourn, Alan (2000), *House* and *Garden*, Faber, London.

Bach, Rebecca Ann (2000), *Colonial Transformations: The Cultural Production of the New Atlantic World, 1580–1640*, Palgrave, London.

Bakhtin, Mikhail, (trans. C. Emerson and M. Holquist) (1981), *The Dialogic Imagination*, University of Texas Press, Austin.

Bakhtin, Mikhail (trans. H. Iswolksy) (1984), *Rabelais and His World*, Indiana University Press.

Bakhtin, Mikhail. (ed. and trans. C. Emerson) (1994), *Problems of Dostoevsky's Poetics*, University of Minnesota Press, Minneapolis and London.

Barish, Jonas A. (1960) *Ben Jonson and the Language of Prose Comedy*, Harvard University Press, Cambridge Mass.

Barnes, P. (1981), *Collected Plays*, Heinemann, London; reprinted as Barnes P. (1989), *Plays One*, Methuen, London.

Barnes, P. (1990), *The Spirit of Man*, Methuen, London.

Barnes, P. (1996), 'Democracy and Deconstruction', *New Theatre Quarterly*, 47, 203–6.

Barnes, P. (1999), *Dreaming*, Methuen, London.

Barton, Anne (1979), '*The New Inn* and the problem of Jonson's late style', *ELR* 9: 395–418.

Barton, Anne (1984), *Ben Jonson, Dramatist*, Cambridge University Press, Cambridge.

Barton, Anne (1994), 'The King Disguised', in *Essays, Mainly Shakespearean*, Cambridge University Press, Cambridge.

Bataille, G. (1962), *Eroticism*, Calder and Boyars, London.

Bataille, G. (1989, 1991), *The Accursed Share*, trans. Robert Hurley, 3 vols. New York, Zone Books, 1988 (vol. 1), 1991 (vols. 2–3).

Baudrillard, Jean (1983), *Simulations*, Semiotext(e), New York.

Baudrillard, Jean (1990), *Fatal Strategies*, Semiotext(e) / Pluto, New York.

Bazin, A. (ed. F. Truffaut) (1982), *The Cinema of Cruelty: From Buñuel to Hitchcock*, Seaver, New York.

Billington, Michael (1990), *Alan Ayckbourn*, 2nd edition, Macmillan, London.

Bordwell, D., Staiger, J. and Thompson, K. (eds) (1985), *Classical Hollywood Comedy*, Routledge, New York and London.

Braun, E. (ed.) (1969), *Meyerhold on Theatre*, Eyre Methuen, London.

Braunmuller, A. R. and Hattaway, M. (1990), *The Cambridge Companion to English Renaissance Drama,* Cambridge University Press, Cambridge.

Brecht, Bertolt (ed. and trans. John Willett) (1992), *Brecht on Theatre*, Methuen, London.

Brome, Richard (1873), *The Dramatic Works*, John Pearson, London.

Bull, John and Gray, Frances (1982), 'Joe Orton', in Hedwig Bock and Albert Wertheim (eds), *Essays on Contemporary British Drama*, Max Hueber, Munich.

Bull, John (2003), 'Joe Orton and Oscar Wilde', in Francesca Coppa (ed.), *A Casebook on Joe Orton*, Routledge, London.

Buck-Morss, Susan (1977), *The Origin of Negative Dialectics*, The Harvester Press, Brighton.

Butler, Martin (1984), *Theatre and Crisis: 1632–42*, Cambridge University Press, Cambridge.

Butler, Martin (1992), 'Late Jonson', in Gordon McMullan and Jonathan Hope (eds), *The Politics of Tragicomedy: Shakespeare and After*, Routledge, London, 166–88.

Castle, Terry (1986), *Masquerade and Civilization: The Carnivalesque in Eighteenth Century Culture and Fiction*, Stanford University Press, Stanford.

Cave, Richard Allen (1991), *Ben Jonson*, Macmillan, Basingstoke and London.

Cave, Richard Allen (1994), 'Cruelty in the Theatre and the Theatre of Cruelty: Observations on Artaud and the Modern Director', in G. Ahrends and H-J. Diller (eds) *Chapters from the History of Stage Cruelty*, Gunter Narr Verlag, Tubingen.

Cave, Richard, Schafer, Elizabeth and Woolland, Brian (1999), *Ben Jonson and Theatre*, Routledge, London.

Cavendish, Margaret (1662), *Playes*, London.

Cavendish, Margaret (1668), *Plays never before Printed*, London.

Cavendish, Margaret (ed. Kate Lilley) (1994), *The Blazing World and Other Writings*, Harmondsworth, Penguin.

Centlivre, Susanna (1872), *The Dramatic Works of the Celebrated Mrs Centlivre with A New Account of her Life*, 3 vols., John Pearson, London.

Chedgzoy, K., Sanders, J. and Wiseman, S. (1998), *Refashioning Ben Jonson*, Macmillan, Basingstoke and London.

Christie I. and Taylor, R. (eds) (1993), *Eisenstein Rediscovered*, Routledge, London.

Cohen, Michael (1995), 'Exemplary Drama: Arden's Shifting Perspective on Sixteenth and Seventeenth Century Predecessors', in Jonathan Wilk (ed.), *John Arden and Margaretta Arden: a Casebook*, Garland, London and New York.

Colepeper, Thomas (1690), 'Adversaria', British Library Harley MSS 7587–7605.

Cotton, Nancy (1980), *Women Playwrights in England 1363-1750*, Bucknell University Press, Lewisburg.

Craig, D.H. (ed.) (1990), *Ben Jonson: The Critical Heritage*, Routledge, London and New York.

Creaser, John (2002), 'Forms of Confusion', in Alexander Leggatt (ed.), *The Cambridge Companion to Shakespearean Comedy*, Cambridge University Press, Cambridge, 81–101.

Croft-Brooke, Rupert (1974), *The Caves of Hercules*, W.H. Allen, London.

Delgado, M.M. and Heritage, P. (eds) (1996), *In Contact With The Gods: Directors Talk Theatre*, Manchester University Press, Manchester and New York.

DiGangi, Mario (1997), *The Homoerotics of Early Modern Drama*, Cambridge University Press, Cambridge.

Donaldson, Ian (1997), *Jonson's Magic Houses: Essays in Interpretation*, Clarendon Press, Oxford, 66–88.

Dollimore, Jonathan (1998), *Death, Desire and Loss in Western Culture*, Allen Lane, The Penguin Press, London.

Dutton, Richard (ed.) (2000), *Ben Jonson*, Longman, Harlow.

Eisenstein, S. *Nonindifferent Nature* (ed. and trans. H. Marshall) (1987), Cambridge University Press, Cambridge.

Eisenstein, S. *Towards a Theory of Montage: Volume 2* (Glenny, M. and Taylor, R. eds) (1991), British Film Institute, London.

Euripides (1973), *The Bacchae and Other Plays*, Penguin, London.

Evans, Robert C. (2000), 'Jonson's Critical Heritage', in Richard Harp and Stanley Stewart (eds), *The Cambridge Companion to Ben Jonson*, Cambridge University Press, Cambridge: 188–201.

Fairclough, H. Rushton (ed. and trans.) (1955), *Horace's Satires, Epistles and Ars Poetica*, Heinemann, London; Harvard Poetry Press, Cambridge, Mass.

The Female Wits Or The Triumvirate of Poets at Rehearsal by Mr W. M. (1704), London.

Findlay, Alison, and Hodgson-Wright, Stephanie with Williams, Gweno (2000), *Women and Dramatic Production 1550–1700*, Pearson, Basingstoke.

Fishman, Jenn (1996), 'Performing Identities: Female Cross-Dressing in *She Ventures and He Wins*,' in *Restoration: Studies in English Literary Culture 1660–1700*, 20: 1, 36–51.

Flaumenhaft, M. (1994), *The Civic Spectacle*, Rowmen and Littlefield, London.

Gair, Reavley (1982), *The Children of Paul's: The Story of a Theatre Company*, Cambridge University Press, Cambridge.

Gambit (1972), No. 22.

Gaskell, William (1960), 'Comic Masks & "The Happy Haven"', *Encore*, Nov / Dec, No.28, p. 19.

Gauci, Perry (2001), *The Politics of Trade: The Overseas Merchant in State and Society 1660–1720*, Oxford University Press, Oxford.

Gildon, John (1702), *A Comparison Between the Two Stages*, London.

Gurr, Andrew (1970), *The Shakespearean Stage*, Cambridge University Press, Cambridge.

Hall, Peter (1983), *Peter Hall's Diaries*, Hamish Hamilton, London.

Haynes, J. (1992), *The Social Relations of Jonson's Theater*, Cambridge University Press, Cambridge.

Head, Richard (1666), *The English Rogue Described, in the Life of Meriton Latroon*: a witty extravagant Being a compleat discovery of the most eminent cheats of both sexes (London, 1666).

Henderson, B. (ed.) (1985), *Preston Sturges: Five Screenplays*, University of California Press, Berkeley, Los Angeles and London.

Herford, C.H., Simpson, Percy and Simpson, Evelyn (eds) (1925–52), 'Ben Jonson', 11 vols., Clarendon Press, Oxford.

Holland, Peter (1997), *English Shakespeares: Shakespeare on the English Stage in the 1990s*, Cambridge University Press, Cambridge.

hooks, bel (1990), *Yearning: Race, Gender and Cultural Politics*, South End Press, Boston; (1991) Turnaround, London.

Hughes, Derek (2001), *The Theatre of Aphra Behn*, Palgrave, Basingstoke.

Hunt, Albert (1974), *Arden: a Study of His Plays*, Eyre Methuen, London.

Innes, C. (1992), *Modern British Drama: 1890–1990*, Cambridge University Press, Cambridge.

Jenkins, H. (1985), '"The Laughingstock of the City": Performance Anxiety, Male Dread and *Unfaithfully Yours*', in *Classical Hollywood Comedy* (D. Bordwell, J. Staiger, and K. Thompson, eds), Routledge, New York and London.

Jonson, Ben, *The Alchemist*, F.H. Mares (ed.) (1966), Revels Plays, Manchester University Press, Manchester.

Jonson, Ben, *Bartholomew Fair*, E.A. Horseman (ed.) (1960), Revels Plays, Manchester University Press, Manchester.

Jonson, Ben, *The Devil is an Ass*, Peter Happé (ed.) (1994), Revels Plays, Manchester University Press, Manchester.

Jonson, Ben, *Epicœne, or The Silent Woman*, Richard Dutton (ed.) 2003, Revels Plays, Manchester University Press, Manchester.

Jonson, Ben, *Every Man in His Humour: A Parallel-Text Edition of the 1601 Quarto and the 1616 Folio*, J.W. Lever (ed.) (1972), Regents Renaissance Drama Series, Edward Arnold, London.

Jonson, Ben, *Every Man out of His Humour*, Helen Ostovich (ed.) (2001), Revels Plays, Manchester University Press, Manchester.

Jonson, Ben, *The Magnetic Lady*, Peter Happé (ed.) (2000), Revels Plays, Manchester University Press, Manchester.

Jonson, Ben, *The New Inn*, Michael Hattaway (ed.) (1984), Revels Plays, Manchester University Press, Manchester.

Jonson, Ben, *Sejanus his Fall*, Philip J. Ayers (ed.) (1990), Revels Plays, Manchester University Press, Manchester.

Jonson, Ben, *Volpone or, The Fox*, R.B. Parker (ed.) (1983), Revels Plays, Manchester University Press, Manchester.

Kalson, Albert E. (1993), *Laughter in the Dark: The Plays of Alan Ayckbourn*, Associated University Presses, London and Toronto.

Kastan, D.S. and Stallybrass, P. (1991) (eds), *Staging the Renaissance*, Routledge, London.

Kleiman, N. (1993), 'Arguments and Ancestors', in I. Christie and R. Taylor (eds), *Eisenstein Rediscovered*, Routledge, London.

Kellner, Douglas (1997), 'Aesthetics, Ethics and Politics in the Films of Spike Lee', in M. Reid (ed.), *Spike Lee's Do the Right Thing*, Cambridge University Press, Cambridge.

Kemp, Philip (2000), 'Ants in his Pants', *Sight and Sound*, 2000: 05.

Killigrew, Thomas (1664), *Comedies and Tragedies*, Henry Herringman, London.

Kinsley, J. (ed.) (1958), *John Dryden's Poems*, 4 vols., Clarendon, Oxford.

Krey, Gary De (1985), *A Fractured Society: The Politics of London in the First Age of Party 1688–1715*, Clarendon Press, Oxford.

Lacey, Stephen (1995), *British Realist Theatre: the New Wave in its Context,1956–65*, Routledge, London.

Lahr, John (1980), *Prick Up Your Ears: The Biography of Joe Orton*, Penguin, London.

Lahr, John (ed.) (1986), *The Orton Diaries*, Penguin, London.

Leach, R. (1989), *Vsevolod Meyerhold*, Cambridge University Press, Cambridge.

Lennep, van W., Avery, E.L., Scouten, A.H., Stone Jr., G.W. and Hogan, C.B. (eds) (1965–68), *The London Stage, 1660–1800*, 5 parts in 11 vols., Illinois University Press, Carbondale.

Levin, Herry (1987), *Playboys and Killjoys*, Oxford University Press, Oxford.

Lowenthal, Cynthia (1996), 'Sticks and Bags, Bodies and Brocade: Essentializing Discourses and the Restoration Playhouse,' in Katherine M. Quinsey (ed.), *Broken Boundaries: Women and Feminism in Restoration Drama*, University Press of Kentucky, Lexington, pp. 219–234.

Lyons, Paddy and Morgan, Fidelis (eds) (1991), *Female Playwrights of the Restoration: Five Comedies*, J. M. Dent, London.

Macdonald, R. (1988), *Shakespeare and Jonson / Jonson and Shakespeare*, University of Nebraska Press, Lincoln, USA and London.

McGrath, John (1990), *The Bone Won't Break*, Methuen, London.

McKeon, Michael (1987), *The Origins of the English Novel 1660–1740,* The Johns Hopkins University Press, Baltimore.

MacLennan, Elizabeth (1990), *The Moon Belongs to Everyone: Making Theatre with 7:84*, Methuen, London.

Madox Ford, Ford (2002), *Critical Essays*, eds Max Saunders and Richard Stang, Carcanet, Manchester.

Mamet, D. (1988), Writing in Restaurants, Faber, London.

Mamet D. (1991), *On Directing Film*, Faber and Faber, London.

Mamet, D. (1996), 'The Shawl', in *David Mamet: Plays 3*, Methuen, London.

Manera, Claudia (1997), *Carnivalesque Disruptions and Political Theatre: Plays by Dario Fo, Franco Rame and Caryl Churchill*, unpublished PhD thesis, University of Reading.

Milling, Jane (1996), 'As The Actress Said to the Politician: The Development of Feminine Oratory in Restoration England', *Women and Theatre: Occasional Papers* 3, 16–29.

Mulryne, Ronnie and Shewring, Margaret (1989), *This Golden Round*, Mulryne and Shewring Ltd, Stratford-upon-Avon.

Noyes, Robert Gale (1935), *Ben Jonson on the English Stage, 1660-1776*, Harvard University Press, Cambridge.

Noyes, Robert Gale (1966), *Ben Jonson on the English Stage 1660–1776*, Harvard Studies in English, Volume XVII, Benjamin Blom, London and New York.

O'Connor, Barry (1995), 'Late Seventeenth-Century Royal Portraiture and Restoration Staging,' *Theatre Notebook* XLIX: 3 152–64.

Orgel, Stephen (ed.) (1969), *Ben Jonson: The Complete Masques*, Yale University Press, Newhaven, Connecticut.

Orgel, Stephen and Strong, Roy (1973), *Inigo Jones: The Theatre of the Stuart Court*, 2 vols., Sotheby Parke Bernet and the University of California Press, London and Berkeley.

Orgel, Stephen (1981), 'What is a Text?', *Research Opportunities in Renaissance Drama*, 26: 3–6.

Orgel, Stephen (1996), *Impersonations: The Performance of Gender in Shakespeare's England*, Cambridge University Press, Cambridge.

Orton, Joe (1976), *Complete Plays*, introduction by John Lahr, Methuen, London.

Ostovich, Helen (ed.) (1997a), *Ben Jonson: Four Comedies*, Addison Wesley Longman, London and New York.

Ostovich, Helen (1997b), 'Mistress and Maid: Women and Friendship in *The New Inn*', *Ben Jonson Journal* 4: 1–26.

Ostovich, Helen (1998), 'Hell for Lovers: Shades of Adultery in *The Devil is an Ass*', in Julie Sanders, with Kate Chedgzoy and Susan Wiseman (eds), *Refashioning Ben Jonson: Gender, Politics and the Jonsonian Canon*, Macmillan, London, 155–82.

Owen, Susan J. (1996), 'Sexual politics and party politics in Behn's drama, 1678–83', in Janet Todd (ed.), *Aphra Behn Studies*, Cambridge University Press, Cambridge.

Pearson, Jacqueline (1988), *The Prostituted Muse: Images of Woman and Women Dramatists 1642–1737*, Harvester Wheatsheaf, Hemel Hempstead.

Pepys, Samuel, *The Diary of Samuel Pepys*, ed. Robert Latham and William Matthews (1970–1983), 11 vols., Bell, London, Vol. II (1970).

Perry, William (ed.) (1950), *The Plays of Nathan Field*, The University of Texas Press, Austin.

Pix, Mary (1698), *The Deceiver Deceived: A Comedy*, London.

Polwhele, Elizabeth, *The Frolicks*, ed. Judith Milhous and Robert D. Hume (1977), Cornell University Press, Ithaca and London.

Potter, Lois (1999), 'The Swan Song of the Stage Historian', in Martin Butler (ed.), *Re-presenting Ben Jonson: Text, History, Performance*, Macmillan, London, 193–209.

Ravenhill, Mark (1996), *Shopping and Fucking*, Methuen, London.

Ravenhill, Mark (1999), *Some Explicit Polaroids*, Methuen, London.

Reid, Mark A. (1997), *Spike Lee's Do the Right Thing*, Cambridge University Press, Cambridge.

Rosenthal, Laura J. (1996), *Playwrights and Plagiarists in Early Modern England: Gender, Authorship, Literary Property*, Cornell University Press, Ithaca and London.

Runge, Laura L. (1997), *Gender and Language in British Literary Criticism, 1660-1790*, Cambridge University Press, Cambridge.

Sanders, Julie (1998a), *Ben Jonson's Theatrical Republics*, Macmillan, Basingstoke.

Sanders, Julie (1998b), ' "A Woman Write a Play!": Jonsonian strategies and the dramatic writings of Margaret Cavendish; or, did the Duchess feel the anxiety of influence,' in S.P. Cerasano, and Marion Wynne-Davies (eds) (1998), *Readings in Renaissance Women's Drama*, Routledge, London, pp. 293–305.

Sanders, Julie (1999a), 'Jonson, *The Sad Shepherd* and the North Midlands', *Ben Jonson Journal*, 6: 49–68.

Sanders, Julie (1999b), 'Midwifery and the New Science in the Seventeenth Century: Language, Print and Theatre', in Erica Fudge, Ruth Gilbert and Susan Wiseman (eds), *At the Borders of the Human: Beasts, Bodies and Natural Philosophy in the early modern period*, Macmillan, London, 74–90.

Sanders, Julie (1999c) ""Twill fit the players yet": Women and theatre in Jonson's late plays' in R. Cave, E. Schafer and B. Woolland, (eds), *Ben Jonson and Theatre: Performance, Practice and Theory*.

Shaw, George Bernard (1934), *The Complete Plays*, Oldhams, London.

Skantze, P.A. (1994), 'The Lady Eve, or Who's on First?', *Women and Theatre*, 2, 73–87.

Speaight, R. (1954), *William Poel and the Elizabethan Revival*, Heinemann, London.

Stallybrass, P. and White, A. (1986), *The Politics and Poetics of Transgression*, Methuen, London.

Sturges, P. (ed. B. Henderson) (1985), *Five Screenplays*, University of California Press, Berkeley, Los Angeles, London.

Sturges, S. (ed.) (1991), *Preston Sturges on Preston Sturges*, Faber and Faber, London and Boston.

Summers, Montague (ed.) (1915), *The Works of Aphra Behn*, 6 vols., William Heinemann, London: A.H. Bullen, Stratford-on-Avon.

Summers, Montague (ed.) (1927), *Complete Works of Thomas Shadwell*, 5 vols., Fortune Press, London.

Swedenberg Jr., H.T. (ed.) (1956–89), *John Dryden's Works*, 20 vols., University of California Press, Berkeley and London.

Taylor, John Russell (ed.) (1965), *New English Dramatists: 8*, Penguin, London.

Thayer, C.G. (1963), *Ben Jonson: Studies in the Plays*, University of Oklahoma Press, Oklahoma.

Thomas, David and Hare, Arnold (eds) (1989), *Restoration and Georgian England 1660–1788*, Cambridge University Press, Cambridge.

Todd, Janet (ed.) (1992–96), *The Works of Aphra Behn*, 7 vols., William Pickering, London.

Todd, Janet (1996), *The Secret Life of Aphra Behn*, Palgrave, Basingstoke.

Wayne, Don. E. (1982), *Drama and Society in the Age of Jonson: An Alternative View*, Renaissance Drama 12: 103–29.

Wilde, Oscar (1954), *Plays*, Penguin, London.

Wilde, Oscar, *The Importance of Being Earnest & Other Plays*, Richard Cave (ed.), (2000), Penguin, London.

Wilson, R. and Dutton, R. (1992), *New Historicism and Renaissance Drama*, Longman, Harlow.

Williams, Carolyn D. (1993), *Pope, Homer, and Manliness*, Routledge, London.

Williams, Raymond (1976), *Keywords: A vocabulary of culture and society*, Fontana, London.

Williams, Raymond (1987), 'A Defence of Realism', in *What I Came to Say*, Verso, London.

Wilson, Scott (1995), *Cultural Materialism: Theory and Practice*, Blackwell, London.

Womack, Peter (1986), *Ben Jonson*, Basil Blackwell, Oxford and New York.

Index